MYTH, RITUAL & RELIGION

VOLUME TWO

MYTH, RITUAL & RELIGION

VOLUME TWO

ANDREW LANG

Myth, Ritual & Religion Vol. II

First published in 1913 by Longman's, Green & Co.,
London

This edition first published in 1996 by Senate,
an imprint of Random House UK Ltd,
Random House, 20 Vauxhall Bridge Road,
London SW1V 2SA

ISBN 1 85958 183 8

Printed and bound in Guernsey by
The Guernsey Press Co Ltd

CONTENTS.

CHAPTER XII.

CHAPTER XIII.

CHAPTER XIV.

CHAPTER XV.

CHAPTER XVI.

CHAPTER XVII.

CHAPTER XVIII.

CHAPTER XIX.

APPENDIX A.

APPENDIX B.

MYTH, RITUAL AND RELIGION.

CHAPTER XII.

GODS OF THE LOWEST RACES.

Savage religion mysterious—Why this is so—Australians in 1688—Sir John Lubbock—Roskoff—Evidence of religion—Mr. Manning—Mr. Howitt—Supreme beings—Mr. Tylor's theory of borrowing—Reply—Morality sanctioned—Its nature—Satirical rite—"Our Father"—Mr. Ridley on a creator—Mr. Langloh Parker—Dr. Roth—Conclusion—Australians' religious.

THE Science of Anthropology can speak, with some confidence, on many questions of Mythology. Materials are abundant and practically undisputed, because, as to their myths, savage races have spoken out with freedom. Myth represents, now the early scientific, now the early imaginative and humorous faculty, playing freely round all objects of thought: even round the Superhuman beings of belief. But, as to his Religion, the savage by no means speaks out so freely. Religion represents his serious mood of trust, dependence or apprehension.

In certain cases the ideas about superhuman Makers and judges are veiled in mysteries, rude sketches of the mysteries of Greece, to which the white man is but seldom admitted. In other cases the highest religious conceptions of the people are in a state of obsolescence, are subordinated to the cult of accessible minor deities, and are rarely mentioned. While sacrifice or service again is done to the lower objects of faith (ghosts or gods developed out of ghosts) the Supreme Being, in a surprising number of instances, is wholly unpropitiated. Having all things, he needs nothing (at all events gets nothing) at men's hands except obedience to his laws; being good, he is not feared; or being obsolescent (superseded, as it seems, by deities who can be bribed) he has shrunk to the shadow of a name. Of the gods too good and great to need anything, the Ahone of the Red Men in Virginia, or the Dendid of the African Dinkas, is an example. Of the obsolescent god, now but a name, the Atahocan of the Hurons was, while the "Lord in heaven" of the Zulus is, an instance. Among the relatively supreme beings revealed only in the mysteries, the gods of many Australian tribes are deserving of observation.

For all these reasons, mystery, absence of sacrifice or idol, and obsolescence, the Religion of savages is a subject much more obscure than their mythology. The truth is that anthropological inquiry is not yet in a position to be dogmatic; has not yet knowledge sufficient for a theory of the Origins of Religion, and the evolution of belief from its lowest stages and earliest germs. Nevertheless such a theory has been framed, and has been already stated.

We formulated the objections to this current hypothesis, and observed that its defenders must take refuge in denying the evidence as to low savage religions, or, if the facts be accepted, must account for them by a theory of degradation, or by a theory of borrowing from Christian sources. That the Australians are not degenerate we demonstrated, and we must now give reasons for holding that their religious conceptions are not borrowed from Europeans.

The Australians, when observed by Dampier on the North-west Coast in 1688, seemed "the miserablest people in the world," without houses, agriculture, metals, or domesticated animals.[1] In this condition they still remain, when not under European influence. Dampier, we saw, noted peculiarities: "Be it little or much they get, every one has his part, as well the young and tender as the old and feeble, who are not able to go abroad, as the strong and lusty". This kind of justice or generosity, or unselfishness, is still inculcated in the religious mysteries of some of the race. "Generosity is certainly one of the native's leading features. He is always accustomed to give a share of his food, or of what he may possess, to his fellows. It may be, of course, objected to this that in doing so he is only following an old-established custom, the breaking of which would expose him to harsh treatment and to being looked on as a churlish fellow. It will, however, be hardly denied that, as this custom expresses the idea that, in this particular matter, every one is supposed to act in a kindly way towards certain individuals: the very existence of such a custom, even if it be only carried out in the hope of securing at some time a *quid pro quo*, shows that the native is alive to the fact that an action which benefits some one else is worthy to be performed. . . . It is with the native a fixed habit to give away part of

[1] *Early Voyages to Australia*, pp. 102-111. Hakluyt Society.

what he has."[1] The authors of this statement do not say that the duty is inculcated, in Central Australia, under religious sanction, in the tribal mysteries. This, however, is the case among the Kurnai, and some tribes of Victoria and New South Wales.[2]

Since Dampier found the duty practised as early as 1688, it will scarcely be argued that the natives adopted this course of what should be Christian conduct from their observations of Christian colonists.

The second point which impressed Dampier was that men and women, old and young, all lacked the two front upper teeth. Among many tribes of the natives of New South Wales and Victoria, the boys still have their front teeth knocked out, when initiated, but the custom does not prevail (in ritual) where circumcision and another very painful rite are practised, as in Central Australia and Central Queensland.

Dampier's evidence shows how little the natives have changed in two hundred years. Yet evidence of progress may be detected, perhaps, as we have already shown. But one fact, perhaps of an opposite bearing, must be noted. A singular painting, in a cave, of a person clothed in a robe of red, reaching to the feet, with sleeves, and with a kind of halo (or set of bandages) round the head, remains a mystery, like similar figures with blue halos or bandages, clothed and girdled. None of the figures had mouths; otherwise, in Sir George Grey's sketches, they have a remote air of Cimabue's work.[3] These designs were by men familiar

[1] Spencer and Gillen, *Natives of Central Australia*, p. 48.

[2] Howitt, *Journal Anthrop. Inst.*, 1885, p. 310.

[3] Grey's *Journals of Expeditions of Discovery* in North-West and

with clothing, whether their own, or that of strangers observed by them, though in one case an unclothed figure carries a kangaroo. At present the natives draw with much spirit, when provided with European materials, as may be seen in Mrs. Langloh Parker's two volumes of *Australian Legendary Tales*. Their decorative patterns vary in character in different parts of the continent, but nowhere do they now execute works like those in the caves discovered by Sir George Grey. The reader must decide for himself how far these monuments alone warrant an inference of great degeneration in Australia, or are connected with religion.

Such are the Australians, men without kings or chiefs, and what do we know of their beliefs?

The most contradictory statements about their religion may be found in works of science. Mr. Huxley declared that "their theology is a mere belief in the existence, powers and dispositions (usually malignant) of ghost-like entities who may be propitiated or scared away; but no cult can be properly said to exist. And in this stage theology is wholly independent of ethics." This, he adds, is "theology in its simplest condition".

In a similar sense, Sir John Lubbock writes: "The Australians have no idea of creation, nor do they use prayers; they have no religious forms, ceremonies or worship. They do not believe in the existence of a Deity, nor is morality in any way connected with their religion, if it can be so called."[1]

Western Australia, in the years 1837-39, vol. i., pp. 200-263. Sir George regarded the pictures as perhaps very ancient. The natives "chaffed" him when he asked for traditions on the subject.

[1] Lubbock, *Origin of Civilisation*, p. 158, 1870. In 1889, for "a deity" "a true Deity".

This remark must be compared with another in the same work (1882, p. 210). "Mr. Ridley, indeed, . . . states that they have a traditional belief in one supreme Creator, called Baiamai, but he admits that most of the witnesses who were examined before the Select Committee appointed by the Legislative Council of Victoria in 1858 to report on the Aborigines, gave it as their opinion that the natives had no religious ideas. It appears, moreover, from a subsequent remark, that Baiamai only possessed "traces" "of the three attributes of the God of the Bible, Eternity, Omnipotence and Goodness".[1]

Mr. Ridley, an accomplished linguist who had lived with wild blacks in 1854-58, in fact, said long ago, that the Australian *Bora*, or Mystery, "involves the idea of dedication to God". He asked old Billy Murri Bundur whether men *worshipped* Baiame at the Bora? "Of course they do," said Billy. Mr. Ridley, to whose evidence we shall return, was not the only affirmative witness. Archdeacon Günther had no doubt that Baiame was equivalent to the Supreme Being, "a remnant of original traditions," and it was Mr. Günther, not Mr. Ridley, who spoke of "traces" of Baiame's eternity, omnipotence and goodness. Mr. Ridley gave similar reports from evidence collected by the committee of 1858. He found the higher creeds most prominent in the interior, hundreds of miles from the coast.

Apparently the reply of Gustav Roskoff to Sir John Lubbock (1880) did not alter that writer's opinion. Roskoff pointed out that Waitz-Gerland, while denying

[1] *Cf. J. A. I.*, 1872, 257-271.

that Australian beliefs were derived from any higher culture, denounced the theory that they have no religion as "entirely false". "Belief in a Good Being is found in South Australia, New South Wales, and the centre of the south-eastern continent."[1] The opinion of Waitz is highly esteemed, and that not merely because, as Mr. Max Müller has pointed out, he has edited Greek classical works. *Avec du Grec on ne peut gâter rien.* Mr. Oldfield, in addition to bogles and a water-spirit, found Biam (Baiame) and Namba-jundi, who admits souls into his Paradise, while Warnyura torments the bad under earth.[2] Mr. Eyre, publishing in 1845, gives Baiame (on the Morrum-bidgee, Biam; on the Murray, Biam-Vaitch-y) as a source of songs sung at dances, and a cause of disease. He is deformed, sits cross-legged, or paddles a canoe. On the Murray he found a creator, Noorele, "all powerful, and of benevolent character," with three unborn sons, dwelling "up among the clouds". Souls of dead natives join them in the skies. Nevertheless "the natives, as far as yet can be ascertained, have no religious belief or ceremonies"; and, though Noorele is credited with "the origin of creation," "he made the earth, trees, water, etc.," a deity, or Great First Cause, "can hardly be said to be acknowledged".[3] Such are the consistent statements of Mr. Eyre! Roskoff also cites Mr. Ridley, Braim, Cunningham, Dawson, and other witnesses, as opposed to Sir John

[1] Waitz-Gerland, *Anthropologie*, vi. 794 *et seq.*

[2] Oldfield, *Translations of Ethnol. Soc.*, iii. 208. On this evidence I lay no stress.

[3] Eyre, *Journals*, ii. pp. 355-358.

Lubbock, and he includes Mr. Tylor.[1] Mr. Tylor, later, found Baiame, or Pei-a-mei, no earlier in literature than about 1840, in Mr. Hale's *United States Exploring Expedition.*[2] Previous to that date, Baiame, it seems, was unknown to Mr. Threlkeld, whose early works are of 1831-1857. He only speaks of Koin, a kind of goblin, and for lack of a native name for God, Mr. Threlkeld tried to introduce Jehova-ka-biruê, and Eloi, but failed. Mr. Tylor, therefore, appears to suppose that the name, Baiame, and, at all events, his divine qualities, were introduced by missionaries, apparently between 1831 and 1840.[3] To this it must be replied that Mr. Hale, about 1840, writes that "when the missionaries first came to Wellington" (Mr. Threlkeld's own district) "Baiame was worshipped there with songs". "These songs or hymns, *according to Mr. Threlkeld*, were passed on" from a considerable distance. It is notorious that songs and dances are thus passed on, till they reach tribes who do not even know the meaning of the words.[4] In this way Baiame songs had reached Wellington before the arrival of the missionaries, and for this fact Mr. Threlkeld (who is supposed not to have known Baiame) is Mr. Hale's authority. In Mr. Tylor's opinion (as I understand it) the word Baiame was the missionary translation of our word "Creator," and derived from *Baia* "to make". Now, Mr. Ridley says that Mr. Greenway "discovered" this *baia* to be the root of Baiame.

[1] Roskoff, *Das Religionswesen der Rohesten Naturvölker*, pp. 37-41.

[2] *Ethnology and Philology*, p. 110. 1846.

[3] Tylor, *The Limits of Savage Religion*, *J. A. I.*, vol. xxi. 1892.

[4] Roth, *Natives of N.-W. Central Queensland*, p. 117.

But what missionary introduced the word before 1840? Not Mr. Threlkeld, for he (according to Mr. Tylor), did not know the word, and he tried Eloi, and Jehova-ka-biruê, while Immanueli was also tried and also failed.[1] Baiame, known in 1840, does not occur in a missionary primer before Mr. Ridley's *Gurre Kamilaroi* (1856), so the missionary primer did not launch Baiame before the missionaries came to Wellington. According to Mr. Hale, the Baiame songs were brought by blacks from a distance (we know how Greek mysteries were also *colportés* to new centres), and the yearly rite had, in 1840, been for three years in abeyance. Moreover, the etymology, *Baia* "to make" has a competitor in "Byamee = Big Man".[2] Thus Baiame, as a divine being, preceded the missionaries, and is not a word of missionary manufacture, while sacred words really of missionary manufacture do not find their way into native tradition. Mr. Hale admits that the ideas about Baiame may "possibly" be of European origin, though the great reluctance of the blacks to adopt any opinion from Europeans makes against that theory.[3]

It may be said that, if Baiame was premissionary, his higher attributes date after Mr. Ridley's labours, abandoned for lack of encouragement in 1858. In 1840, Mr. Hale found Baiame located in an isle of the seas, like Circe, living on fish which came to his call. Some native theologians attributed Creation to his Son, Burambin, the Demiurge, a common savage form of Gnosticism.

[1] Ridley, speaking of 1855. Lang's *Queensland*, p. 435.

[2] Mrs. Langloh Parker, *More Australian Legendary Tales*. 1898. Glossary.

[3] *Op. cit.*, p. 110.

On the nature of Baiame, we have, however, some curious early evidence of 1844-45. Mr. James Manning, in these years, and earlier, lived "near the outside boundaries of settlers to the south". A conversation with Goethe, when the poet was eighty-five, induced him to study the native beliefs. "No missionaries," he writes, "ever came to the southern district at any time, and it was not till many years later that they landed in Sydney on their way to Moreton Bay, to attempt, in vain, to Christianise the blacks of that locality, before the Queensland separation from this colony took place." Mr. Manning lost his notes of 1845, but recovered a copy from a set lent to Lord Audley, and read them, in November, 1882, to the Royal Society of New South Wales. The notes are of an extraordinary character, and Mr. Manning, perhaps unconsciously, exaggerated their Christian analogies, by adopting Christian terminology. Dean Cowper, however, corroborated Mr. Manning's general opinion, by referring to evidence of Archdeacon Günther, who sent a grammar, with remarks on "Bhaimè, or Bhaiamè," from Wellington to Mr. Max Müller. "He received his information, he told me, from some of the oldest blacks, who, he was satisfied, could not have derived their ideas from white men, as they had not then had intercourse with them." Old savages are not apt to be in a hurry to borrow European notions. Mr. Manning also averred that he obtained his information with the greatest difficulty. "They required such secrecy on my part, and seemed so afraid of being heard even in the most secret places, that, in one or two cases, I have seen them almost tremble in speaking." One native, after carefully examining doors and windows, "stood in a wooden fireplace, and spoke in a tone little above a whisper, and confirmed what I had before heard". Another stipulated that silence must be observed, otherwise the European hands might question his wife, in which case he would be obliged to kill her. Mr. Howitt also found that the name of Darumulun (in religion) is too sacred to be spoken except almost in whispers, while the total exclusion of women from mysteries and religious knowledge, on pain of death, is admitted to be universal among the tribes.[1] Such secrecy, so widely diffused, is hardly compatible with humorous imposture by the natives.

There is an element of humour in all things. Mr. Manning, in 1882, appealed to his friend, Mr. Mann, to give testimony to the excellency of Black Andy, the native from whom he derived most of his notes, which were corroborated by other black witnesses. Mr. Mann arose and replied that "he had never met one aborigine who had any true belief in a Supreme Being". On cross-examination, they always said that they had got their information from a missionary or other resident. Black Andy was not alluded to by Mr. Mann, who regarded all these native religious ideas as filtrations from European sources. Mr. Palmer, on the other hand, corroborated Mr. Manning, who repeated the expression of his convictions.[2] Such, then, is the perplexed condition of the evidence.

[1] Howitt, *J. A. I.*, xiii. 193.

[2] Mr. Mann told a story of native magic, viewed by himself, which might rouse scepticism among persons not familiar with what these conjurers can do.

It may be urged that the secrecy and timidity of Mr. Manning's informants, corresponding with Mr. Howitt's experience, makes for the affirmative side; that, in 1845, when Mr. Manning made his notes, missionaries were scarce, and that a native "cross-examined" by the sceptical and jovial Mr. Mann, would probably not contradict. (Lubbock, *O. of C.*, p. 4.) Confidence is only won by sympathy, and one inquirer will get authentic legends and folk-lore from a Celt, while another of the ordinary English type will totally fail. On this point Mr. Manning says: "Sceptics should consider how easy it might be for intelligent men to pass almost a life-time among the blacks in any quarter of this continent without securing the confidence even of the best of the natives around them, through whom they might possibly become acquainted with their religious secrets, secrets which they dare not reveal to their own women at all, nor to their adult youths until the latter have been sworn to reticence under that terrifiying ceremony which my notes describe". In the same way Mrs. Langloh Parker found that an European neighbour would ask, "but have the blacks any legends?" and we have cited Mr. Hartt on the difficulty of securing legends on the Amazon, while Mr. Sproat had to live long among, and become very intimate with, the tribes of British Columbia, before he could get any information about their beliefs. Thus, the present writer is disinclined to believe that the intelligence offered to Mr. Manning with shy secrecy in 1845 was wholly a native copy of recently acquired hints on religion derived from Europeans, especially as Mr.

Howitt, who had lived long among the Kurnai, and had written copiously on them, knew nothing of their religion, before, about 1882, he was initiated and admitted to the knowledge like that of Mr. Manning in 1845 The theory of borrowing is also checked by the closely analogous savage beliefs reported from North America before a single missionary had arrived, and from Africa. For the Australian, African and American ideas have a common point of contact, not easily to be explained as deduced from Christianity.

According, then, to Mr. Manning, the natives believed in a being called Boyma, who dwells in heaven, "immovably fixed in a crystal rock, with only the upper half of a supernatural body visible". Now, about 1880, a native described Baiame to Mr. Howitt as "a very great old man with a beard," and with crystal pillars growing out of his shoulders which prop up a supernal sky. This vision of Baiame was seen by the native, apparently as a result of the world-wide practice of crystal-gazing.[1] Mr. Tylor suspects "the old man with the beard" as derived from Christian artistic representations, but old men are notoriously the most venerated objects among the aborigines. Turning now to Mrs. Langloh Parker's *More Australian Legendary Tales* (p. 90), we find Byamee "fixed to the crystal rock on which he sat in Bullimah" (Paradise). Are we to suppose that some savage caught at Christian teaching, added this feature of the crystal rock from "the glassy sea" of the Apocalpyse, or from the great white throne, and succeeded in securing wide acceptance and long

[1] *J. A. I.*, xvi. p. 49, 50.

persistence for a notion borrowed from Europeans? Is it likely that the chief opponents of Christianity everywhere, the Wirreenuns or sorcerers, would catch at the idea, introduce it into the conservative ritual of the Mysteries, and conceal it from women and children who are as open as adults to missionary influence? Yet from native women and children the belief is certainly concealed.

Mr. Manning, who prejudices his own case by speaking of Boyma as "the Almighty," next introduces us to a "Son of God" equal to the father as touching his omniscience, and otherwise but slightly inferior. Mr. Eyre had already reported on the unborn sons of Noorele, "there is no mother". The son of Boyma's name is Grogoragally. He watches over conduct, and takes the good to Ballima (Bullimah in Mrs. Langloh Parker), the bad to Oorooma, the place of fire (*gumby*). Mr. Eyre had attested similar ideas of future life of the souls with Noorele. (Eyre, ii. 357.) In Mrs. Langloh Parker's book a Messenger is called "the All-seeing Spirit," apparently identical with her Wallahgooroonbooan, whose voice is heard in the noise of the *tundun*, or bull-roarer, used in the Mysteries.[1] Grogoragally is unborn of any mother. He is represented by Mr. Manning as a mediator between Boyma and the race of men. Here our belief is apt to break down, and most people will think that Black Andy was a well-instructed Christian catechumen. This occurred to Mr. Manning, who put it plainly to Andy. He replied that the existence of names in the native language for the

[1] *More Legendary Tales*, p. 86.

sacred persons and places proved that they were not of European origin. "White fellow no call budgery place (paradise) 'Ballima,' or other place 'Oorooma,' nor God 'Boyma,' nor Son 'Grogoragally,' only we black fellow think and call them that way in our own language, before white fellow came into the country." A son or deputy of the chief divine being is, in fact, found among the Kurnai and in other tribes. He directs the mysteries. Here, then, Andy is backed by Mr. Howitt's aboriginal friends. Their deity sanctioned morality "before the white men came to Melbourne" (1835) and was called "Our Father" at the same date.[1] Several old men insisted on this, as a matter of their own knowledge. They were initiated before the arrival of Europeans. Archdeacon Günther received the same statements from old aborigines, and Mr. Palmer, speaking of other notions of tribes of the North, is perfectly satisfied that none of their ideas were derived from the whites.[2] In any case, Black Andy's intelligence and logic are far beyond what most persons attribute to his race. If we disbelieve him, it must be on the score, I think, that he consciously added European ideas to names of native origin. On the other hand, analogous ideas, not made so startling as in Mr. Manning's Christian terminology, are found in many parts of Australia.

Mr. Manning next cites Moodgeegally, the first man, immortal, a Culture Hero, and a messenger of Boyma's. There are a kind of rather mediæval fiends, Waramolong, who punish the wicked (murderers, liars and breakers of marriage laws) in Gumby. Women do not

[1] *J. A. I.*, xiii. p. 192, 193. [2] *Op. cit.*, p. 290.

go to Ballima, Boyma being celibate, and women know nothing of all these mysteries ; certainly this secrecy is not an idea of Christian origin. If women get at the secret, the whole race must be exterminated, men going mad and slaying each other. This notion we shall see is corroborated. But if missionaries taught the ideas, women must know all about them already. Mr. Manning's information was confirmed by a black from 300 miles away, who called Grogoragally by the name of Boymagela. There are no prayers, except for the dead at burial: corroborated by Mrs. Langloh Parker's beautiful Legend of Eerin. "Byamee," the mourners cry, "let in the spirit of Eerin to Bullimah. Save him from Eleänbah wundah, abode of the wicked. For Eerin was faithful on earth, faithful to the laws you left us!"[1] The creed is taught to boys when initiated, with a hymn which Mr. Manning's informant dared not to reveal. He said angrily that Mr. Manning already knew more than any other white man. Now, to invent a hymn could not have been beyond the powers of this remarkable savage, Black Andy. The "Sons" of Baiame answer, we have seen, to those ascribed to Noorele, in Mr. Eyre's book. They also correspond to Daramulun where he is regarded as the son of Baiame, while the Culture Hero, Moodgeegally, founder of the Mysteries, answers to Tundun, among the Kurnai.[2] We have, too, in Australia, Dawed, a subordinate where Mangarrah is the Maker in the Larrakeah tribe.[3] In some cases, responsibility for evil, pain, and punishment, are shifted from the good Maker on to the

[1] *More Australian Tales*, p. 96. [2] Howitt, *J. A. I.*, 1885, p. 313.
[3] *J. A. I.*, Nov., 1894, p. 191.

shoulders of his subordinate. This is the case, in early Virginia, with Okeus, the subordinate of the Creator, the good Ahone.[1] We have also, in West Africa, the unpropitiated Nyankupon, with his active subordinate, who has human sacrifices, Bobowissi;[2] and Mulungu, in Central Africa, "possesses many powerful servants, but is himself kept a good deal behind the scenes of earthly affairs, like the gods of Epicurus".[3] The analogy, as to the Son, interpreter of the divine will, in Apollo and Zeus (certainly not of Christian origin !) is worth observing. In the Andaman Islands, Mr. Mann, after long and minute inquiry from the previously uncontaminated natives, reports on an only son of Puluga, "a sort of archangel," who alone is permitted to live with his father, whose orders it is his duty to make known to the *moro-win*, his sisters, ministers of Puluga, the angels, that is, inferior ministers of Puluga's will.[4]

It is for science to determine how far this startling idea of the Son is a natural result of a desire to preserve the remote and somewhat inaccessible and otiose dignity of the Supreme Being from the exertion of activity; and how far it is a savage refraction of missionary teaching, even where it seems to be anterior to missionary influences, which, with these races, have been almost a complete failure. The subject abounds in difficulty, but the sceptic must account for the marvellously rapid acceptance of the European ideas by the most conservative savage class, the doctors

[1] William Strachey, Hakluyt Society, chapter vii., date, 1612.

[2] Ellis, *Religion of the Tshi-speaking Races.*

[3] Macdonald, *Africana*, vol. i. p. 67.

[4] *J. A. I.*, xii. p. 158.

or sorcerers; for the admission of the ideas into the most conservative of savage institutions, the Mysteries; for the extreme reticence about the ideas in presence of the very Europeans from whom they are said to have been derived; and in some cases for the concealment of the ideas from the women, who, one presumes, are as open as the men to missionary teaching. It is very easy to talk of "borrowing," not so easy to explain these points on the borrowing theory, above all, when evidence is frequent that the ideas preceded the arrival of Christian teachers.

On this crucial point, the question of borrowing, I may cite Mr. Mann as to the Andamanese beliefs. Mr. Mann was for eleven years in the islands, and for four years superintended our efforts to "reclaim" some natives. He is well acquainted with the South Andaman dialect, and has made studies of the other forms of the language. This excellent witness writes: "It is extremely improbable that their legends were the result of the teaching of missionaries or others". They have no tradition of any foreign arrivals, and their reputation (undeserved) as cannibals, with their ferocity to invaders, "precludes the belief" that any one ever settled there to convert or instruct them. "Moreover, to regard with suspicion, as some have done, the genuineness of such legends argues ignorance of the fact that numerous other tribes, in equally remote or isolated localities, have, when first discovered, been found to possess similar traditions on the subject under consideration." Further, "I have taken special care not only to obtain my information on each point from those who are considered by their fellow tribesmen as authorities, but [also from those] who, from having had little or no intercourse with other races, were in entire ignorance regarding any save their own legends," which, "they all agree in stating, were handed down to them by their first parent, To-mo, and his immediate descendants".[1] What Mr. Mann says concerning the unborrowed character of Andaman beliefs applies, of course, to the yet more remote and inaccessible natives of Australia.

In what has been, and in what remains to be said, it must be remembered that the higher religious ideas attributed to the Australians are not their only ideas in this matter. Examples of their wild myths have already been offered, they are totemists, too, and fear, though they do not propitiate, ghosts. Vague spirits unattached are also held in dread, and inspire sorcerers and poets,[2] as also does the god Bunjil.[3]

Turning from early accounts of Australian religion, say from 1835 to 1845, we look at the more recent reports. The best evidence is that of Mr. Howitt, who, with Mr. Fison, laid the foundations of serious Australian anthropology in *Kamilaroi and Kurnai* (1881). In 1881, Mr. Howitt, though long and intimately familiar with the tribes of Gippsland, the Yarra, the Upper Murray, the Murumbidgee, and other districts, had found no trace of belief in a moral Supreme

[1] *J. A. I.*, xii. pp. 156, 157.

[2] *Ibid.*, xvi., pp. 330, 331. On Bunjil.

[3] In *Folk-Lore*, December, 1898, will be found an essay, by Mr. Hartland, on my account of Australian gods. Instancing many wild or comic myths (some of them unknown to me when I wrote *The Making of Religion*), Mr. Hartland seems to argue that these destroy the sacredness of other co-existing native beliefs of a higher kind. But, on this theory, what religion *is* sacred? All have contradictory myths. See Introduction.

Being. He was afterwards, however, initiated, or less formally let into the secret, by two members of Brajerak (wild) black fellows, not of the same tribe as the Kurnai. The rites of these former aborigines are called Kuringal. Their supreme being is Daramulun "believed in from the sea-coast across to the northern boundary claimed by the Wolgal, about Yass and Gundagai, and from Omeo to at least as far as the Shoalhaven River. . . . He was not, as it seems to me, everywhere thought to be a malevolent being, but he was dreaded as one who could severely punish the trespasses committed against these tribal ordinances and customs, whose first institution is ascribed to him. . . . It was taught also that Daramulun himself watched the youths from the sky, prompt to punish by sickness or death the breach of his ordinances." These are often mere taboos; an old man said: "I could not eat Emu's eggs. *He* would be very angry, and perhaps I should die." It will hardly be argued that the savages have recently borrowed from missionaries this conception of Daramulun, as the originator and guardian of tribal taboos. Opponents must admit him as of native evolution in that character at least.

The creed of Daramulun is not communicated to women and children. "It is said that the women among the Ngarego and Wolgal knew only that a great being lived beyond the sky, and that he was spoken of by them as Papang (Father). This seemed to me when I first heard it to bear so suspicious a resemblance to a belief derived from the white men, that I thought it necessary to make careful and repeated inquiries. My Ngarego and Wolgal informants, two of them old men, strenuously maintained that it was so before the white men came." They themselves only learned the doctrine when initiated, as boys, by the old men of that distant day. The name Daramulun, was almost whispered to Mr. Howitt, and phrases were used such as "He," "the man," "the name I told you of". The same secrecy was preserved by a Woi-worung man about Bunjil, or Pund-jel, "though he did not show so much reluctance when repeating to me the 'folk-lore' in which the 'Great Spirit' of the Kulin plays a part". "He" was used, or gesture signs were employed by this witness, who told how his grandfather had warned him that Bunjil watched his conduct from a star, "he can see you and all you do down here,"—"before the white men came to Melbourne" (1835).[1]

Are we to believe that this mystic secrecy is kept up, as regards white men, about a Being first heard of from white men? And is it credible that the "old men," the holders of tribal traditions, and the most conservative of mortals, would borrow a new divinity from "the white devils," conceal the doctrine from the women (as accessible to missionary teaching as themselves), adopt the new Being as the founder of the antique mysteries, and introduce him into the central rite? And can the natives have done so steadily, ever since about 1840 at least? To believe all this is to illustrate the credulity of scepticism.

Mr. Howitt adds facts about tribes "from Twofold Bay to Sydney, and as far west, at least, as Hay". Here, too, Daramulun instituted the rites; his voice is

[1] *J. A. I.*, xiii., 1884, pp. 192, 193.

heard in the noise of the whirling *mudji* (bull-roarer). "The muttering of thunder is said to be his voice 'calling to the rain to fall, and make the grass grow up green'." Such are "the very words of Umbara, the minstrel of the tribe".[1]

At the rites, respect for age, for truth, for unprotected women and married women, and other details of sexual morality, is inculcated partly in obscene dances. A magic ceremony, resembling mesmeric passes, and accompanied by the word "Good" (*nga*) is meant to make the boys acceptable to Daramulun. A temporary image of him is made on raised earth (to be destroyed after the rites), his attributes are then explained. "This is the Master (Biamban) who can go anywhere and do anything."[2] An old man is buried, and rises again. "This ceremony is most impressive." "The opportunity is taken of impressing on the mind of youth, in an indelible manner, those rules of conduct which form the moral law of the tribe." "There is clearly a belief in a Great Spirit, or rather an anthropomorphic Supernatural Being, the Master of All, whose abode is above the sky, and to whom are attributed powers of omnipotence and omnipresence, or, at any rate, the power "to do anything and go anywhere. . . . To his direct ordinance are attributed the social and moral laws of the community." Mr. Howitt ends, "I venture to assert that it can no longer be maintained that [the Australians] have no belief which can be called religious—that is, in the sense of beliefs which govern tribal and individual morality under a supernatural sanction".[3] Among the rites is one which

[1] *J. A. I.*, 1884, p. 446. [2] *Op. cit.*, p. 453. [3] *J. A. I.*, 1884, p. 459.

"is said to be intended to teach the boys to speak the straightforward truth, and the *kabos* (mystagogues) thus explain it to them ".[1]

It is, perhaps, unfortunate that Mr. Howitt does not give a full account of what the morality thus sanctioned includes. Respect for age, for truth, for unprotected women, and for nature (as regards avoiding certain unnatural vices) are alone spoken of, in addition to taboos which have no relation to developed morality. Mr. Palmer, in speaking of the morality inculcated in the mysteries of the Northern Australians, adds to the elements of ethics mentioned by Mr. Howitt in the south, the lesson "not to be quarrelsome". To each lad is given, "by one of the elders, advice so kindly, fatherly and impressive, as often to soften the heart, and draw tears from the youth".[2] So far, the morality religiously sanctioned is such as men are likely to evolve, and probably no one will maintain that it must have been borrowed from Europeans. It is argued that the morality is only such as the tribes would naturally develop, mainly in the interests of the old (the ruling class) and of social order (Hartland, *op. cit.*, pp. 316-329). What else did any one ever suppose the *mores* of a people to be, *plus* whatever may be allowed for the effects of kindliness, or love, which certainly exists? I never hinted at morals divinely and supernormally revealed. All morality had been denied to the Australians. Yet in the religious rites they are "taught to speak the straightforward truth"! As regards women, there are parts of Australia where disgusting laxity prevails, except

[1] *J. A. I.*, xiii. 444. [2] *Ibid.*, xiii. 296.

in cases prohibited by the extremely complex rules of forbidden degrees. Such parts are Central Australia and North-west Central Queensland.[1]

Another point in Mr. Howitt's evidence deserves notice. He at first wrote "The Supreme Being who is believed in by all the tribes I refer to here, either as a benevolent or more frequently as a malevolent being, it seems to me represents the defunct headman". We have seen that Mr. Howitt came to regard "malevolence" as merely the punitive aspect of the "Supreme Being". As to the theory that such a being represents a dead headman, no proof is anywhere given that ghosts of headmen are in any way propitiated. Even "corpse-feeding" was represented to Mr. Dawson by intelligent old blacks, as "white fellows' gammon".[2] Mrs. Langloh Parker writes to me that she, when she began to study the blacks, "had, I must allow, a prejudice in favour of Mr. Herbert Spencer's theory—it seemed so rational, but, accepting my savages' evidence, I must discard it". As to "offerings of food to the dead," Mrs. Langloh Parker found that nothing was offered except food "which happened to be in the possession of the corpse," at his decease.

For these reasons it is almost inconceivable that the "Supreme Being" should "represent a dead headman," as to dead men of any sort no tribute is paid. Mr. Howitt himself appears to have abandoned the hypothesis that Daramulun represents a dead headman, for he speaks of him as the "Great Spirit," or rather an "anthropomorphic Supernatural Being".[3] A Great

[1] Spencer and Gillen, and Roth.

[2] Dawson, *Aborigines of Australia.* [3] *J. A. I.*, 1884, p. 458.

Spirit might, conceivably, be developed out of a little spirit, even out of the ghost of a tribesman. But to the conception of a "supernatural anthropomorphic being," the idea of "spirit" is not necessary. Men might imagine such an entity before they had ever dreamed of a ghost.

Having been initiated into the secrets of one set of tribes, Mr. Howitt was enabled to procure admission to those of another group of "clans," the Kurnai. For twenty-five years the Jeraeil, or mystery, had been in abeyance, for they are much in contact with Europeans. The old men, however, declared that they exactly reproduced (with one confessed addition) the ancestral ceremonies. They were glad to do it, for their lads "now paid no attention either to the words of the old men, or to those of the missionaries".[1]

This is just what usually occurs. When we meet a savage tribe we destroy the old bases of its morality and substitute nothing new of our own. "They pay no attention to the words of the missionaries," but loaf, drink and gamble like station hands "knocking down a cheque".

Consequently a rite unknown before the arrival of Europeans is now introduced at the Jeraeil. Swift would have been delighted by this ceremony. "It was thought that the boys, having lived so much among the whites, had become selfish and no longer willing to share that which they obtained by their own exertions, or had given to them, with their friends." The boys were, therefore, placed in a row, and the initiator or mystagogue stooped over the first boy, and, muttering

[1] *J. A. I.*, 1885, p. 304.

some words which I could not catch, he kneaded the lad's stomach with his hands. This he did to each one successively, and by it the Kurnai supposed the "greediness" (πλεονεξία) "of the youth would be expelled".[1]

So far from unselfishness being a doctrine borrowed by the Kurnai from Christians, and introduced into their rites, it is (as we saw in the case of the Arunta of Central Australia) part of the traditional morality —"the good old ancestral virtues," says Mr. Howitt— of the tribes. A special ceremony is needed before unselfishness can be inspired among blacks who have lived much among adherents of the Gospel.

Thus "one satiric touch" seems to demonstrate that the native ethics are not of missionary origin.

After overcoming the scruples of the old men by proving that he really was initiated in the Kuringal, Mr. Howitt was admitted to the central rite of the Kurnai "showing the Grandfather". The essence of it is that the *mystae* have their heads shrouded in blankets. These are snatched off, the initiator points solemnly to the sky with his throwing stick (which propels the spears) and then points to the Tundun, or bull-roarer. This object (ῥόμβος) was also used in the Mysteries of ancient Greece, and is still familiar in the rites of savages in all quarters of the world.

"The ancestral beliefs" are then solemnly revealed. It seems desirable to quote freely the "condensed" version of Mr. Howitt. "Long ago there was a great Being called Mungan-ngaur." Here a note adds that Mungan means "Father," and "ngaur" means "Our".

[1] *Op. cit.*, pp. 310, 311.

"He has no other name among the Kurnai. In other tribes the Great Supreme Being, besides being called 'father,' has a name, for example Bunjil, Baiame, Daramulun." "This Being lived on the earth, and taught the Kurnai . . . all the arts they know. He also gave them the names they bear. Mungan-gnaur had a son" (the Sonship doctrine already noticed by Mr. Manning) "named Tundun (the bull-roarer), who was married, and who is the direct ancestor—the Weintwin or father's father—of the Kurnai. Mungan-ngaur instituted the Jeraeil (mysteries) which was conducted by Tundun, who made the instruments" (a large and a small bull-roarer, as also in Queensland) "which bear the name of himself and his wife.

"Some tribal traitor impiously revealed the secrets of the Jeraeil to women, and thereby brought down the anger of Mungan upon the Kurnai. He sent fire which filled the wide space between earth and sky. Men went mad, and speared one another, fathers killing their children, husbands their wives, and brethren each other." This corroborates Black Andy. "Then the sea rushed over the land, and nearly all mankind were drowned. Those who survived became the ancestors of the Kurnai. . . . Tundun and his wife became porpoises" (as Apollo in the Homeric hymn became a dolphin), "Mungan left the earth, and ascended to the sky, where he still remains."[1]

Here the Son is credited with none of the mediatorial attributes in Mr. Manning's version, but universal massacre, as a consequence of revealing the esoteric doctrine, is common to both accounts.

[1] *Op. cit.*, pp. 313, 314.

Morals are later inculcated.

1. "To listen to and obey the old men.

2. "To share everything they have with their friends

3. "To live peaceably with their friends.

4. "Not to interfere with girls or married women.

5. "To obey the food restrictions until they are released from them by the old men." [As at Eleusis.]

These doctrines, and the whole belief in Mungan-ngaur, "the Kurnai carefully concealed from me," says Mr. Howitt, "until I learned them at the Jeraeil".[1] Mr. Howitt now admits, in so many words, that Mungan-ngaur "is rather the beneficent father, and the kindly though severe headman of the whole tribe . . . than the malevolent wizard". . . . He considers it "perhaps indicative of great antiquity, that this identical belief forms part of the central mysteries of a tribe so isolated as the Kurnai, as well as of those of the tribes which had free communication one with another".

As the morals sanctioned by Mungan-ngaur are simply the extant tribal morals (of which unselfishness is a part, as in Central Australia), there seems no reason to attribute them to missionaries—who are quite unheeded. This part of the evidence may close with a statement of Mr. Howitt's: "Beyond the vaulted sky lies the mysterious home of that great and powerful Being who is Bunjil, Baiame, or Daramulun in different tribal languages, but who in all is known by a name, the equivalent of the only one used by the Kurnai, which is Mungan-ngaur, Our Father".[2]

[1] *Op. cit.*, 321, note 2. [2] *J. A. I.*, xvi. 54.

Other affirmative evidence might be adduced. Mr. Ridley, who wrote primers in the Kamilaroi language as early as in 1856 (using Baiame for God), says: "In every part of Australia where I have conversed with the aborigines, they have a traditional belief in one Supreme Creator," and he wonders, as he well may, at the statement to the contrary in the *Encyclopædia Britannica*, which rests solely on the authority of Dr. Lang, in Queensland. Of names for the Supreme Being, Mr. Ridley gives Baiame, Anamba; in Queensland, Mumbal (Thunder) and, at Twofold Bay, "Dhurumbulum, which signifies, in the Namoi, a sacred staff, originally given by Baiame, and is used as the title of Deity".[1]

By "staff" Mr. Ridley appears to indicate the Tundun, or bull-roarer. This I venture to infer from Mr. Matthews' account of the Wiradthuri (New South Wales) with whom Dhuramoolan is an extinct bugbear, not answering to Tundun among the Kurnai, who is subordinate, as son, to Mungan-ngaur, and is associated with the mystic bull-roarer, as is Gayandi, the voice of the Messenger of Baiame, among Mrs. Langloh Parker's informants.[2] In one tribe, Daramulun used to carry off and eat the initiated boys, till he was stopped and destroyed by Baiame. This myth can hardly exist, one may suppose, among such tribes as consider Daramulun to preside over the mysteries. Living in contact with the Baiame-worshipping Kamilaroi, the Wiradthuri appear to make a jest of the power of Daramulun, who (we have learned) is said to have died, while his "spirit"

[1] *J. A. I.*, ii. (1872), 268, 270. [2] *Ibid.*, xxv. 298.

dwells on high.[1] Mr. Greenway also finds Turramulan to be subordinate to Baiame, who "sees all, and knows all, if not directly, through Turramulan, who presides at the Bora. . . . Turramulan is mediator in all the operations of Baiame upon man, and in all man's transactions with Baiame. Turramulan means "leg on one side only," "one-legged". Here the mediatorial aspect corroborates Mr. Manning's information.[2] I would suggest, *periculo meo*, that there may have been some syncretism, a Baiame-worshipping tribe adopting Daramulun as a subordinate and mediator; or Baiame may have ousted Daramulun, as Zeus did Cronos.

Mr. Ridley goes on to observe that about eighteen years ago (that is, in 1854) he asked intelligent blacks "if they knew Baiame". The answer was: "Kamil zaia zummi Baiame, zaia winuzgulda," "I have not seen Baiame, I have heard or perceived him". The same identical answer was given in 1872 "by a man to whom I had never before spoken". "If asked who made the sky, the earth, the animals and man, they always answer 'Baiame'." Varieties of opinion as to a future life exist. All go to Baiame, or only the good (the bad dying eternally), or they change into birds![3]

Turning to North-west Central Queensland we find Dr. Roth (who knows the language and is partly initiated) giving Mul-ka-ri as "a benevolent, omnipresent, supernatural being. Anything incomprehensible." He offers a sentence: "Mulkari tikkara ena" = "Lord (who dwellest) among the sky". Again:

[1] *J. A. I.*, xii. 194. [2] *Ibid.*, vii. 242. [3] *Ibid.*, ii. 269.

"Mulkari is the supernatural power who makes everything which the blacks cannot otherwise account for; he is a good, beneficent person, and never kills any one". He initiates medicine men. His home is in the skies. He once lived on earth, and there was a culture-hero, inventing magic and spells. That Mulkari is an ancestral ghost as well as a beneficent Maker I deem unlikely, as no honours are paid to the dead. "Not in any way to refer to the dead appears to be an universal rule among all these tribes."[1] Mulkari has a malignant opposite or counterpart.

Nothing is said by Dr. Roth as to inculcation of these doctrines at the Mysteries, nor do Messrs. Spencer and Gillen allude to any such being in their accounts of Central Australian rites, if we except the "self-existing" "out of nothing" Ungambikula, sky-dwellers.

One rite "is supposed to make the men who pass through it more kindly," we are not told why.[2] We have also an allusion to "the great spirit Twangirika," whose voice (the women are told) is heard in the noise of the bull-roarer.[3] "The belief is fundamentally the same as that found in all Australian tribes," write the authors, in a note citing Tundun and Daramulun. But they do not tell us whether the Arunta belief includes the sanction, by Twangirika, of morality. If it does not, have the Central Australians never developed the idea, or have they lost it? They have had quite as much experience of white men (or rather much more) than the believers in Baiame or Bunjil, "before the white men came to Melbourne," and, if one set of

[1] Roth, pp. 14, 36, 116, 153, 158, 165.

[2] Spencer and Gillen, p. 369. [3] *Ibid.*, p. 246.

tribes borrowed ideas from whites, why did not the other?

The evidence here collected is not exhaustive. We might refer to Pirnmeheal, a good being, whom the blacks loved before they were taught by missionaries to fear him.[1] Mr. Dawson took all conceivable pains to get authentic information, and to ascertain whether the belief in Pirnmeheal was pre-European. He thinks it was original. The idea of "god-borrowing" is repudiated by Manning, Günther, Ridley, Greenway, Palmer, Mrs. Langloh Parker and others, speaking for trained observers and (in several cases) for linguists, studying the natives on the spot, since 1845. It is thought highly improbable by Mr. Hale (1840). It is rejected by Waitz-Gerland, speaking for studious science in Europe. Mr. Howitt, beginning with distrust, seems now to regard the beliefs described as of native origin. On the other hand we have Mr. Mann, who has been cited, and the great authority of Mr. E. B. Tylor, who, however, has still to reply to the arguments in favour of the native origin of the beliefs which I have ventured to offer. Such arguments are the occurrence of Baiame before the arrival of missionaries; the secrecy, as regards Europeans, about ideas derived (Mr. Tylor thinks) from Europeans; the ignorance of the women on these heads; the notorious conservatism of the "doctors" who promulgate the creed as to ritual and dogma, and the other considerations which have been fully stated. In the meanwhile I venture to think, subject to correction, that, while Black Andy may have exaggerated, or Mr. Manning

[1] Dawson, *The Australian Aborigines.*

may have coloured his evidence by Christian terminology, and while mythical accretions on a religious belief are numerous, yet the lowest known human race has attained a religious conception very far above what savages are usually credited with, and has not done so by way of the "ghost-theory" of the anthropologists. In this creed sacrifice and ghost-worship are absent.[1]

It has seemed worth while to devote space and attention to the Australian beliefs, because the vast continent contains the most archaic and backward of existing races. We may not yet have a sufficient collection of facts microscopically criticised, but the evidence here presented seems deserving of attention. About the still more archaic but extinct Tasmanians and their religion, evidence is too scanty, too casual, and too conflicting for our purpose.[2]

[1] These Australian gods are confusing.

1. Daramulun is supreme among the Coast Murring. *J. A. I.*, xiv. 432-459.

2. Baiame is supreme, Daramulun is an extinct bugbear, among the Wiradthuri. *J. A. I.*, xxv. 298.

3. Baiame is supreme, Daramulun is "mediator," among the Kamilaroi. *J. A. I.*, vii. 242.

[2] See Ling Roth's *Tasmanians.*

CHAPTER XIII.

GODS OF THE LOWEST RACES.

Bushmen gods—Cagn, the grasshopper?—Hottentot gods—"Wounded knee," a dead sorcerer—Melanesian gods—Qat and the spider—Aht and Maori beasts-gods and men-gods — Samoan form of animal-gods — One god incarnate in many animal shapes—One for each clan—They punish the eating of certain animals.

PASSING from Australia to Africa, we find few races less advanced than the Bushmen (*Sa-n*, "settlers," in Nama). Whatever view may be taken of the past history of the Bushmen of South Africa, it is certain that at present they are a race on a very low level of development. "Even the Hottentots," according to Dr. Bleek, "exceed the Bushmen in civilisation and political organisation."[1]

Before investigating the religious myths of the Bushmen, it must be repeated that, as usual, their religion is on a far higher level than their mythology. The conception of invisible or extra-natural powers, which they entertain and express in moments of earnest need, is all unlike the tales which they tell about their own

[1] See Waitz, *Anthrop. Nat. Völk*, ii. 323-329. **Our main authorities at present for Bushman myths are contained in *A Brief Account of Bushman Folk-lore*, Bleek, London, 1875; and in *A Glimpse into the Mythology of the Maluti Bushmen*, by Mr. Orpen, Chief Magistrate, St. John's Territory, *Cape Monthly Magazine*, July, 1874. Some information may also be gleaned from the *South African Folk-lore Journal*, 1879-80.**

gods, if gods such mythical beings may be called. Thus Livingstone says: "On questioning intelligent men among the Bakwains as to their former knowledge of good and evil, of God and the future state, they have scouted the idea of any of them ever having been without a tolerably clear conception on all these subjects".[1] Their ideas of sin were the same as Livingstone's, except about polygamy, and apparently murder. Probably there were other trifling discrepancies. But "they spoke in the same way of the direct influence exercised by God in giving rain in answer to the prayers of the rain-makers, and in granting deliverance in times of danger, as they do now, before they ever heard of white men". This was to be expected. In short, the religion of savages, in its childlike and hopeful dependence on an invisible friend or friends, in its hope of moving him (or them) by prayer, in its belief that he (or they) "make for righteousness," is absolutely human. On the other side, as in the myths of Greece or India, stand the absurd and profane anecdotes of the gods.

We now turn to a Bushman's account of the religious myths of his tribe. Shortly after the affair of Langalibalele, Mr. Orpen had occasion to examine an unknown part of the Maluti range, the highest mountains in South Africa. He engaged a scout named Qing, son of a chief of an almost exterminated clan of hill Bushmen. He was now huntsman to King Nqusha, Morosi's son, on the Orange River, and *had never seen a white man, except fighting*. Thus Qing's evidence could not be much affected by European

[1] *Missionary Travels*, p. 158.

communications. Mr. Orpen secured the services of Qing, who was a young man and a mighty hunter. By inviting him to explain the wall-pictures in caves, Mr. Orpen led him on to give an account of Cagn, the chief mythical being in Bushman religion. "Cagn made all things, and we pray to him," said Qing. "At first he was very good and nice, but he got spoilt through fighting so many things." "The prayer uttered by Qing, 'in a low imploring voice,' ran thus: 'O Cagn, O Cagn, are we not your children? Do you not see our hunger? Give us food.'" Where Cagn is Qing did not know, "but the elands know. Have you not hunted and heard his cry when the elands suddenly run to his call?"[1] Now comes in myth. Cagn has a wife called Coti. How came he into the world? "Perhaps with those who brought the sun; . . . only the initiated men of that dance know these things."[2] Cagn had two sons, Cogaz and Gcwi. He and they were "great chiefs," but used stone-pointed digging sticks to grub up edible roots! Cagn's wife brought forth a fawn, and, like Cronus when Rhea presented him with a foal, Cagn was put to it to know the nature and future fortunes of this child of his. To penetrate the future he employed the ordinary native charms and sorcery. The remainder of the myth accounts for the origin of elands and for their inconvenient wildness. A daughter of Cagn's married "snakes who were also men," the

[1] Another Bushman prayer, a touching appeal, is given in Alexander's *Expedition*, ii. 125, and a Khoi-Khoi hymn of prayer is in Hahn, pp. 56, 57.

[2] *Cf. Custom and Myth*, pp. 41, 42. It appears that the Bushmen, like the Egyptians and Greeks, hand down myths through esoteric societies, with dramatic mysteries.

eternal confusion of savage thought. These snakes became the people of Cagn. Cagn had a tooth which was "great medicine"; his force resided in it, and he lent it to people whom he favoured. The birds (as in Odin's case) were his messengers, and brought him news of all that happened at a distance.[1] He could turn his sandals and clubs into dogs, and set them at his enemies. The baboons were once men, but they offended Cagn, and sang a song with the burden, "Cagn thinks he is clever"; so he drove them into desolate places, and they are accursed till this day. His strong point was his collection of charms, which, like other Bushmen and Hottentots, he kept "in his belt". He could, and did, assume animal shapes; for example, that of a bull-eland. The thorns were once people, and killed Cagn, and the ants ate him, but his bones were collected and he was revived. It was formerly said that when men died they went to Cagn, but it has been denied by later Bushmen sceptics.

Such is Qing's account of Cagn, and Cagn in myth is plainly but a successful and idealised medicine-man whose charms actually work. Dr. Bleek identifies his name with that of the mantis insect. This insect is the chief mythological personage of the Bushmen of the western province. |*Kággen* his name is written. Dr. Bleek knew of no prayer to the mantis, but was acquainted with addresses to the sun, moon and stars. If Dr. Bleek's identification is correct, the Cagn of

[1] Compare with the separable vigour of Cagn, residing in his tooth, the European and Egyptian examples of a similar myth—the lock of hair of Minos, the hair of Samson—in introduction to Mrs. Hunt's Grimm's *Household Stories*, p. lxxv.

Qing is at once human and a sort of grasshopper, just as Pund-jel was half human, half eagle-hawk.

"The most prominent of the mythological figures," says Dr. Bleek, speaking of the Bushmen, "is the mantis." His proper name is |Kaggẹn, but if we call him Cagn, the interests of science will not seriously suffer. His wife is the "Dasse Hyrax". Their adopted daughter is the porcupine, daughter of ||*Khwái hemm*, the All-devourer. Like Cronus, and many other mythological persons, the All-devourer has the knack of swallowing all and sundry, and disgorging them alive. Dr. Bleek offers us but a wandering and disjointed account of the mantis or Cagn, who is frequently defeated by other animals, such as the suricat. Cagn has one point at least in common with Zeus. As Zeus was swallowed and disgorged by Cronus, so was Cagn by ||*Khwái hemm.* As Indra once entered into the body of a cow, so did Cagn enter into the body of an elephant. Dr. Bleek did not find that the mantis was prayed to, as Cagn was by Qing. The moon (like sun and stars) is, however, prayed to, and "the moon belongs to the mantis," who, indeed, made it out of his old shoe! The chameleon is prayed to for rain on occasion, and successfully.

The peculiarity of Bushman mythology is the almost absolute predominance of animals. Except "an old woman," who appears now and then in these incoherent legends, their myths have scarcely one human figure to show. Now, whether the Bushmen be deeply degenerate from a past civilisation or not, it is certain that their myths are based on their actual condition of thought, unless we prefer to say that their intellectual condition is derived from their myths. We have already derived the constant presence and personal action of animals in myth from that savage condition of the mind in which "all things, animate or inanimate, human, animal, vegetable or inorganic, seem on the same level of life, passion and reason" (chap. iii.). Now, there can be no doubt that, whether the Bushman mind has descended to this stage or not, in this stage it actually dwells at present. As examples we may select the following from Dr. Bleek's *Bushman Folk-lore. Díalkwãin* told how the death of his own wife was "foretold by the springbok and the gemsbok". Again, for examples of living belief in community of nature with animals, Díalkwãin mentioned an old woman, a relation and friend of his own, who had the power "of turning herself into a lioness". Another Bushman, Kábbo, retaining, doubtless, his wide-awake mental condition in his sleep, "dreamed of lions which talked". Another informant explained that lions talk like men "by putting their tails in their mouth".

This would have pleased Sydney Smith, who thought that "if lions would meet and growl out their observations to each other," they might sensibly improve in culture. Again, "all things that belong to the mantis can talk," and most things do belong to that famous being. In "News from Zululand,"[1] in a myth of the battle of Isandlwana, a blue-buck turns into a young man and attacks the British. These and other examples demonstrate that the belief in the personal

[1] *Folk-lore Journal of South Africa*, i. iv. 83.

and human character and attributes of animals still prevails in South Africa. From that living belief we derive the personal and human character and attributes of animals, which, remarkable in all mythologies, is perhaps specially prominent in the myths of the Bushmen.

Though Bushman myth is only known to us in its outlines, and is apparently gifted with even more than the due quantity of incoherence, it is perhaps plain that animals are the chief figures in this African lore, and that these Bushmen gods, if ever further developed, will retain many traces of their animal ancestry.

From the Bushmen we may turn to their near neighbours, the Hottentots or Khoi-Khoi. Their religious myths have been closely examined in Dr. Hahn's *Tsuni Goam, the Supreme Being of the Khoi-Khoi*. Though Dr. Hahn's conclusions as to the origin of Hottentot myth differ entirely from our own, his collection and critical study of materials, of oral traditions, and of the records left by old travellers are invaluable. The early European settlers at the Cape found the Khoi-Khoi, that is, "The Men," a yellowish race of people, who possessed large herds of cattle, sheep and goats.[1] The Khoi-Khoi, as nomad cattle and sheep farmers, are on a much higher level of culture than the Bushmen, who are hunters.[2] The languages of the two peoples leave "no more doubt as to their primitive relationship" (p. 7). The wealth of the Khoi-Khoi was considerable and unequally distributed, a respectable proof of nascent civilisation. The

[1] *Op. cit.*, pp. 1, 32. [2] *Ibid.*, p. 5.

rich man was called *gou aob*, that is "fat". In the same way the early Greeks called the wealthy "*ἄνδρες τῶν παχέων*".[1] As the rich man could afford many wives (which gives him a kind of "commendation" over men to whom he allots his daughters), he "gradually rose to the station of a chief".[2] In domestic relations, Khoi-Khoi society is "matriarchal" (pp. 19-21).[3] All the sons are called after the mother, the daughters after the father. Among the arts, pottery and mat-making, metallurgy and tool-making are of ancient date. A past stone age is indicated by the use of quartz knives in sacrifice and circumcision. In Khoi-Khoi society seers and prophets were "the greatest and most respected old men of the clan" (p. 24). The Khoi-Khoi of to-day have adopted a number of Indo-European beliefs and customs, and "the Christian ideas introduced by missionaries have amalgamated . . . with the national religious ideas and mythologies," for which reasons Dr. Hahn omits many legends which, though possibly genuine, might seem imported (pp. 30, 31).

A brief historical abstract of what was known to old travellers of Khoi-Khoi religion must now be compiled from the work of Dr. Hahn.

In 1655 Corporal Müller found adoration paid to great stones on the side of the paths. The worshippers pointed upwards and said *Hette hie*, probably "Heitsi Eibib," the name of a Khoi-Khoi extra-natural being. It appears (p. 37) that Heitsi Eibib "has changed

[1] Herodotus, v. 30. [2] *Op. cit.*, p. 16.

[3] But speaking of the wife, Kolb calls "the poor wretch" a "drudge, exposed to the insults of her children".—English transl., p. 162.

names" in parts of South Africa, and what was his worship is now offered "to ǀ Garubeb, or Tsui i Goab".

In 1671 Dapper found that the Khoi-Khoi "believe there is one who sends rain on earth; . . . they also believe that they themselves can make rain and prevent the wind from blowing". Worship of the moon and of "erected stones" is also noticed. In 1691 Nicolas Witsen heard that the Khoi-Khoi adored a god which Dr. Hahn (p. 91) supposes to have been "a peculiar-shaped stone-fetish," such as the Basutos worship and spit at. Witsen found that the "god" was daubed with red earth, like the Dionysi in Greece. About 1705 Valentyn gathered that the people believed in "a great chief who dwells on high," and a devil; "but in carefully examining this, it is nothing else but their *somsomas* and *spectres*" (p. 38). We need not accept that opinion. The worship of a "great chief" is mentioned again in 1868. In 1719 Peter Kolb, the German Magister, published his account of the Hottentots, which has been done into English.[1] Kolb gives Gounja Gounja, or Gounja Ticqvoa, as the divine name; "they say he is a good man, who does nobody any hurt, . . . and that he dwells far above the moon".[2] This corresponds to the Australian Pirnmeheal. Kolb also noted propitiation of an evil power. He observed that the Khoi-Khoi worship the mantis insect, which, as we have seen, is the chief mythical character among the Bushmen.[3] Dr. Hahn remarks, "Strangely enough the Namaquas also call it ǀ Gaunab, as they call the enemy of Tsui i

[1] Second edition, London, 1738. [2] Engl. transl., i. 95.

[3] Engl. transl., i. 97, gives a picture of Khoi-Khoi adoring the mantis.

Goab ".[1] In Kolb's time, as now, the rites of the Khoi (except, apparently, their worship at dawn) were performed beside cairns of stones. If we may credit Kolb, the Khoi-Khoi are not only most fanatical adorers of the mantis, but "pay a religious veneration to their saints and men of renown departed". Thunberg (1792) noticed cairn-worship and heard of mantis-worship. In 1803 Lichtenstein saw cairn-worship. With the beginning of the present century we find in Appleyard, Ebner and others Khoi-Khoi names for a god, which are translated "Sore-Knee" or "Wounded-Knee". This title is explained as originally the name of a "doctor or sorcerer" of repute, "invoked even after death," and finally converted into a deity. His enemy is Gaunab, an evil being, and he is worshipped at the cairns, below which he is believed to be buried.[2] About 1842 Knudsen considered that the Khoi-Khoi believed in a dead medicine-man, Heitsi Eibib, who could make rivers roll back their waves, and then walk over safely, as in the *märchen* of most peoples. He was also, like Odin, a "shape-shifter," and he died several times and came to life again.[3] Thus the numerous graves of Heitsi Eibib are explained by his numerous deaths. In Egypt the numerous graves of Osiris were explained by the story that he was mutilated, and each limb buried in a different place. Probably both the Hottentot and the Egyptian legend were invented to account for the many worshipped cairns attributed to the same corpse.

[1] Page 42; compare pp. 92, 125.

[2] Alexander, *Expedition*, i. 166; Hahn, *op. cit.*, pp. 69, 50, where Moffat is quoted.

[3] Hahn, p. 56.

We now reach the myths of Heitsi Eibib and Tsui ||Goab collected by Dr. Hahn himself. According to the evidence of Dr. Hahn's own eyes, the working religion of the Khoi-Khoi is "a firm belief in sorcery and the arts of living medicine-men on the one hand, and, on the other, belief in and adoration of the powers of the dead" (pp. 81, 82, 112, 113). Our author tells us that he met in the wilds a woman of the "fat" or wealthy class going to pray at the grave and to the manes of her own father. "We Khoi-Khoi always, if we are in trouble, go and pray at the graves of our grandparents and ancestors." They also sing rude epic verses, accompanied by the dance in honour of men distinguished in the late Namaqua and Damara war. Now it is alleged by Dr. Hahn that prayers are offered at the graves of Heitsi Eibib and Tsui Goab, as at those of ancestors lately dead, and Heitsi Eibib and Tsui Goab within living memory were honoured by song and dance, exactly like the braves of the Damara war.

The obvious and natural inference is that Heitsi Eibib and Tsui Goab were and are regarded by their worshippers as departed but still helpful ancestral warriors or medicine-men. We need not hold that they ever were actual living men; they may be merely idealised figures of Khoi-Khoi wisdom and valour. Here, as elsewhere, Animism, ghost-worship, is potent, and, in proportion, theism declines.

Here Dr. Hahn offers a different explanation, founded on etymological conjecture and a philosophy of religion. According to him, the name of Tsui Goab originally meant, not wounded knee, but red dawn. The dawn was worshipped as a symbol or suggestion of the infinite, and only by forgetfulness and false interpretation of the original word did the Khoi-Khoi fall from a kind of pure theosophy to adoration of a presumed dead medicine-man. As Dr. Hahn's ingenious hypothesis has been already examined by us,[1] it is unnecessary again to discuss the philological basis of his argument.

Dr. Hahn not only heard simple and affecting prayers addressed to Tsui Goab, but learned from native informants that the god had been a chief, a warrior, wounded in his knee in battle with Gaunab, another chief, and that he had prophetic powers. He still watches the ways of men (p. 62) and punishes guilt. Universal testimony was given to the effect that Heitsi Eibib also had been a chief from the East, a prophet and a warrior. He apportioned, by blessings and curses, their present habits to many of the animals. Like Odin, he was a "shape-shifter," possessing the medicine-man's invariable power of taking all manner of forms. He was on one occasion born of a cow, which reminds us of a myth of Indra. By another account he was born of a virgin who tasted a certain kind of grass. This legend is of wonderfully wide diffusion among savage and semi-civilised races.[2] The tales about Tsui Goab and Heitsi Eibib are chiefly narratives of combats with animals and with the evil power in a nascent dualism, Gaunab, "at first a ghost," according to Hahn (p. 85), or "certainly nobody else

[1] *Custom and Myth*, pp. 197-211.

[2] *Le Fils de la Vierge*, H. de Charency, Havre, 1879. A tale of incest by Heitsi Eibib, may be compared with another in Muir's *Sanskrit Texts*, iv. 39.

but the Night" (pp. 125, 126). Here there is some inconsistency. If we regard the good power, Tsui Goab, as the Red Dawn, we are bound to think the evil power, Gaunab, a name for the Night. But Dr. Hahn's other hypothesis, that the evil power was originally a malevolent ghost, seems no less plausible. In either case, we have here an example of the constant mythical dualism which gives the comparatively good being his perpetual antagonist—the Loki to his Odin, the crow to his eagle-hawk. In brief, Hottentot myth is pretty plainly a reflection of Hottentot general ideas about ancestor worship, ghosts, sorcerers and magicians, while, in their *religious* aspect, Heitsi Eibib or Tsui Goab are guardians of life and of morality, fathers and friends.

A description of barbarous beliefs not less scholarly and careful than that compiled by Dr. Hahn has been published by the Rev. R. H. Codrington.[1] Mr. Codrington has studied the myths of the Papuans and other natives of the Melanesian group, especially in the Solomon Islands and Banks Island. These peoples are by no means in the lowest grade of culture ; they are traders in their way, builders of canoes and houses, and their society is interpenetrated by a kind of mystic hierarchy, a religious *Camorra*. The Banks Islanders[2] recognise two sorts of intelligent extra-natural beings—the spirits of the dead and powers which have never been human. The former are *Tamate*, the latter *Vui*—ghosts and *genii*, we might call them. Vuis are classed by Mr. Codrington as "corporeal" and

[1] *Journal Anthrop. Inst.*, February, 1881.
[2] *Op. cit.*, p. 267.

"incorporeal," but he thinks the corporeal Vuis have not *human* bodies. Among corporeal Vuis the chief are the beings nearest to gods in Melanesian myths—the half god, half "culture-hero," I Qat, his eleven brothers, and his familiar and assistant, Marawa. These were members of a race anterior to that of the men of to-day, and they dwelt in Vanua Levu. Though now passed away from the eyes of mortals, they are still invoked in prayer. The following appeal by a voyaging Banks Islander resembles the cry of the shipwrecked Odysseus to the friendly river:—

"Qat! Marawa! look down upon us; smooth the sea for us two, that I may go safely on the sea. Beat down for me the crests of the tide-rip; let the tide-rip settle down away from me; beat it down level that it may sink and roll away, and I may come to a quiet landing-place."

Compare the prayer of Odysseus:—

"'Hear me, O king, whosoever thou art; unto thee am I come as to one to whom prayer is made, while I flee the rebukes of Poseidon from the deep. . . .' So spake he, and the god straightway stayed his stream and withheld his waves, and made the water smooth before him, and brought him safely to the mouth of the river."

But for Qat's supernatural power and creative exploits,[1] "there would be little indeed to show him other than a man". He answers almost precisely to Maui, the "the culture-hero" of New Zealand. Qat's mother either was, or, like Niobe, became a stone.

[1] See "Savage Myths of the Origin of Things".

He was the eldest (unlike Maui) of twelve brothers, among whom were Tongaro the Wise and Tongaro the Fool. The brothers were killed by an evil gluttonous power like Kwai Hemm and put in a food chest. Qat killed the foe and revived his brothers, as the sons of Cronus came forth alive from their father's maw. His great foe—for of course he had a foe—was Qasavara, whom he destroyed by dashing him against the solid firmament of sky. Qasavara is now a stone (like the serpent displayed by Zeus at Aulis [1]), on which sacrifices are made. Qat's chief friend is Marawa, a spider, or a Vui in the shape of a spider. The divine mythology of the Melanesians, as far as it has been recovered, is meagre. We only see members of a previous race, "magnified non-natural men," with a friendly insect working miracles and achieving rather incoherent adventures.

Much on the same footing of civilisation as the Melanesians were the natives of Tonga in the first decade of this century. The Tongan religious beliefs were nearly akin to the ideas of the Samoans and of the Solomon Islanders. In place of Vuis they spoke of Hotooas (Atuas), and like the Vuis, those spiritual beings have either been purely spiritual from the beginning or have been incarnate in humanity and are now ghosts, but ghosts enjoying many of the privileges of gods. All men, however, have not souls capable of a separate existence, only the *Egi* or nobles, possess a spiritual part, which goes to Bolotoo, the land of gods and ghosts, after death, and enjoys "power similar to that of the original gods, but less".

[1] *Iliad*, ii. 315-318.

It is open to philosophers of Mr. Herbert Spencer's school to argue that the "original gods" were once ghosts like the others, but this was not the opinion of the Tongans. They have a supreme Creator, who alone receives no sacrifice.[1] Both sorts of gods appear occasionally to mankind—the primitive deities particularly affect the forms of "lizards, porpoises and a species of water-snake, hence those animals are much respected".[2] Whether each stock of Tongans had its own animal incarnation of its special god does not appear from Mariner's narrative. The gods took human morality under their special protection, punishing the evil and rewarding the good, in this life only, not in the land of the dead. When the comfortable doctrine of eternal punishment was expounded to the Tongans by Mariner, the poor heathen merely remarked that it "was very bad indeed for the Papalangies" or foreigners. Their untutored minds, in their pagan darkness, had dreamed of no such thing. The Tongans themselves are descended from some gods who set forth on a voyage of discovery out of Bolotoo. Landing on Tonga, these adventurers were much pleased with the island, and determined to stay there; but in a few days certain of them died. They had left the deathless coasts for a world where death is native, and, as they had eaten of the food of the new realm, they would never escape the condition of mortality. This has been remarked as a widespread belief. Persephone became enthralled to Hades after tasting the mystic pomegranate of the underworld.

[1] Mariner, ii. 205.

[2] Mariner's *Tonga Islands*, Edin., 1827, ii. 99-101.

In Samoa Siati may not eat of the god's meat, nor Wainamoinen in Pohjola, nor Thomas the Rhymer in Fairyland. The exploring gods from Bolotoo were in the same way condemned to become mortal and people the world with mortal beings, and all about them should be *méa máma*, subject to decay and death.[1] It is remarkable, if correctly reported, that the secondary gods, or ghosts of nobles, cannot reappear as lizards, porpoises and water-snakes; this is the privilege of the original gods only, and may be an assumption by them of a conceivably totemistic aspect. The nearest approach to the idea of a permanent supreme deity is contained in the name of Táli y Toobo—"wait there, Toobo"—a name which conveys the notion perhaps of permanence or eternity. "He is a great chief from the top of the sky to the bottom of the earth."[2] He is invoked both in war and peace, not locally, but "for the general good of the natives". He is the patron, not of any special stock or family, but of the house in which the royal power is lodged for the time. Alone of gods he is unpropitiated by food or libation, indicating that he is not evolved out of a hungry ghost. Another god, Toobo Toty or Toobo the Mariner, may be a kind of Poseidon. He preserves canoes from perils at sea. On the death of the daughter of Finow, the king in Mariner's time, that monarch was so indignant that he threatened to kill the priest of Toobo Toty. As the god is believed to inspire the priest, this was certainly a feasible way of getting at the god. But Toobo Toty was beforehand with Finow, who died himself before

[1] Mariner, ii. 115. [2] *Ibid.*, ii. 205.

he could carry the war into Bolotoo.[1] This Finow was a sceptic; he allowed that there were gods, because he himself had occasionally been inspired by them; "but what the priests tell us about their power over mankind I believe to be all false". Thus early did the conflict of Church and State declare itself in Tonga. Human sacrifices were a result of priestcraft in Tonga, as in Greece. Even the man set to kill a child of Toobo Toa's was moved by pity, and exclaimed *O iaooé chi vale!* ("poor little innocent!") The priest demanded this sacrifice to allay the wrath of the gods for the slaying of a man in consecrated ground.[2] Such are the religious ideas of Tonga; of their mythology but little has reached us, and that is under suspicion of being coloured by acquaintance with the stories of missionaries.

The Maoris, when first discovered by Europeans, were in a comparatively advanced stage of barbarism. Their society had definite ranks, from that of the Rangatira, the chief with a long pedigree, to the slave. Their religious hymns, of great antiquity, have been collected and translated by Grey, Taylor, Bastian and others. The mere possession of such hymns, accurately preserved for an unknown number of years by oral tradition, proves that the mythical notions of the Maoris have passed through the minds of professed bards and early physical speculators. The verses, as Bastian has observed (*Die Heilige Sage der Polynesier*), display a close parallel to the roughest part of the early Greek cosmogonies, as expounded by Hesiod. Yet in the Maori hymns there are metaphysical ideas

[1] Mariner, i. 307, ii. 107. [2] Compare the ἄγος of the Alcmæonidæ.

and processes which remind one more of Heraclitus than of Hesiod, and perhaps more of Hegel than of either. Whether we are to regard the abstract conceptions or the rude personal myths of gods such as A, the Beyond All, as representing the earlier development of Maori thought, whether one or the other element is borrowed, not original, are questions which theorists of different schools will settle in their own way to their own satisfaction. Some hymns represent the beginning of things from a condition of thought, and Socrates might have said of the Maori poets as he did of Anaxagoras, that compared with other early thinkers, they are " like sober men among drunkards ". Thus one hymn of the origins runs thus :—

From the conception the increase,
From the increase the swelling,
From the swelling the thought,
From the thought the remembrance,
From the remembrance the desire.
The word became fruitful,
It dwelt with the feeble glimmering,
It brought forth Night.

From the nothing the begetting,

. . . .

It produced the atmosphere which is above us.

. . . .

The atmosphere above dwelt with the glowing sky,
Forthwith was produced the sun.
Then the moon sprang forth.
They were thrown up above as the chief eyes of heaven,
Then the heavens became light.

. . . .

The sky which floats above dwelt with Hawaiki,[1]
And produced (*certain islands*).

[1] The islands of Hawaiki, being then the only land known, is put for *Papa*, the earth.

Then follow genealogies of gods, down to the chief in whose family this hymn was traditional.[1]

Other hymns of the same character, full of such metaphysical and abstract conceptions as "the proceeding from the nothing," are quoted at great length.

These extracts are obviously speculative rather than in any sense mythological. The element of myth just shows itself when we are told that the sky dwelt with the earth and produced certain islands. But myth of a familiar character is very fully represented among the Maoris. Their mythical gods, though "mixed up with the spirits of ancestors," are great natural powers, first Heaven and Earth, Rangi and Papa, the parents of all. These are conceived as having originally been united in such a close embrace, the Heaven lying on the Earth, that between their frames all was darkness, and in darkness the younger gods, Atua, O-te-po, their children, were obliged to dwell. These children or younger gods (answering to the Cronidæ) were the god of war (Tumatauenga), the forest-god (Tane Mahuta), in shape a tree, the wind-god (Tawhiri Matea), the gods of cultivated and natural fruits, the god of ocean (Tangaroa). These gods were unable to endure the dungeon and the darkness of their condition, so they consulted together and said: "Let us seek means whereby to destroy Heaven and Earth, or to separate them from each other". The counsel of Tane Mahuta prevailed: "Let one go upwards and become a stranger to us; let the other remain below and be a parent to us". Finally, Tane Mahuta rent asunder Heaven and Earth, pushing Heaven up where he has ever since

[1] Taylor, *New Zealand*, pp. 110-112.

remained. The wind-god followed his father, abode with him in the open spaces of the sky, and thence makes war on the trees of the forest-god, his enemy. Tangaroa went, like Poseidon, to the great deep, and his children, the reptiles and fishes, clove part to the waters, part to the dry land. The war-god, Tŭ, was more of a human being than the other gods, though his "brethren" are plants, fish and reptiles. Still, Tŭ is not precisely the first man of New Zealand.

Though all these mythical beings are in a sense departmental gods, they yield in renown to a later child of their race, Maui, the great culture-hero, who is an advanced form of the culture-heroes, mainly theriomorphic, of the lower races.[1]

Maui, like many heroes of myth, was a youngest son. He was prematurely born (a similar story comes in the Brahmanic legend of the Adityas); his mother wrapped him up in her long hair and threw him out to sea. A kinsman rescued him, and he grew up to be much the most important member of his family, like Qat in his larger circle of brethren. Maui it was who snared the sun, beat him,[2] and taught him to run his appointed course, instead of careering at will and at any pace he chose about the heavens. He was the culture-hero who invented barbs for spears and

[1] Te-Heu-Heu, a powerful chief, described to Mr. Taylor the departmental character of his gods. "Is there one maker of things among Europeans? Is not one a carpenter, another a blacksmith, another a shipbuilder? So it was in the beginning. One made this, another that. Tane made trees, Ru mountains, Tangaroa fish, and so forth." Taylor, *New Zealand*, p. 108, note.

[2] The sun, when beaten, cried out and revealed his great name, exactly as Indra did in his terror and flight after slaying the serpent. Taylor, *op. cit.*, p. 131.

hooks; he turned his brother into the first dog, whence dogs are sacred, he fished New Zealand out of the sea; he stole fire for men. How Maui performed this feat, and how he "brought death into the world and all our woe," are topics that belong to the myths of *Death* and of the *Fire-Stealer*.[1] Maui could not only change men into animals, but could himself assume animal shapes at will.

Such is a brief account of the ancient traditions of mythical Maori gods and of the culture-hero. In practice, the conception of *Atua* (or a kind of extra-natural power or powers) possesses much influence in New Zealand. All manner of spirits in all manner of forms are *Atuas*. "A great chief was regarded as a malignant god in life, and a still worse one after death."[2] Again, "after Maui came a host of gods, each with his history and wonderful deeds. . . . These were ancestors who became deified by their respective tribes,"[3]—a statement which must be regarded as theoretical. It is odd enough, if true, that Maru should be the war-god of the southern island, and that the planet Mars is called after him Maru. "There were also gods in human forms, and others with those of reptiles. . . . At one period there seems to have been a mixed offspring from the same parents. Thus while Tawaki was of the human form, his brethren were *taniwa* and sharks; there were likewise mixed marriages among them." These legends are the natural result of that lack of distinction between man and the other things in the world

[1] See *La Mythologie*, A. L., Paris, 1886.
[2] Taylor, *op. cit.*, pp. 134, 135. [3] *Op. cit.*, p. 136.

which, as we demonstrated, prevails in early thought. It appears that the great mythical gods of the Maoris have not much concern with their morality. The myths are "but a magnified history of their chiefs, their wars, murders and lusts, with the addition of some supernatural powers"—such as the chiefs are very apt to claim.[1] In the opinion of a competent observer, the gods, or Atua, who are feared in daily life, are "spirits of the dead," and *their* attention is chiefly confined to the conduct of their living descendants and clansmen. They inspire courage, the leading virtue. When converted, the natives are said not to expel, but merely to subordinate their Atua, "believing Christ to be a more powerful Atua".[2] The Maoris are perhaps the least elevated race in which a well-developed polytheism has obscured almost wholly that belief in a moral Maker which we find among the lowest savages who have but a rudimentary polytheism. When we advance to ancient civilised peoples, like the Greeks, we shall find the archaic Theism obscured, or obliterated, in a similar way.

In the beliefs of Samoa (formerly called the Navigators' Islands, and discovered by a Dutch expedition in 1722) may be observed a most interesting moment in the development of religion and myth. In many regions it has been shown that animals are worshipped as totems, and that the gods are invested with the shape of animals. In the temples of higher civilisations will be found divine images still retaining in human

[1] *Op. cit.*, p. 137.

[2] Shortland, *Trad. and Superst. of New Zealanders*, 1856, pp. 83-85.

form certain animal attributes, and a minor worship of various beasts will be shown to have grouped itself in Greece round the altars of Zeus, or Apollo, or Demeter. Now in Samoa we may perhaps trace the actual process of the "transition," as Mr. Tylor says, "from the spirit inhabiting an individual body to the deity presiding over all individuals of a kind". In other words, whereas in Australia or America each totem-kindred reveres each animal supposed to be of its own lineage—the "Cranes" revering all cranes, the "Kangaroos" all kangaroos—in Samoa the various clans exhibit the same faith, but combine it with the belief that one spiritual deity reveals itself in each separate animal, as in a kind of avatar. For example, the several Australian totem-kindreds do not conceive that Pund-jel incarnates himself in the emu for one stock, in the crow for another, in the cockatoo for a third, and they do not by these, but by other means, attain a religious unity, transcending the diversity caused by the totemic institutions. In Samoa this kind of spiritual unity is actually reached by various stocks.

The Samoans were originally spoken of by travellers as the "godless Samoans," an example of a common error. Probably there is no people whose practices and opinions, if duly investigated, do not attest their faith in something of the nature of gods. Certainly the Samoans, far from being "godless," rather deserve the reproach of being "in all things too superstitious". "The gods were supposed to appear in some *visible incarnation*, and the particular thing in which his god was in the habit of appearing was to the Samoan an object of veneration."[1] Here we find that the religious sentiment has already become more or less self-conscious, and has begun to reason on its own practices. In pure totemism it is their kindred animal that men revere. The Samoans explain their worship of animals, not on the ground of kinship and common blood or "one flesh" (as in Australia), but by the comparatively advanced hypothesis that a spiritual power is *in* the animal. "One, for instance, saw his god in the eel, another in the shark, another in the turtle, another in the dog, another in the owl, another in the lizard," and so on, even to shell-fish. The creed so far is exactly what Garcilasso de la Vega found among the remote and ruder neighbours of the Incas, and attributed to the pre-Inca populations. "A man," as in Egypt, and in totemic countries generally, "would eat freely of what was regarded as the incarnation of the god of another man, but the incarnation of his own god he would consider it death to injure or eat. The god was supposed to avenge the insult by taking up his abode in that person's body, and causing to generate there the very thing which he had eaten until it produced death. The god used to be heard within the man, saying, "I am killing this man; he ate my incarnation". This class of tutelary deities they called *aitu fale*, or "gods of the house," gods of the stock or kindred. In totemistic countries the totem is respected *per se*, in Samoa the animal is worshipful because a god abides within him. This appears to be a theory by which the reflective Samoans have explained to themselves what was once pure totemism.

[1] Turner's *Samoa*, p. 17.

Not only the household, but the village has its animal gods or god incarnate in an animal. As some Arab tribes piously bury dead gazelles, as Athenians piously buried wolves, and Egyptians cats, so in Samoa "if a man found a dead owl by the roadside, and if that happened to be the incarnation of his village god, he would sit down and weep over it, and beat his forehead with a stone till the blood came. This was supposed to be pleasing to the deity. Then the bird would be wrapped up and buried with care and ceremony, as if it were a human body. This, however, was not the death of the god." Like the solemnly sacrificed buzzard in California, like the bull in the Attic *Diipolia*, "he was supposed to be yet alive and incarnate in all the owls in existence".[1]

In addition to these minor and local divinities, the Samoans have gods of sky, earth, disease and other natural departments.[2] Of their origin we only know that they fell from heaven, and all were incarnated or embodied in birds, beasts, plants, stones and fishes. But they can change shapes, and appear in the moon when she is not visible, or in any other guise they choose. If in Samoa the sky-god was once on the usual level of sky-gods elsewhere, he seems now to be degenerate.

[1] τὸν τεθνεῶτα ἀναστησάντων ἐν ᾗπερ ἀπέθανε θυσίᾳ. Porph., *De Abst.*, ii. 29; *Samoa*, p. 21.

[2] I am careful not to call Samoan sacred animals "Totems," to which Mr. Tylor justly objects, but I think the Samoan belief has Totemistic origins.

CHAPTER XIV.

AMERICAN DIVINE MYTHS.

Novelty of the "New World"—Different stages of culture represented there—Question of American Monotheism—Authorities and evidence cited—Myths examined: Eskimo, Ahts, Thlinkeets, Iroquois, the Great Hare—Dr. Brinton's theory of the hare—Zuñi myths—Transition to Mexican mythology.

THE divine myths of the vast American continent are a topic which a lifetime entirely devoted to the study could not exhaust. At best it is only a sketch in outline that can be offered in a work on the development of mythology in general. The subject is the more interesting as anything like systematic borrowing of myths from the Old World is all but impossible, as has already been argued in chapter xi. America, it is true, may have been partially "discovered" many times; there probably have been several points and moments of contact between the New and the Old World. Yet at the time when the Spaniards landed there, and while the first conquests and discoveries were being pursued, the land and the people were to Europeans practically as novel as the races and territories of a strange planet.[1] But the New World only revealed the old stock of humanity in many of its familiar stages of culture,

[1] Réville, *Hibbert Lectures*, 1884, p. 8.

and, consequently, with the old sort of gods, and myths, and creeds.

In the evolution of politics, society, ritual, and in all the outward and visible parts of religion, the American races ranged between a culture rather below the ancient Egyptian and a rudeness on a level with Australian or Bushman institutions. The more civilised peoples, Aztecs and Peruvians, had many peculiarities in common with the races of ancient Egypt, China and India; where they fell short was in the lack of alphabet or syllabary. The Mexican MSS. are but an advanced picture-writing, more organised than that of the Ojibbeways; the Peruvian Quipus was scarcely better than the Red Indian wampum records. Mexicans and Peruvians were settled in what deserved to be called cities; they had developed a monumental and elaborately decorated architecture; they were industrious in the arts known to them, though ignorant of iron. Among the Aztecs, at least, weapons and tools of bronze, if rare, were not unknown. They were sedulous in agriculture, disciplined in war, capable of absorbing and amalgamating with conquered tribes.

In Peru the ruling family, the Incas, enjoyed all the sway of a hierarchy, and the chief Inca occupied nearly as secure a position, religious, social and political, as any Rameses or Thothmes. In Mexico, doubtless, the monarch's power was at least nominally limited, in much the same way as that of the Persian king. The royal rule devolved on the elected member of an ancient family, but once he became prince he was surrounded by imposing ceremony. In both these two civilised peoples the priesthood enjoyed great power, and in Mexico, though not so extensively, if at all, in Peru, practised an appalling ritual of cannibalism and human sacrifice. It is extremely probable, or rather certain, that both of these civilisations were younger than the culture of other American peoples long passed away, whose cities stand in colossal ruin among the forests, whose hieroglyphs seem undecipherable, and whose copper-mines were worked at an unknown date on the shore of Lake Superior. Over the origin and date of those "crowned races" it were vain to linger here. They have sometimes left the shadows of names—Toltecs and Chichimecs—and relics more marvellous than the fainter traces of miners and builders in Southern and Central Africa. The rest is silence. We shall never know why the dwellers in Palenque deserted their majestic city while "the staircases were new, the steps whole, the edges sharp, and nowhere did traces of wear and tear give certain proof of long habitation".[1]

On a much lower level than the great urban peoples, but tending, as it were, in the same direction, and presenting the same features of state communism in their social arrangements, were, and are, the cave and cliff dwellers, the agricultural village Indians (Pueblo Indians) of New Mexico and Arizona. In the sides of the cañons towns have been burrowed, and men have dwelt in them like sand-martins in a sand-bank. The traveller views "perpendicular cliffs everywhere riddled with human habitations, which resemble the cells of a honeycomb more than anything else". In lowland

[1] Nadaillac, *Prehistoric America*, p. 323.

villages the dwellings are built of clay and stone. "The San Juan valley is strewn with ruins for hundreds of miles; some buildings, three storeys high, of masonry, are still standing."[1] The Moquis, Zuñis and Navahos of to-day, whose habits and religious rites are known from the works of Mr. Cushing, Mr. Matthews, and Captain John G. Bourke, are apparently descendants of "a sedentary, agricultural and comparatively cultivated race," whose decadence perhaps began "before the arrival of the Spaniards".[2]

Rather lower in the scale of culture than the settled Pueblo Indians were the hunter tribes of North America generally. They dwelt, indeed, in collections of wigwams which were partially settled, and the "long house" of the Iroquois looks like an approach to the communal system of the Pueblos.[3] But while such races as Iroquois, Mandans and Ojibbeways cultivated the maize plant, they depended for food more than did the Pueblo peoples on success in the chase. Deer, elk, buffalo, the wild turkey, the bear, with ducks and other birds, supplied the big kettle with its contents. Their society was totemistic, as has already been described; kinship, as a rule, was traced through the female line; the Sachems or chiefs and counsellors were elected, generally out of certain totem-kindreds; the war-chiefs were also elected when

[1] Nadaillac, p. 222.

[2] *Ibid.*, p. 257. See Bourke's *Snake-Dance of the Natives of Arizona*, and the fifth report of the Archæological Institute of America, with an account of the development of Pueblo buildings. It seems scarcely necessary to discuss Mr. Lewis Morgan's attempt to show that the Aztecs of Cortes's time were only on the level of the modern Pueblo Indians.

[3] Mr. Lewis Morgan's valuable *League of the Iroquois* and the *Iroquois Book of Rites* (Brinton, Philadelphia, 1883) may be consulted.

a military expedition started on the war-path; and Jossakeeds or medicine-men (the title varied in different dialects) had no small share of secular power. In war these tribes displayed that deliberate cruelty which survived under the Aztec rulers as the enormous cannibal ritual of human sacrifice. A curious point in Red Indian custom was the familiar institution of scalping the slain in war. Other races are head-hunters, but scalping is probably peculiar to the Red Men and the Scythians.[1]

On a level, yet lower than that of the Algonkin and other hunter tribes, are the Ameriean races whom circumstances have driven into desolate infertile regions; who live, like the Ahts, mainly on fish; like the Eskimos, in a world of frost and winter; or like the Fuegians, on crustaceans and seaweed. The minute gradations of culture cannot be closely examined here, but the process is upwards, from people like the Fuegians and Diggers, to the builders of the kitchen-middens—probably quite equals of the Eskimos[2]—and so through the condition of Ahts,

[1] Herodotus, iv. 64. The resemblance between Scythian and Red Indian manners exercised the learned in the time of Grotius. It has been acutely remarked by J. G. Müller, that in America one stage of society, as developed in the Old World, is absent. There is no pastoral stage. The natives had neither domesticated kine, goats nor sheep. From this lack of interest in the well-being of the domesticated lower animals he is inclined to deduce the peculiarly savage cruelty of American war and American religion. Sympathy was undeveloped. Possibly the lack of tame animals may have encouraged the prevalence of human sacrifice. The Brahmana shows how, in Hindostan, the lower animals became vicarious substitutes for man in sacrifice, as the fawn of Artemis or the ram of Jehovah took the place of Iphigenia or of Isaac. *Cf.* J. G. Müller, *Geschichte der Amerikanischen Urreligionen*, pp. 22, 23.

[2] Nadaillac, *Prehistoric America*, p. 66.

Thlinkeets, Cahrocs and other rude tribes of the North-west Pacific Coast, to that of Sioux, Blackfeet, Mandans, Iroquois, and then to the settled state of the Pueblo folk, the southern comforts of the Natchez, and finally to the organisation of the Mayas, and the summit occupied by the Aztecs and Incas.

Through the creeds of all these races, whether originally of the same stock or not, run many strands of religious and mythical beliefs—the very threads that are woven into the varied faiths of the Old World. The dread of ghosts; the religious adoration paid to animals; the belief in kindred and protecting beasts; the worship of inanimate objects, roughly styled fetishes; a certain reverence for the great heavenly bodies, sun, moon and Pleiades; a tendency to regard the stars, with all other things and phenomena, as animated and personal—with a belief in a Supreme Creator, these are the warp, as it were, of the fabric of American religion.[1] In one stage of culture one set of those ideas may be more predominant than in another stage, but they are present in all. The zoomorphic or theriomorphic mythologies and creeds are nowhere more vivacious than in America. Not content with the tribal zoomorphic guardian and friend, the totem, each Indian was in the habit of seeking for a special animal protector of his own. This being, which he called his Manitou, revealed itself to him in the long fasts of that savage sacrament which consecrates the entrance on full manhood. Even in the elaborate religions of the civilised races, Peruvians

[1] The arguments against the borrowing of the Creator from missionaries have already been stated.

and Aztecs, the animal deities survive, and sacred beasts gather in the shrine of Pachacamac, or a rudimentary remnant of ancestral beak or feather clings to the statue of Huitzilopochtli. But among the civilised peoples, in which the division of labour found its place and human ranks were minutely discriminated, the gods too had their divisions and departments. An organised polytheism prevailed, and in the temples of Centeotl and Tlazolteotl, Herodotus or Pausanias would have readily recognised the Demeter and the Aphrodite of Mexico.

There were departmental gods, and there was even an obvious tendency towards the worship of one spiritual deity, the Bretwalda of all the divine kings, a god on his way to becoming single and supreme. The religions and myths of America thus display, like the myths and religions of the Old World, the long evolution of human thought in its seeking after God. The rude first draughts of Deity are there, and they are by no means effaced in the fantastic priestly designs of departmental divinities.

The question of a primitive American monotheism has been more debated than even that of the "Henotheism" of the Aryans in India. On this point it must be said that, in a certain sense, probably any race of men may be called monotheistic, just as, in another sense, Christians who revere saints may be called polytheistic.[1] It has been constantly set forth in this work that, in moments of truly religious thought, even the lowest tribes turn their minds

[1] Gaidoz, *Revue Critique*, March, 1887.

towards a guardian, a higher power, something which watches and helps the race of men. This mental approach towards the powerful friend is an aspiration, and sometimes a dogma; it is religious, not mythological; it is monotheistic, not polytheistic. The Being appealed to by the savage in moments of need or despair may go by a name which denotes a hawk, or a spider, or a grasshopper, but we may be pretty sure that little thought of such creatures is in the mind of the worshipper in his hour of need.[1] Again, the most ludicrous or infamous tales may be current about the adventures and misadventures of the grasshopper or the hawk. He may be, as mythically conceived, only one out of a crowd of similar magnified non-natural men or lower animals. But neither his companions nor his legend are likely to distract the thoughts of the Bushman who cries to Cagn for food, or of the Murri who tells his boy that Pund-jel watches him from the heavens, or of the Solomon Islander who appeals to Qat as he crosses the line of reefs and foam. Thus it may be maintained that whenever man turns to a guardian not of this world, not present to the senses, man is for the moment a theist, and often a monotheist. But when we look from aspiration to doctrine, from the solitary ejaculation to ritual, from religion to myth, it would probably be vain to suppose

[1] There are exceptions, as when the Ojibbeway, being in danger, appeals to his own private protecting Manitou, perhaps a wild duck; or when the Zuñi cries to "Ye animal gods, my fathers!" (*Bureau of Ethnol.*, 1880-81, p. 42.) Thus we can scarcely agree entirely with M. Maurice Vernes when he says, "All men are monotheistic in the fervour of adoration or in moments of deep thought". (*L'Histoire des Religions*, Paris, 1887, p. 61.) The tendency of adoration and of speculation is, however, monotheistic.

that an uncontaminated belief in one God only, the maker and creator of all things, has generally prevailed, either in America or elsewhere. Such a belief, rejecting all minor deities, consciously stated in terms and declared in ritual, is the result of long ages and efforts of the highest thought, or, if once and again the intuition of Deity has flashed on some lonely shepherd or sage like an inspiration, his creed has usually been at war with the popular opinions of men, and has, except in Islam, won its disciples from the learned and refined. America seems no exception to so general a rule.

An opposite opinion is very commonly entertained, because the narratives of missionaries, and even the novels of Cooper and others, have made readers familiar with such terms as "the Great Spirit" in the mouths of Pawnees or Mohicans. On the one hand, taking the view of borrowing, Mrs. E. A. Smith says: "'The Great Spirit,' so popularly and poetically know as 'the God of the Red Man,' and 'the happy hunting-ground,' generally reported to be the Indian's idea of a future state, are both of them but their ready conception of the white man's God and heaven".[1] Dr, Brinton, too,[2] avers that "the Great Spirit" is a post-Christian conception. "In most cases these terms are entirely of modern origin, coined at the suggestion of missionaries, applied to the white man's God. . . . The Jesuits' *Relations* state positively that there was no one immaterial God recognised by

[1] *Bureau of Ethnology's Second Report*, p. 52.

[2] *Myths of the New World*, New York, 1876, p. 53.

the Algonkin tribes, and that the title 'The Great Manito' was introduced first by themselves in its personal sense." The statement of one missionary cannot be taken, of course, to bind all the others. The Père Paul le Jeune remarks: "The savages give the name of Manitou to whatsoever in nature, good or evil, is superior to man. Therefore when we speak of God, they sometimes call him 'The Good Manitou,' that is, 'The Good Spirit'."[1] The same Père Paul le Jeune[2] says that by Manitou his flock meant *un ange ou quelque nature puissante. Il y'en a de bons et de mauvais.* The evidence of Père Hierosme Lallemant[3] has already been alluded to, but it may be as well to repeat that, while he attributes to the Indians a kind of unconscious religious theism, he entirely denies them any monotheistic dogmas. With Tertullian, he writes, *Exclamant vocem naturaliter Christianam.* "To speak truth, these peoples have derived from their fathers no knowledge of a god, and before we set foot in their country they had nothing but vain fables about the origin of the world. Nevertheless, savages as they were, there did abide in their hearts a secret sentiment of divinity, and of a first principle, author of all things, whom, not knowing, they yet invoked. In the forest, in the chase, on the water, in peril by sea, they call him to their aid." This guardian, it seems, receives different names in different circumstances. Myth comes in; the sky is a God; a Manitou dwelling in the north sends ice and snow; another dwells in the waters, and many in the

[1] *Relations de la Nouvelle France*, 1637, p. 49.
[2] *Relations*, 1633, p. 17. [3] 1648, p. 77.

winds.[1] The Père Allouez[2] says, "They recognise no sovereign of heaven or earth". Here the good father and all who advocate a theory of borrowing are at variance with Master Thomas Heriot, "that learned *Mathematician*" (1588). In Virginia "there is one chiefe god, that has beene from all eternitie," who "made other gods of a principall order".[3] Near New Plymouth, Kiehtan was the chief god, and the souls of the just abode in his mansions.[4] We have already cited Ahone, and shown that he and the other gods found by the first explorers, are certainly not of Christian origin.

A curious account of Red Indian religion may be extracted from a work styled *A Narrative of the Captivity and Adventures of John Tanner during a Thirty Years' Residence among the Indians* (New York, 1830). Tanner was caught when a boy, and lived as an Indian, even in religion. The Great Spirit constantly appears in his story as a moral and protecting deity, whose favour and help may be won by

[1] The Confessions of Kah-ge-ga-gah Bowh, a converted Crane of the Ojibbeways, may be rather a suspicious document. Kah, to shorten his noble name, became a preacher and platform-speaker of somewhat windy eloquence, according to Mr. Longfellow, who had heard him. His report is that in youth he sought the favour of the Manitous (*Mon-e-doos* he calls them), but also revered *Ke-sha-mon-e-doo*, the benevolent spirit, "who made the earth with all its variety and smiling beauty". But his narrative is very unlike the Indian account of the manufacture of the world by this or that animal, already given in "Myths of the Origin of Things". The benevolent spirit, according to Kah's father, a medicine-man, dwelt in the sun (Copway, *Recollections of a Forest Life*, London, *s. a.* pp. 4, 5). Practical and good-natured actions of the Great Spirit are recorded on p. 35. He directs starving travellers by means of dreams.

[2] *Relations*, 1667, p. 1. [3] Arber, *Captain John Smith*, p. 321.

[4] *Op. cit.*, p. 768.

prayers, which are aided by magical ceremonies and dances. Tanner accepted and acted on this part of the Indian belief, while generally rejecting the medicine-men, who gave themselves out for messengers or avaters of the Great Spirit. Tanner had frequent visions of the Great Spirit in the form of a handsome young man, who gave him information about the future. "Do I not know," said the appearance, "when you are hungry and in distress? I look down upon you at all times, and it is not necessary you should call me with such loud cries" (p. 189).

Almost all idea of a tendency towards monotheism vanishes when we turn from the religions to the myths of the American peoples. Doubtless it may be maintained that the religious impulse or sentiment never wholly dies, but, after being submerged in a flood of fables, reappears in the philosophic conception of a pure deity entertained by a few of the cultivated classes of Mexico and Peru. But our business just now is with the flood of fables. From north to south the more general beliefs are marked with an early dualism, and everywhere are met the two opposed figures of a good and a bad extra-natural being in the shape of a man or beast. The Eskimos, for example, call the better being Torngarsuk. "They don't all agree about his form or aspect. Some say he has no form at all; others describe him as a great bear, or as a great man with one arm, or as small as a finger. He is immortal, but might be killed by the intervention of the god *Crepitus*."[1] "The other great but malignant spirit is a nameless female," the

[1] The circumstances in which this is possible may be sought for in Crantz, *History of Greenland*, London, 1767, vol. i. p. 206

wife or mother of Torngarsuk. She dwells under the sea in a habitation guarded by a Cerberus of her own, a huge dog, which may be surprised, for he sleeps for one moment at a time. Torngarsuk is not the maker of all things, but still is so much of a deity that many, "when they hear of God and his omnipotence, are readily led to the supposition that probably we mean their Torngarsuk". All spirits are called Torngak, and *soak* = *great*; hence the good spirit of the Eskimos in his limited power is "the Great Spirit".[1] In addition to a host of other spirits, some of whom reveal themselves affably to all, while others are only accessible to Angakut or medicine-men, the Eskimos have a Pluto, or Hades, or Charos of their own. He is meagre, dark, sullen, and devours the bowels of the ghosts. There are spirits of fire, water, mountains, winds; there are dog-faced demons, and the souls of abortions become hideous spectres, while the common ghost of civilised life is familiar. The spirit of a boy's dead mother appeared to him in open day, and addressed him in touching language: "Be not afraid; I am thy mother, and love thee!" for here, too, in this frozen and haunted world, love is more strong than death.[2]

Eskimo myth is practical, and, where speculative, is concerned with the fortunes of men, alive or dead, as far as these depend on propitiating the gods or extra-natural beings. The Eskimo myth of the origin of death would find its place among the other legends of this sort.[3] As a rule, Eskimo myth, as far as it has been investigated, rather resembles that of the

[1] Crantz, *op. cit.*, i. 207, note. [2] *Op. cit.*, i. 209

[3] *Cf. Modern Mythology*, "The Origin of Death".

Zulus. *Märchen* or romantic stories are very common; tales about the making of things and the actions of the pre-human beings are singularly scarce. Except for some moon and star myths, and the tale of the origin of death, hardly any myths, properly so called, are reported. "Only very scanty traces," says Rink, "have been found of any kind of ideas having been formed as to the origin and early history of the world and the ruling powers or deities."[1]

Turning from the Eskimos to the Ahts of Vancouver's Island, we find them in possession of rather a copious mythology. Without believing exactly in a *supreme*, they have the conception of a *superior* being, Quawteaht, no mere local nor tribal deity, but known in every village, like Osiris in Egypt. He is also, like Osiris and Baiame, the chief of a beautiful, far-off, spiritual country, but he had his adventures and misadventures while he dwelt on earth. The malevolent aspect of things—storms, disease and the rest—is either Quawteaht enraged, or the manifestation of his opponent in the primitive dualism, Tootooch or Chay-her, the Hades or Pluto of the Ahts. Like Hades, Chay-her is both a person and a place—the place of the dead discomforted, and the ruler of that land, a boneless form with a long grey beard. The exploits of Quawteaht in the beginning of things were something between those of Zeus and of Prometheus.

[1] He adds that this "seems sufficiently to show that such mythological speculations have been, in respect to other nations, also the product of a later stage of culture". That this position is erroneous is plain from the many myths here collected from peoples lower in culture than the Eskimos. *Cf.* Rink, *Tales and Traditions of the Eskimos.*

"He is the general framer—I do not say creator of all things, though some special things are excepted."[1] Quawteaht, in the legend of the loon (who was once an injured Indian, and still wails his wrongs), is represented as conscious of the conduct of men, and as prone to avenge misdeeds.[2] In person Quawteaht was of short stature, with very strong hairy arms and legs.[3] There is a touch of unconscious Darwinism in this description of "the first Indian". In Quawteaht mingle the rough draughts of a god and of an Adam, a creator and a first man. This mixture is familiar in the Zulu Unkulunkulu. Unlike Prometheus, Quawteaht did not steal the seed of fire. It was stolen by the cuttlefish, and in some legends Quawteaht was the original proprietor. Like most gods, he could assume the form of the beasts, and it was in the shape of a great whale that he discomfited his opponent Tootooch.[4] It does not appear that Tootooch receives any worship or adoration, such as is offered to the sun and moon.

Leaving the Ahts for the Thlinkeets, we find Yehl, the god or hero of the introduction of the arts, who, like the Christ of the Finnish epic or Maui in New Zealand, was born by a miraculous birth. His mother was a Thlinkeet woman, whose boys had all been slain. As she wandered disconsolate by the sea-shore, a dolphin or whale, taking pity upon her, bade her drink a little salt water and swallow a pebble. She did so, and in due time bore a child, Yehl, the hero of the Thlinkeets. Once, in his youth, Yehl shot a

[1] Sproat, *Savage Life*, London, 1868, p. 210.
[2] *Op. cit.*, p. 182. [3] *Ibid.*, p. 179. [4] *Ibid.*, p. 177.

supernatural crane, skinned it, and whenever he wished to fly, clothed himself in the bird's skin. Yet he is always known as a raven. Hence there is much the same confusion between Yehl and the bird as between Amun in Egypt and the ram in whose skin he was once pleased to reveal himself to a mortal. In Yehl's youth occurred the deluge, produced by the curse of an unfriendly uncle of his own; but the deluge was nothing to Yehl, who flew up to heaven, and anchored himself to a cloud by his beak till the waters abated. Like most heroes of his kind, Yehl brought light to men. The heavenly bodies in his time were kept in boxes by an old chief. Yehl, by an ingenious stratagem, got possession of the boxes. To fly up to the firmament with the treasure, to open the boxes, and to stick stars, sun and moon in their proper places in the sky, was to the active Yehl the work of a moment.

Fire he stole, like Prometheus, carrying a brand in his beak till he reached the Thlinkeet shore. There the fire dropped on stones and sticks, from which it is still obtained by striking the flints or rubbing together the bits of wood. Water, like fire, was a monopoly in those days, and one Khanukh kept all of it in his own well. Khanukh was the ancestor of the Wolf family among the Thlinkeets, as Yehl is the first father of the stock called Ravens. The wolf and raven thus answer to the mythic creative crow and cockatoo in Australian mythology, and take sides in the primitive dualism. When Yehl went to steal water from Khanukh, the pair had a discussion, exactly like that between Joukahainen and Wainamoinen in the epic of the Finns, as to which of them had been longer in the world. "Before the world stood in its place, I was there," says Yehl; and Wainamoinen says, "When earth was made, I was there; when space was unrolled, I launched the sun on his way". Similar boasts occur in the poems of Empedocles and of Taliesin. Khanukh, however, proved to be both older and more skilled in magic than Yehl. Yet the accomplishment of flying once more stood Yehl in good stead, and he carried off the water, as Odin, in the form of a bird, stole Suttung's mead, by flying off with it in his beak. Yehl then went to his own place.[1]

In the myths of the other races on the North-west Pacific Coast nothing is more remarkable than the theriomorphic character of the heroes, who are also to a certain extent gods and makers of things.

The Koniagas have their ancestral bird and dog, demiurges, makers of sea, rivers, hills, yet subject to "a great deity called Schljam Schoa," of whom they are the messengers and agents.[2] The Aleuts have their primeval dog-hero, and also a great old man, who made people, like Deucalion, and as in the Macusi myth, by throwing stones over his shoulder.[3]

Concerning the primal mythical beings of the great hunter and warrior tribes of America, Algonkins, Hurons and Iroquois, something has already been said in the chapter on "Myths of the Origin of Things".

[1] Bancroft, iii. 100-102 [Holmberg, *Eth. Skiz.*, p. 61].

[2] *Ibid.*, 104, quoting Dall's *Alaska*, p. 405, and Lisiansky's *Voyage*, pp. 197, 198.

[3] Brett's *Indians of Guiana*, p. 384.

It is the peculiarity of such heroes or gods of myth as the opposing Red Indian good and evil deities that they take little part in the affairs of the world when once these have been started.[1] Ioskeha and Tawiscara, the good and bad primeval brothers, have had their wars, and are now, in the opinion of some, the sun and the moon.[2] The benefits of Ioskeha to mankind are mainly in the past; as, for example, when, like another Indra, he slew the great frog that had swallowed the waters, and gave them free course over earth.[3] Ioskeha is still so far serviceable that he "makes the pot boil," though this may only be a way of recalling the benefits conferred on man by him when he learned from the turtle how to make fire. Ioskeha, moreover, is thanked for success in the chase, because he let loose the animals from the cave in which they lived at the beginning. As they fled he spoiled their speed by wounding them with arrows; only one escaped, the wind-swift wolf. Some devotees regarded Ioskeha as the teacher of agriculture and the giver of great harvests of maize. In 1635 Ioskeha was seen, all meagre and skeleton-like, tearing a man's leg with his

[1] Erminie Smith, in *Report of Bureau of Ethnology*, 1880-81, publishes a full, but not very systematic, account of Iroquois gods of to-day. Thunder, the wind, and echo are the chief divine figures. The Titans or Jotuns, the opposed supernatural powers, are giants of stone. "Among the most ancient of the deities were their most remote ancestors, certain animals who later were transformed into human shapes, the name of the animals being preserved by their descendants, who have used them to designate their gentes or clans." The Iroquois have a strange and very touching version of the myth of Orpheus and Eurydice (*op. cit.*, p. 104). It appears to be native and unborrowed; all the details are pure Iroquois.

[2] *Relations de la Nouvelle France*, 1636, p. 102.

[3] *Ibid.*, p. 103.

teeth, a prophecy of famine. A more agreeable apparition of Ioskeha is reported by the Père Barthelemy Vimont.[1] When an Iroquois was fishing, "a demon appeared to him in the shape of a tall and beautiful young man. 'Be not afraid,' said this spirit; 'I am the master of earth, whom you Hurons worship under the name of Ioskeha; the French give me the erroneous name of Jesus, but they know me not.'" Ioskeha then gave some directions for curing the small-pox. The Indian's story is, of course, coloured by what he knew of missionary teaching, but the incident should be compared with the "medicine dream" of John Tanner.

The sky, conceived as a person, held a place rather in the religion than in the mythology of the Indians. He was approached with prayer and sacrifice, and "they implored the sky in all their necessities".[2] "The sky hears us," they would say in taking an oath, and they appeased the wrath of the sky with a very peculiar semi-cannibal sacrifice.[3]

What Ioskeha was to the Iroquois, Michabo or Manibozho was to the Algonkin tribes. There has been a good deal of mystification about Michabo or Manibozho, or Messou, who was probably, in myth, a hare *sans phrase*, but who has been converted by philological processes into a personification of light or dawn. It has already been seen that the wild North Pacific peoples recognise in their hero and demiurge animals of various species; dogs, ravens, muskrats

[1] *Relations*, 1640, p. 92. [2] *Op. cit.*, 1636, p. 107.

[3] For Pawnees and Blackfeet see Grinnell, *Pawnee and Blackfoot Legends* (2 vols.).

and coyotes have been found in this lofty estimation, and the Utes believe in "Cin-au-av, the ancient of wolves".[1] It would require some labour to derive all the ancient heroes and gods from misconceptions about the names of vast natural phenomena like light and dawn, and it is probable that Michabo or Manibozho, the Great Hare of the Algonkins, is only a successful apotheosised totem like the rest. His legend and his dominion are very widely spread. Dr. Brinton himself (p. 153) allows that the great hare is a totem. Perhaps our earliest authority about the mythical great hare in America is William Strachey's *Travaile into Virginia*.[2]

Among other information as to the gods of the natives, Strachey quotes the remarks of a certain Indian: "We have five gods in all; our chief god appears often unto us in the likeness of a mighty great hare; the other four have no visible shape, but are indeed the four wynds". An Indian, after hearing from the English the Biblical account of the creation, explained that "our god, who takes upon him the shape of a hare, . . . at length devised and made divers men and women". He also drove away the cannibal Manitous. "That godlike hare made the water and the fish and a great deare." The other four gods, in envy, killed the hare's deer. This is curiously like the Bushman myth of Cagn, the mantis insect, and his favourite eland. "The godly hare's house" is at the place of sun-rising; there the souls of good Indians "feed on delicious fruits with that

[1] Powell, in *Bureau of Ethnology*, 1879-80, p. 43.

[2] *Circa* 1612; reprinted by the Hakluyt Society.

great hare," who is clearly, so far, the Virginian Osiris.[1] Dr. Brinton has written at some length on "this chimerical beast," whose myth prevails, he says, "from the remotest wilds of the North-west to the coast of the Atlantic, from the southern boundary of Carolina to the cheerless swamps of Hudson's Bay. . . The totem" (totem-kindred probably is meant) "clan which bore his name was looked up to with peculiar respect." From this it would appear that the hare was a totem like another, and had the same origin, whatever that may have been. According to the Père Allouez, the Indians "ont en veneration toute particulière, une certaine beste chimerique, qu'ils n'ont jamais veuë sinon en songe, ils l'appellent Missibizi," which appears to be a form of Michabo and Manibozho.[2]

In 1670 the same Père Allouez gives some myths about Michabo. "C'est-à-dire le grand lièvre," who made the world, and also invented fishing-nets. He is the master of life, and can leap eight leagues at one bound, and is beheld by his servants in dreams. In 1634 Père Paul le Jeune gives a longer account of Messou, "a variation of the same name," according to Dr. Brinton, as Michabo. This Messou reconstructed the drowned world out of a piece of clay brought him by an otter, which succeeded after the failure of a raven sent out by Messou. He afterwards married a muskrat, by whom he became the father of a flourishing

[1] *History of Travaile*, pp. 98, 99. This hare we have alluded to in vol. i. p. 184, but it seems worth while again to examine Dr. Brinton's theory more closely.

[2] *Relations*, 1667, p. 12.

family. "Le brave reparateur de l'univers est le frère aisné de toutes les bestes," says the mocking missionary.[1] Messou has the usual powers of shape-shifting, which are the common accomplishments of the medicine-man or conjuror, *se transformant en mille sortes d'animaux*.[2] He is not so much a creator as a demiurge, inferior to a mysterious being called Atahocan. But Atahocan is obsolescent, and his name is nearly equivalent to an old wife's fable, a story of events *au temps jadis*.[3] "Le mot *Nitatohocan* signifie, 'Je dis un vieux conte fait à plaisir'."

These are examples of the legends of Michabo or Manibozho, the great hare. He appears in no way to differ from the other animals of magical renown, who, in so many scores of savage myths, start the world on its way and instruct men in the arts. His fame may be more widely spread, but his deeds are those of eagle, crow, wolf, coyote, spider, grasshopper, and so forth, in remote parts of the world. His legend is the kind of legend whose origin we ascribe to the credulous fancy of early peoples, taking no distinction between themselves and the beasts. If the hare was indeed the totem of a successful and honoured kindred, his elevation is perfectly natural and intelligible.

Dr. Brinton, in his *Myths of the New World* (New York, 1876), adopts a different line of explanation. Michabo, he says, "was originally the highest divinity recognised by them, powerful and beneficent beyond all others, maker of the heavens and the world". We gladly welcome him in that capacity in religion. But

[1] *Relations*, 1634, p. 13. [2] *Op. cit.*, 1633, p. 16.
[3] *Op. cit.*, 1634, p. 13.

it has already been shown that Michabo is only, in myth, the *reparateur de l'univers*, and that he has a sleeping partner—a deity retired from business. Moreover, Dr. Brinton's account of Michabo, "powerful and beneficent beyond all others, maker of the heavens and the world," clashes with his own statement, that "of monotheism as displayed in the one personal definite God of the Semitic races" (to whom Dr. Brinton's description of Michabo applies) "there is not a single instance on the American continent".[1] The residences and birthplaces of Michabo are as many as those of the gods of Greece. It is true that in some accounts, as in Strachey's, "his bright home is in the *rising* sun". It does not follow that the hare had any original connection with the dawn. But this connection Dr. Brinton seeks to establish by philological arguments. According to this writer, the names (Manibozho, Nanibozhu, Missibizi, Michabo, Messou) "all seem compounded, according to well-ascertained laws of Algonkin euphony, from the words corresponding to *great* and *hare* or *rabbit*, or the first two perhaps from *spirit* and *hare*".[2] But this seeming must not be trusted. We must attentively examine the Algonkin root *wab*, when it will appear "that in fact there are two roots having this sound. One is the initial syllable of the word translated hare or rabbit, but the other means *white*, and from it is derived the words for the east, the dawn, the light, the day, and the morning. Beyond a doubt (*sic*) this is the compound in the names Michabo and Manibozho, which therefore mean the great light, the spirit of light, of the dawn, or

[1] *Relations*, pp. 53, 176. [2] *Op. cit.*, p. 178.

the east." Then the war of Manibozho became the struggle of light and darkness. Finally, Michabo is recognised by Dr. Brinton as "the not unworthy personification of the purest conceptions they possessed concerning the Father of All,"[1] though, according to Dr. Brinton in an earlier passage, they can hardly be said to have possessed such conceptions.[2] We are not responsible for these inconsistencies. The degeneracy to the belief in a "mighty great hare," a "chimerical beast," was the result of a misunderstanding of the root *wab* in their own language by the Algonkins, a misunderstanding that not only affected the dialects in which the root *wab* occurred in the hare's name, but those in which it did not!

On the whole, the mythology of the great hunting and warrior tribes of North America is peopled by the figures of ideal culture-heroes, partly regarded as first men, partly as demiurges and creators. They waver in outward aspect between the beautiful youths of the "medicine-dreams" and the bestial guise of totems and protecting animals. They have a tendency to become identified with the sun, like Osiris in Egypt, or with the moon. They are adepts in all the arts of the medicine-man, and they are especially addicted to animal metamorphosis. In the long winter evenings, round the camp-fire, the Indians tell such grotesque tales of their pranks and adventures as the Greeks told of their gods, and the Middle Ages of the saints.[3]

[1] *Relations*, p. 183. [2] *Op. cit.*, p. 53.

[3] A full collection of these, as they survive in oral tradition, with an obvious European intermixture, will be found in Mr. Leland's *Algonquin Legends*, London, 1884, and in Schoolcraft's *Hiawatha Legends*, London, 1856. See especially the Manibozho legend.

The stage in civilisation above that of the hunter tribes is represented in the present day by the settled Pueblo Indians of New Mexico and Arizona. Concerning the faith of the Zuñis we fortunately possess an elaborate account by Mr. Frank Cushing.[1] Mr. Cushing was for long a dweller in the clay *pueblos* of the Zuñis, and is an initiated member of their sacred societies. He found that they dealt at least as freely in metaphysics as the Maoris, and that, like the Australians, "they suppose sun, moon and stars, the sky, earth and sea, in all their phenomena and elements, and all inanimate objects, as well as plants, animals and men, to belong to one great system of all conscious and interrelated life, in which the degrees of relationship seem to be determined largely, if not wholly, by the degrees of resemblance". This, of course, is stated in terms of modern self-conscious speculation. When much the same opinions are found among the Kamilaroi and Kurnai of Australia, they are stated thus: "Some of the totems divide not mankind only, but the whole universe into what may almost be called gentile divisions".[2] "Everything in nature is divided between the classes. The wind belongs to one and the rain to another. The sun is Wutaroo and the moon is Yungaroo. . . . The South Australian savage looks upon the universe as the great tribe, to one of whose divisions he himself belongs, and all things, animate or inanimate, which belong to his class are parts of the body corporate, whereof he himself is part. They are almost parts of himself"

[1] *Report of Bureau of Ethnology*, Washington, 1880-81.
[2] *Kamilaroi and Kurnai*, p. 167.

(p. 170). Mrs. Langloh Parker, in a letter to me, remarks that Baiame alone is outside of this conception, and is common to all classes, and totems, and class divisions.

Manifestly this is the very condition of mind out of which mythology, with all existing things acting as *dramatis personæ*, must inevitably arise.

The Zuñi philosophy, then, endows all the elements and phenomena of nature with personality, and that personality is blended with the personality of the beast "whose operations most resemble its manifestation". Thus lightning is figured as a serpent, and the serpent holds a kind of mean position between lightning and man. Strangely enough, flint arrow-heads, as in Europe, are regarded as the gift of thunder, though the Zuñis have not yet lost the art of making, nor entirely abandoned, perhaps, the habit of using them. Once more, the supernatural beings of Zuñi religion are almost invariably in the shape of animals, or in monstrous semi-theriomorphic form. There is no general name for the gods, but the appropriate native terms mean "creators and masters," "makers," and "finishers," and "immortals". All the classes of these, including the class that specially protects the animals necessary to men, "are believed to be related by blood". But among these essences, the animals are nearest to man, most accessible, and therefore most worshipped, sometimes as mediators. But the Zuñi has mediators even between him and his animal mediators, and these are fetishes, usually of stone, which accidentally resemble this or that beast-god in shape. Sometimes, as in the Egyptian sphinx, the natural resemblance of a stone to a living form has been accentuated and increased by art. The stones with a natural resemblance to animals are most valued when they are old and long in use, and the orthodox or priestly theory is that they are petrifactions of this or that beast. Flint arrow-heads and feathers are bound about them with string.

All these beliefs and practices inspire the Zuñi epic, which is repeated, at stated intervals, by the initiated to the neophytes. Mr. Cushing heard a good deal of this archaic poem in his sacred capacity. The epic contains a Zuñi cosmogony. Men, as in so many other myths, originally lived in the dark places of earth in four caverns. Like the children of Uranus and Gæa, they murmured at the darkness. The "holder of the paths of life," the sun, now made two beings out of his own substance; they fell to the earth, armed with rainbow and lightning, a shield and a magical flint knife. The new-comers cut the earth with a flint-knife, as Qat cut the palpable dark with a blade of red obsidian in Melanesia. Men were then lifted through the hole on the shield, and began their existence in the sunlight, passing gradually through the four caverns. Men emerged on a globe still very wet; for, as in the Iroquois and other myths, there had been a time when "water was the world". The two benefactors dried the earth and changed the monstrous beasts into stones. It is clear that this myth accounts at once for the fossil creatures found in the rocks and for the merely accidental resemblance to animals of stones now employed as fetishes.[1] In the stones is

[1] *Report*, etc., p. 15.

believed to survive the "medicine" or magic, the spiritual force of the animals of old.

The Zuñis have a culture-hero as usual, Po'shai-an-k'ia, who founded the mysteries, as Demeter did in Greece, and established the sacred orders. He appeared in human form, taught men agriculture, ritual, and then departed. He is still attentive to prayer. He divided the world into regions, and gave the animals their homes and functions, much as Heitsi Eibib did in Namaqualand. These animals carry out the designs of the culture-hero, and punish initiated Zuñis who are careless of their religious duties and ritual. The myths of the sacred beasts are long and dismal, chiefly ætiological, or attempts to account by a fictitious narrative for the distribution and habits of the various creatures. Zuñi prayers are mainly for success in the chase; they are directed to the divine beasts, and are reinforced by magical ceremonies. Yet a prayer for sport may end with such a truly religious petition as this: "Grant me thy light; give me and my children a good trail across life". Again we read: "This day, my fathers, ye animal gods, although this country be filled with enemies, render me precious. . . . Oh, give ye shelter of my heart from them!" Yet in religious hymns the Zuñis celebrate Ahonawilona, "the Maker and Container of All, the All Father," the uncreated, the unbegotten, who "thought himself out into space". Here is monotheism among fetishists.[1]

The faith of the Zuñis, with its metaphysics, its devoutness and its magic ritual, may seem a kind of

[1] Cushing, *Report*, *Ethnol. Bureau*, 1891-92, p. 379.

introduction to the magic, the ritual and the piety of the ancient Aztecs. The latter may have grown, in a long course of forgotten ages, out of elements like those of the Zuñi practice, combined with the atrocious cruelty of the warrior tribes of the north. Perhaps in no race is the extreme contrast between low myth, and the highest speculation, that of "the Eternal thinking himself out into space," so marked as among the Zuñis. The highly abstract conception of Ahonawilona was unknown to Europeans when this work first appeared.

CHAPTER XV.

MEXICAN DIVINE MYTHS.

European eye-witnesses of Mexican ritual—Diaz, his account of temples and Gods—Sahagun, his method—Theories of the god Huitzilopochtli—Totemistic and other elements in his image and legend—Illustrations from Latin religion—"God-eating"—The calendar—Other gods—Their feasts and cruel ritual—Their composite character—Parallels from ancient classical peoples—Moral aspects of Aztec gods.

THE religion of the Mexicans was a compound of morality and cruelty so astonishing that its two aspects have been explained as the contributions of two separate races. The wild Aztecs from the north are credited with having brought to a high pitch of organised ritual the ferocious customs of the Red Indians. The tortures which the tribes inflicted on captives taken in war were transmuted into the cannibal sacrifices and orgies of bloodshed with which the Aztec temples reeked. The milder elements, again, the sense of sin which found relief in confession and prayer, are assigned to the influence of Mayas, and especially of Toltecs, a shadowy and perhaps an imaginary people. Our ignorance of Mexican history before the Spanish conquest is too deep to make any such theory of the influence of race on religion in Mexico more than merely plausible. The facts of ritual and of myth are better known, thanks to the observations of such an honest soldier as Bernal Diaz and such a learned missionary as Sahagun. The author of the *Historia General de las Cosas de Nueva España* was a Spanish Franciscan, and one of the earliest missionaries (1529) in Mexico. He himself describes the method by which he collected his information about the native religion. He summoned together the chief men of one of the provinces, who, in turn, chose twelve old men well seen in knowledge of the Mexican practices and antiquities. Several of them were also scholars in the European sense, and had been taught Latin. The majority of the commission collected and presented "pictures which were the writings formerly in use among them," and the "grammarians" or Latin-learned Aztecs wrote in European characters and in Aztec the explanations of these designs. When Sahagun changed his place of residence, these documents were again compared, re-edited and enlarged by the assistance of the native gentlemen in his new district, and finally the whole was passed through yet a third "sieve," as Sahagun says, in the city of Mexico. The completed manuscript had many ups and downs of fortune, but Sahagun's book remains a source of almost undisputed authenticity.

Probably no dead religion whose life was among a people ignorant of syllabaries or of the alphabet is presented to us in a more trustworthy form than the religion of Mexico. It is necessary, however, to discount the *theories* of Sahagun and his converts, who though they never heard of Euhemerus, habitually applied the euhemeristic doctrine to their facts. They decided that the gods of the Aztecs had once been living men and conjurors, worshipped after their decease. It is possible, too, that a strain of Catholic piety has found its way into the long prayers of the heathen penitents, as reported by Sahagun.[1] Sahagun gives us a full account of the Mexican mythology. What the gods, as represented by idols and adored in ritual, were like, we learn from a gallant Catholic soldier, Bernal Diaz.[2] "Above the altars," he writes, "were two shapes like giants, wondrous for height and hugeness. The first on the right was Huichilobos (Huitzilopochtli), their god of war. He had a big head and trunk, his eyes great and terrible, and so inlaid with precious stones that all his head and body shone with stars thereof. Great snakes of gold and fine stones were girdled about his flanks; in one hand he held a bow, and arrows in the other, and a little idol called his page stood by his side. . . . Thereby also were braziers, wherein burned the hearts of three Indians, torn from their bodies that very day, and the smoke of them and the savour of incense were the sacrifice. The walls of this oratory were black and dripping with gouts of blood, and likewise the floor that stank horribly." Such was the aspect of a Mexican shrine before the Spaniards introduced their faith.

As to the mythical habits of the Aztec Olympians in general, Sahagun observes that "they were friends of disguise, and changed themselves often into birds

[1] For a brief account of Sahagun and the fortunes of his book, see Bancroft, *Native Races of the Pacific States*, iii. 231, note 61. The references here to Sahagun's own work are to the translation by MM. Jourdanet and Siméon, published by Masson, Paris, 1880. Bernal Diaz is referred to in the French edition published by M. Lemerre in 1879.

[2] *Véridique Histoire*, chap. xcii.

or savage beasts". Hence he, or his informants, infer that the gods have originally been necromancers or medicine-men, now worshipped after death; a natural inference, as magical feats of shape-shifting are commonly ascribed everywhere to witches and warlocks. As a matter of fact, the Aztec gods, though bedizened with the attributes of mortal conjurors, and with the fur and feathers of totems, are, for the most part, the departmental deities of polytheism, each ruling over some province of nature or of human activity. Combined with these are deities who, in their origin, were probably ideal culture-heroes, like Yehl, or Qat, or Prometheus. The long and tedious myths of Quetzalcoatl and Tezcatlipoca appear to contain memories of a struggle between the gods or culture-heroes of rival races. Such struggles were natural, and necessary, perhaps, before a kind of syncretism and a general tolerance could unite in peace the deities of a realm composed of many tribes originally hostile. In a cultivated people, made up out of various conquered and amalgamated tribes, we must expect polytheism, because their Olympus is a kind of divine representative assembly. Anything like monotheism, in such a state, must be the result of philosophic reflection. "A laughable matter it is," says Bernal Diaz, "that in each province the Indians have their gods, and the gods of one province or town are of no profit to the people of another. Thus have they an infinite number of idols, to each of which they sacrifice."[1] He might have described, in the same words, the local gods of the Egyptian nomes, for a similar state of things preceded,

[1] Bernal Diaz, chap. xcii.

and to some extent survived, the syncretic efforts of Egyptian priesthood. Meanwhile, the *Teocallis*, or temples of Mexico, gave hospitable shelter to this mixed multitude of divinities. Hard by Huitzilopochtli was Tezcatlipoca (Tezcatepuca, Bernal calls him), whose chapel "stank worse than all the shambles of Castile". He had the face of a bear and shining eyes, made of mirrors called *Tezcut*. He was understood by Bernal to be the Mexican Hades, or warden of the dead. Not far off was an idol, half-human and half-lizard, "the god of fruits and harvest, I remember not his name," and all his chapel walls dripped blood.

In the medley of such a pantheon, it is difficult to arrange the deities on any principle of order. Beginning with Huitzilopochtli, as perhaps the most famous, it is to be observed that he indubitably became and was recognised as a god of battles, and that he was also the guide and protector who (according to the Aztec painted scriptures) led the wandering fathers through war and wilderness to the promised land of Mexico. His birth was one of those miraculous conceptions which we have seen so frequently in the myths and *märchen* of the lower and the higher races. It was not by swallowing a berry, as in Finland, but by cherishing in her bosom a flying ball of feathers that the devout woman, Coatlicue, became the mother of Huitzilopochtli. All armed he sprang to the light, like Athene from the head of Zeus, and slew his brothers that had been born by natural generation. From that day he received names of dread, answering to *Deimos* and *Phobos*.[1] By another myth, euhemer-

[1] Clavigero, *Storia Ant. del Mexico*, ii. 17, 19; Bancroft, iii. 290.

istic in character, Huitziton (the name is connected with *huitzilin*, the humming-bird) was the leader of the Aztecs in their wanderings. On his death or translation, his skull gave oracles, like the head of Bran in the Welsh legend. Sahagun, in the first page of his work, also euhemerises Huitzilopochtli, and makes him out to have been a kind of Hercules *doublé* with a medicine-man; but all this is mere conjecture

The position of Huitzilopochtli as a war-god, guardian and guide through the wilderness is perfectly established, and it is nearly as universally agreed that his name connects him with the humming-bird, which his statue wore on its left foot. He also carried a green bunch of plumage upon his head, shaped like the bill of a small bird. Now, as J. G. Müller has pointed out, the legend and characteristics of Huitzilopochtli are reproduced, by a coincidence startling even in mythology, in the legend and characteristics of Picus in Latium. Just as Huitzilopochtli wore the humming-bird indicated by his name on his foot, so Picus was represented with the woodpecker of his name on his head.[1]

[1] J. G. Müller, *Uramerik. Rel.*, p. 595. On the subject of Picus one may consult Ovid, *Metamorph*, xiv. 314. Here the story runs that Circe loved Picus, whom she met in the woods. He disdained her caresses, and she turned him into the woodpecker, "with his garnet head".

"Et fulvo cervix præcingitur auro."

According to Virgil (*Æn.*, vii. 187), the statue of this Picus was settled in an old Laurentian temple or palace of unusual sanctity, surrounded by images of the earlier gods. The woodpeckers, *pici*, are known *Martio cognomine*, says Pliny (10, 18, 20, § 40), and so connected with the Roman war-god, *Picus Martius*.

In his *Römische Mythologie*, i. 336, 337, Preller makes no use of these materials for comparison, though the conduct and character of the other beast of war, the wolf, as guide and protector of the Hirpi (*wolves*), and

In these Latin legends, as in the legends of Huitzilopochtli, the basis, as J. G. Müller sees, is the bird—the humming-bird in one case, the woodpecker in the other. The bird is then euhemerised or brought into anthropomorphic form. It is fabled that he was originally a man (like Picus before Circe enchanted him to a bird's shape), or, in Mexico, a man named Huitziton, who during the Aztec migrations heard and pursued a little bird that cried "Tinni," that is, "Follow, follow".[1] Now we are all familiar with classical legends of races that were guided by a bird or beast to their ultimate seats. Müller mentions Battus and the raven, the Chalcidians and the dove, the Cretans and the dolphin, which was Apollo, Cadmus and the cow ; the Hirpi, or wolves, who followed the wolf. In the same way the Picini followed the woodpecker, *Picus*, from whom they derived their name, and carried a woodpecker on their banners. Thus we may connect both the Sabine war-gods and the bird of the Mexican war-gods with the many guiding and protecting animals which occur in fable. Now a guiding and protecting animal is almost a synonym for a totem. That the Sabine woodpecker had been a totem may be pretty certainly established on the evidence of Plutarch. The people called by his name (Picini) declined, like totemists everywhere, to eat their holy bird, in this case the woodpecker.[2]

worshipped by them with wolf-dances, is an obvious survival of totemism. The Picini have their animal leader, Picus, the woodpecker, the Hirpi have their animal leader, the wolf, just as the humming-bird was the leader of the Aztecs.

[1] Bancroft, iii. 69, note, quoting Torquemada. [2] *Quæst. Rom.*, xxi.

The inference is that the humming-bird whose name enters into that of Huitzilopochtli, and whose feathers were worn on his heel, had been the totem of an Aztec kindred before Huitzilopochtli, like Picus, was anthropomorphised. On the other hand, if Huitzilopochtli was once the Baiame of the Aztecs, their Guide in their wanderings, he might, in myth, be mixed up with a totem or other worshipful animal. "Before this god was represented in human form, he was merely a little humming-bird, Huitziton; but as the anthropomorphic processes advanced, the bird became an attribute, emblem, or symbol of the deity."[1] If Huitzilopochtli is said to have given the Aztecs fire, that boon is usually regarded by many races, from Normandy to Australia, as the present given to men by a bird; for example, the fire-crested wren.[2] Thus understood, the ornithological element in Huitzilopochtli is purely totemic. While accepting the reduction of him to a humming-bird, M. Réville ingeniously concludes that he was "a derivative form of the sun, and especially of the sun of the fair season". If the bird was worshipped, it was not as a totem, but as "the divine messenger of the spring," like "the plover among the Latins".[3]

Attempts have been made, with no great success, to discover the cosmical character of the god from the

[1] J. G. Müller, *op. cit.*, p. 596.

[2] Bosquet, *La Normandie Merveilleuse*, Paris, 1845; Brough Smyth, *Aborigines of Victoria*, vol. i.; Kuhn, *Herabkunft*, p. 109; *Journal Anthrop. Inst.*, November, 1884; Sproat, *Savage Life* (the cuttlefish), p. 178; Bancroft, iii. 100.

[3] *Hibbert Lectures*, 1884, English trans., pp. 54, 55. The woodpecker seems a better Latin example than the plover.

nature of his feasts. The Mexican calendar, "the Aztec year," as described at considerable length by Sahagun, was a succession of feasts, marked by minute and elaborate rites of a magical character. The gods of rain were frequently propitiated, so was the goddess of maize, the mountain god, the mother of the gods, and many other divinities. The general theory of worship was the adoration of a deity, first by innumerable human sacrifices, next by the special sacrifice of a man for male gods, of a woman for each goddess. The latter victims were regarded as the living images or incarnations of the divinities in each case; for no system of worship carried farther the identification of the god with the sacrifice, and of both with the officiating priest. The connection was emphasised by the priest's wearing the newly-flayed skins of the victims, just as in Greece, Egypt and Assyria the fawn-skin, or bull-hide, or goat-skin, or fish-skin of the victims is worn by the celebrants. Finally, an image of the god was made out of paste, and this was divided into morsels and eaten in a hideous sacrament by those who communicated.[1]

From the special ritual of Huitzilopochtli Mr. Tylor conjectures that this "inextricable compound parthe-

[1] Copious details as to the sacraments, human sacrifices, paste figures of gods, and identity of god and victim, will be found in Sahagun's second and third books. The *magical* character of the ritual deserves particular attention. See many examples of gods made of flour and eaten in Liebrecht's *Zur Volkskunde*, "Der aufgegessene Gott," p. 436. It will be noted that the feasts of the corn goddess, like the rites of Demeter, were celebrated with torch-dances. The ritual of the month Quecholli (iii. 33, 144) is a mere medicine hunt, as Tanner and the Red Indians call it, a procuring of magical virtue for the arrows, as in the Zuñi mysteries to-day. Compare *Report of Bureau of Ethnology*, vol. ii., "Zuñi Prey Gods".

nogenetic" god may have been originally "a nature deity whose life and death were connected with the year".[1] This theory is based on the practice at the feast called *Panquetzaliztli*.[2] "His paste idol was shot through with an arrow," says Mr. Tylor, "and being thus killed, was divided into morsels and eaten; wherefore the ceremony was called *Teoqualo*, or 'god-eating,' and this was associated with the winter solstice." M. Réville says that this feast coincided with our month of December, the beginning of the cold and dry season, Huitzilopochtli would die with the verdure, the flowers and all the beauteous adornments of spring and summer; but like Adonis, like Osiris, and so many other solar deities, he only died to live and to return again. Before identifying him with the sun, it may be remarked that the Aztec feast of the return of the gods was celebrated in the twelfth month and the paste sacrifice of Huitzilopochtli was in the fifteenth.

There were eighteen months in the Aztec year, and the year began on the 2nd of February. The return of the gods was, therefore, in September, and the paste sacrifice of Huitzilopochtli in December. Clearly the god who dies in the winter solstice cannot be thought to "return" late in September. Huitzilopochtli had another feast on the first day of the ninth month, that is, between June and July, when much use was made of floral decorations, and "they offered him the first flowers of the year," although flowers were used two months earlier, in the seventh month and in the fourth month.[3] But the Mexican calendar is hard to deal

[1] *Primitive Culture*, ii. 307; Clavigero, *Messico*, ii. 17, 81.
[2] Sahagun, ii. 15, and Appendix, iii. 2, 3. [3] *Ibid.*, ii. 9.

with. Müller places the feasts of Huitzilopochtli in the middle of May, the middle of August, and the middle of December.[1] He combines his facts with a legend which made Huitzilopochtli to be the son of the goddess of vegetation. J. G. Müller's whole argument is learned and acute, but errs probably in attempting to extract a consecutive symbolical sense out of the chaos of myth. Thus he writes: "When the myth makes the god the son of the mother of plants, it divides his essence from that of his mother, and thus Huitzilopochtli, however closely akin to the plant world, is not the plant world itself". This is to consider more curiously than the myth-makers. The name of the patron goddess of the flower-wearers in feasts was Coatlicue or Coatlan, which is also the name of the mother of Huitzilopochtli; its meaning is "serpent petticoated".[2] When Müller goes on to identify Huitzilopochtli with the bunch of feathers that fell into his mother's breast before his birth, and that again with the humming-bird, and that again with the honey-sucking bird as the "means of fructifying the plants," and, finally, with the *männliche befruchtende Naturkraft*, we have left myth far behind, and are in a region of symbolism and abstract thought, where one conjecture is as good as another. The hypothesis is that men, feeling a sense of religious reverence for the germinal force in Nature, took the humming-bird for its emblem, and so evolved the myth of the birth of Huitzilopochtli, who at once fructifies and is born from the bosom of vernal Nature. It would be rash and wrong to deny that such ideas are mixed in the

[1] *Uramerik. Rel.*, p. 602.

[2] Sahagun, ii. 3.

medley of myth. But, as a rule, the sacred animal (as the humming-bird) is sacred first in itself, probably as a totem or as a guide and protector, and the symbolical sense is a forced interpretation put later on the facts.[1] We can hardly go farther, with safety, than the recognition of mingled aspects and elements in Huitzilopochtli as the totem, the tribal god, the departmental war-god, and possibly he is the god of the year's progress and renewal. His legend and ritual are a conglomerate of all these things, a mass of ideas from many stages of culture.

An abstract comparatively brief must suffice for the other Aztec deities.

Tezcatlipoca is a god with considerable pretensions to an abstract and lofty divinity. His appearance was not prepossessing; his image, as Bernal has described it, wore the head of a bear, and was covered with tiny mirrors.[2] Various attributes, especially the mirror and a golden ear, showed him forth as the beholder of the conduct of men and the hearer of prayer. He was said, while he lived on earth, to have been a kind of Ares in the least amiable aspect of the god, a maker of wars and discord.[3] Wealth and power were in his gift. He was credited with ability to destroy the world when he chose. Seats were consecrated to him in the streets and the public places; on these might no man sit down. He was one of the two gods whose

[1] Compare Maspero on "Egyptian Beast-Gods," *Rev. de l'Hist. des Rel.*, vol. i. and chapter *postea*, on "Egyptian Divine Myths".

[2] The name means "shining mirror". Acosta makes him the god of famine and pestilence (p. 353).

[3] Sahagun, i. 3.

extraordinary birth, and death by "happy despatch," that their vitality might animate the motionless sun, have already been described.[1] Tezcatlipoca, like most of the other gods, revived, and came back from the sky to earth. At a place called Tulla he encountered another god or medicine-man, Quetzalcoatl, and their legends become inextricably entangled in tales of trickery, animal metamorphosis, and perhaps in vague memories of tribal migrations. Throughout Tezcatlipoca brought grief on the people called Toltecs, of whom Quetzalcoatl was the divine culture-hero.[2] His statues, if we may believe Acosta, did him little credit. "In Cholula, which is a commonwealth of Mexico, they worship a famous idoll, which was the god of merchandise. . . . It had the forme of a man, but the visage of a little bird with a red bill and above a combe full of wartes."[3]

A ready way of getting a view of the Mexican Pantheon is to study Sahagun's two books on the feasts of the gods, with their ritual. It will become manifest that the worship was a worship, on the whole, of departmental gods of the elements, of harvest, of various human activities, such as love and commerce, and war and agriculture. The nature of the worship, again, was highly practical. The ceremonies, when not mere offerings of human flesh, were commonly representations on earth of desirable things which the gods were expected to produce in the heavenly sphere. The common type of all such magical ceremonies, whereby

[1] *Antea*, "Myths of the Origins of Things". [2] Sahagun, iii. 5, 6.

[3] Acosta, *Naturall and Morall Historie of the East and West Indies*, London, 1604.

like is expected to produce like, has been discussed in the remarks on magic (chapter iv.). The black smoke of sacrifice generates clouds ; the pouring forth of water from a pitcher (as in the Attic Thesmophoria) induces the gods to pour forth rain. Thus in Mexico the rain-god (Tlaloc, god of waters) was propitiated with sacrifices of children. "If the children wept and shed abundant tears, they who carried them rejoiced, being convinced that rain would also be abundant."[1] The god of the maize, again (Cinteotl, son of the maize-goddess), had rites resembling those of the Greek Pyanepsion and Eiresione. The Aztecs used to make an image of the god, and offer it all manner of maize and beans.[2] Curiously enough, the Greeks also regarded their Pyanepsion as a bean-feast. A more remarkable analogy is that of the Peruvian Mama Cora, the figure of a goddess made of maize, which was asked "if it hath strength sufficient to continue until the next year," and of which the purpose was, "that the seed of the maize may not perish".[3] This corn image of the corn goddess, preserved through all the year and replaced in the next year by a fresh image, is the Attic *Εἰρεσιώνη*, a branch of olive hung with a loaf and with all the fruits of the season, and set up to stand for all the year in front of each house. "And it remains for a year, and when it is dry and withered next year they make a fresh one."[4] Children were sacrificed in Mexico to this deity. In the rites of a goddess of

[1] Sahagun. ii. 2, 3.
[2] *Ibid.*, ii. 4, 24.
[3] Acosta, *Hist. Nat.*, 1604, p. 413.
[4] See Schol. in Aristoph. *Plut.*, 1054, and other texts, quoted by Mannhardt, *Antike Wald und Feld Cultus*, ii. 221, note 3.

harvest, as has been said, torches were borne by the dancers, as in the Eleusinia; and in European and Oriental folk-lore.[1] Demeter was the Greek harvest goddess, in whose rites torches had a place. One of her names is Demeter Erinnys. Mr. Max Müller recognises Erinnys as the dawn. Schwartz connects Demeter Erinnys with the thunderstorm. The torch in the hand of Demeter is the lightning, according to Schwartz. It is interesting, whether the torch be the torch of dawn, or of storm, or neither, to see the prevalence of these torch festivals in rural rites in Mexico, Greece and modern Europe. The idea of the peasants is that the lights scare away evil spirits.[2] In the Mexican rite, a woman, representing the goddess and dressed in her ornaments, was sacrificed. The same horrid ceremony accompanied the feast of the mother of the gods, Teteo Innan.[3] In this rite the man who represented the son of the goddess wore a mask of the skin from the thigh of the female victim who had personated the goddess herself. The wearing of the skin established a kinship between the man and the woman, as in the many classical, ancient and savage rituals where the celebrants wear the hides of the sacrificed beasts. There was a god of storm called "cloudy serpent," Mixcoatl, whose rites were not more humane. The Mexican Aphrodite was named *Tlaçolteotl*,[4] "the impure". About her character the Aztecs had no illusions. She listened to the

[1] Mannhardt, *op. cit.*, ii. 263, i. 501, 502; Schwartz, *Prähistorisch Anthropologische Studien*, p. 79.

[2] Compare the French *jour des brandons.*

[3] See Sahagun, ii. 30.

[4] *Ibid.*, i. 12.

confessions of the most loathsome sinners, whom she perhaps first tempted to err, and then forgave and absolved. Confession was usually put off till people had ceased to be likely to sin. She is said to have been the wife of Tlaloc, carried off by Tezcatlipoca. "She must have been the aquatic vegetation of marshy lands," says M. Réville, "possessed by the god of waters till the sun dries her up and she disappears." This is an amusing example of modern ingenuity. It resembles M. Réville's assertion that Tlaloc, the rain-god, "had but one eye, which shows that he must be ultimately identified as an ancient personification of the rainy sky, whose one eye is the sun". A rainy sky has usually no "eye" at all, and, when it has, in this respect it does not differ from a cloudless sky.

A less lovely set of Olympians than the Aztec gods it is difficult to conceive. Yet, making every allowance for Catholic after-thoughts, there can be no doubt that the prayers, penances and confessions described at length by Sahagun indicate a firm Mexican belief that even these strange deities "made for righteousness," loved good, and, in this world and the next, punished evil. However it happened, whatever accidents of history or of mixture of the races in the dim past caused it, the Aztecs carried to extremes the religious and the mythical ideas. They were exceedingly pious in their attitude of penitence and prayer; they were more fierce and cruel in ritual, more fantastic in myth, than the wildest of tribes, tameless and homeless, ignorant of agriculture or of any settled and assured existence. Even the Inquisition of the Spanish of the sixteenth century was an improvement on the unheard-of abominations of Mexican ritual. As in all fully developed polytheisms of civilised races among the Aztecs we lose sight of the moral primal Being of low savage races. He is obscured by deities of a kind not yet evolved in the lowest culture.

CHAPTER XVI.

THE MYTHOLOGY OF EGYPT.

Antiquity of Egypt—Guesses at origin of the people—Chronological views of the religion—Permanence and changes—Local and syncretic worship—Elements of pure belief and of totemism—Authorities for facts—Monuments and Greek reports—Contending theories of modern authors—Study of the gods, their beasts, their alliances and mutations—Evidence of ritual—A study of the Osiris myth and of the development of Osiris—Savage and theological elements in the myth—Moral aspect of the religion—Conclusion.

EVEN to the ancients Egypt was antiquity, and the Greeks sought in the dateless mysteries of the Egyptian religion for the fountain of all that was most mysterious in their own. Curiosity about the obscure beginnings of human creeds and the first knowledge of the gods was naturally aroused by that spectacle of the Pantheon of Egypt. Her highest gods were abstractions, swathed, like the INVOLUTI of the Etrurians, in veils of mystic doctrine; yet in the most secret recess of her temples the pious beheld "a crocodile, a cat, or a serpent, a beast rolling on a purple couch".[1] In Egypt, the earlier ages and the later times beheld a land dominated by the thought of death, whose shadow falls on the monarch on his crowning day, whose whisper bids him send to far-off shores for the granite and the alabaster of the tomb.

[1] Clem. Alex., *Pædagog.*, iii. 2 (93).

As life was ruled by the idea of death; so was fact conquered by dream, and all realities hastened to lose themselves in symbols; all gods rushed to merge their identity in the sun, as moths fly towards the flame of a candle. This spectacle of a race obedient to the dead and bowing down before the beasts, this procession of gods that were their own fathers and members together in Ra, wakened the interest of the Greeks, who were even more excited by the mystery of extreme age that hid the beginnings of Egypt. Full of their own memories and legends of tribal movements, of migrations, of invasions, the Greeks acknowledged themselves children of yesterday in face of a secular empire with an origin so remote that it was scarcely guessed at in the conjectures of fable. Egypt presented to them, as to us, the spectacle of antique civilisation without a known beginning. The spade of to-day reveals no more than the traditions of two thousand years ago. The most ancient relics of the earliest dynasty are the massive works of an organised society and an accomplished art. There is an unbridged interval between the builders of the mysterious temple hard by the Sphinx and their predecessors, the chippers of palæolithic flint axes in the river drift. We know not whence the Egyptians came; we only trifle with hypotheses when we conjecture that her people are of an Asiatic or an African stock; we know not whether her gods arose in the fertile swamps by Nile-side, or whether they were borne in arks, like the Huitzilopochtli of Mexico, from more ancient seats by the piety of their worshippers. Yet as one great river of mysterious source flows throughout all Egypt, so through the brakes and jungles of her religion flows one great myth from a distant fountain-head, the myth of Osiris.[1]

The questions which we have to ask in dealing with the mythology of Egypt come under two heads: First, What was the nature of Egyptian religion and myth? Secondly, How did that complex mass of beliefs and practices come into existence?

The question, *What was the religion of Egypt?* is far from simple. In a complete treatise on the topic, it would be necessary to ask in reply, At what period, in what place, and among what classes of society did the religion exist which you wish to investigate? The ancient Egyptian religion had a lifetime so long that it almost requires to be meted by the vague measures of geological time. It is historically known to us, by the earliest monuments, about the date at which Archbishop Usher fixed the Creation. Even then, be it noticed, the religion of Egypt was old and full-grown; there are no historical traces of its beginnings. Like the material civilisation, it had been fashioned by the unrecorded *Sheshoa Hor*, "the

[1] As to the origin of the Egyptians, the prevalent belief among the ancients was that they had descended the Nile from the interior of Africa. *Cf.* Diodorus Siculus, iii. 8. Modern theorists occasionally lean in this direction. Dümichen, *Geschichte des Alten Ægyptiens*, i. 118. Again, an attempt has been made to represent them as successful members of a race whereof the Bushmen of South Africa are the social failures. M. Maspero conceives, once more, that the Egyptians were "proto-Semitic," ethnologically related to the people of Eastern Asia, and the grammar of their language has Semitic affinities. But the connection, if it ever existed, is acknowledged to be extremely remote. Maspero, *Hist. de l'Orient*, 4th edit., p. 17. De Rougé writes, "Tout nous ramène vers la parenté primitive de Mitsraim (Egyptains) et de Canaan" (*Recherches sur les Monuments*, p. 11).

servants of Horus," patriarchs dwelling with the blessed. In the four or five thousand years of its later existence, Egyptian religion endured various modifications.[1] It was a conservative people, and schooled by the wisdom of the sepulchre. But invaders, Semitic, Ethiopian and Greek, brought in some of their own ideas. Priestly colleges developed novel dogmas, and insensibly altered ritual. The thought of hundreds of generations of men brooded, not fruitlessly, over the problems of the divine nature. Finally, it is likely that in Egypt, as elsewhere, the superstitions of the least educated and most backward classes, and of subject peoples on a lower level of civilisation, would again and again break up, and win their way to the surface of religion. Thus a complete study of Egyptian faiths would be *chronological*—would note the setting and rising of the stars of elder and later deities.

The method of a systematic history of Egyptian religion would not be regulated by chronology alone. Topographical and social conditions would also claim attention. The favoured god or gods of one nome (administrative district), or of one town, or of one sacred metropolis, were not the gods of another

[1] Professor Lieblein, maintaining this view, opposes the statement of Mr. Le Page Renouf, who writes: "The earliest monuments which have been discovered present to us the very same fully developed civilisation and the same religion as the later monuments" (*Hib. Lectures*, 1880, p. 81). But it is superfluous to attack a position which Mr. Le Page Renouf does not appear really to hold. He admits the existence of development and evolution in Egyptian religious thought. "I believe, therefore, that, after closely approaching the point at which polytheism might have turned into monotheism, the religious thought of Egypt turned aside into a wrong track" (*op. cit.*, p. 235).

metropolis, or town, or nome, though some deities were common to the whole country. The fundamental character might be much the same in each case, but the titles, and aspects, and ritual, and accounts of the divine genealogy varied in each locality. Once more, the "syncretic" tendency kept fusing into one divine name and form, or into a family triad of gods (mother, father and son), the deities of different districts, which, beneath their local peculiarities, theologians could recognise as practically the same.

While political events and local circumstances were thus modifying Egyptian religion, it must never be forgotten that the different classes of society were probably by no means at one in their opinions. The monuments show us what the kings believed, or at least what the kings practised, record the prayers they uttered and the sacrifices they offered. The tombs and the papyri which contain the *Book of the Dead* and other kindred works reveal the nature of belief in a future life, with the changes which it underwent at different times. But the people, the vast majority, unlettered and silent, cannot tell us what *they* believed, or what were their favourite forms of adoration. We are left to the evidence of amulets, of books of magic, of popular tales, surviving on a papyrus here and there, and to the late testimony of Greek writers—Herodotus, Diodorus, the author of the treatise *De Osiride et Iside*, and others. While the clergy of the twentieth dynasty were hymning the perfections of Ammon Ra— "so high that man may not attain unto him, dweller in the hidden place, him whose image no man has beheld"—the peasant may have been worshipping, like a modern Zulu, the serpents in his hovel, or may have been adoring the local sacred cat of his village, or flinging stones at the local sacred crocodile of his neighbours. To the enlightened in the later empire, perhaps to the remotest unknown ancestors also, God was self-proceeding, self-made, manifest in the deities that were members together in him of godhead. But the peasant, if he thinks of the gods at all, thinks of them walking the earth, like our Lord and the saints in the Norse nursery tales, to amuse themselves with the adventures of men. The peasant spoke of the Seven Hathors, that come like fairy godmothers to the cradle of each infant, and foretell his lot in life.[1]

It is impossible, of course, to write here a complete history of Egyptian religion, as far as it is to be extracted from the books and essays of learned moderns; but it has probably been made clear that when we speak of the religion and mythology of Egypt, we speak of a very large and complicated subject. Plainly this is a topic which the lay student will find full of pitfalls, and on which even scholars may well arrive at contradictory opinions. To put the matter briefly, where one school finds in the gods and the holy menagerie of Egyptian creeds the corruption of a primitive

[1] Compare Maspero, *Hist. de l'Orient.*, 4th edit., pp. 279-288, for the priestly hymns and the worship of beasts. "The lofty thoughts remained the property of a small number of priests and instructed people; they did not penetrate the mass of the population. Far from that, the worship of animals, goose, swallow, cat, serpent, had many more followers than Ammon Ra could count." See also Tiele, *Manuel de l'Hist. des Rel.*, Paris, 1880, pp. 46, 47. For the folk-lore of wandering gods see Maspero, *Contes Egyptiens*, Paris, 1882, p. 17.

monotheism, its opponents see a crowd of survivals from savagery combined with clearer religious ideas, which are the long result of civilised and educated thought.[1] Both views may be right in part.

After this preamble let us endeavour to form a general working idea of what Egyptian religion was as a whole. What kind of religion did the Israelites see during the sojourn in Egypt, or what presented itself to the eyes of Herodotus? Unluckily we have no such eye-witnesses of the earlier Egyptian as Bernal Diaz was of the Aztec temples. The Bible says little that is definite about the theological "wisdom of

[1] The English leader of the former school, the believer in a primitive purity, corrupted and degraded but not extinguished, is Mr. Le Page Renouf (*Hibbert Lectures*, London, 1879). It is not always very easy to make out what side Mr. Le Page Renouf does take. For example, in his *Hibbert Lectures*, p. 89, he speaks somewhat sympathetically of the "very many eminent scholars, who, with full knowledge of all that can be said to the contrary, maintain that the Egyptian religion is essentially monotheistic". He himself says that "a power without a name or any mythological characteristic is constantly referred to in the singular number, and can only be regarded as the object of that *sensus numinis*, or immediate perception of the Infinite," which is "the result of an intuition as irresistible as the impressions of our senses". If this be not primitive instinctive monotheism, what is it? Yet Mr. Le Page Renouf says that Egyptian polytheism, after closely approaching the point where it might have become monotheism, went off on a wrong track; so the Egyptians after all were polytheists, not monotheists (*op. cit.*, p. 235). Of similar views are the late illustrious Vicomte de Rougé, M. Mariette, M. Pierret, and Brugsch Pasha (*Rel. und Myth. der Alten Egypter*, vol. i., Leipzig, 1884). On the other side, on the whole regarding Egyptian creeds as a complex mass of early uncivilised and popular ideas, with a later priestly religion tending towards pantheism and monotheism, are M. Maspero, Professor Tiele, Professor Lieblein (English readers may consult his pamphlet, *Egyptian Religion*, Leipzig, 1884), M. Edward Meyer, (*Geschichte des Alterthums*, Stuttgart, 1884), Herr Pietschmann (*Zeitschrift für Ethnologie*, Berlin, 1878, art. "Fetisch Dienst"), and Professor Tiele (*Manuel de l'Histoire des Religions*, Paris, 1880, and *History of Egyptian Religion*, English translation, 1882).

the Egyptians". When confronted with the sacred beasts, Herodotus might have used with double truth the Greek saw: "A great ox has trod upon my tongue".[1] But what Herodotus hinted at or left unsaid is gathered from the evidence of tombs and temple walls and illuminated papyri.

One point is certain. Whatever else the religion of Egypt may at any time have been, it struck every foreign observer as polytheism.[2] Moreover, it was a polytheism like another. The Greeks had no difficulty, for example, in recognising amongst these beast-headed monsters gods analogous to their own. This is demonstrated by the fact that to almost every deity of Egypt they readily and unanimously assigned a Greek divine name. Seizing on a certain aspect of Osiris and of his mystery-play, they made him Dionysus; Hor became Apollo; Ptah, Hephæstus; Ammon Ra, Zeus; Thoth, Hermes, and so on with the rest. The Egyptian deities were recognised as divine beings, with certain (generally ill-defined) departments of Nature and of human activity under their care. Some of them, like Seb (earth) and Nut (heaven), were esteemed elemental forces or phenomena, and were identified with the same personal phenomena or forces, Uranus and Gæa, in the Greek system, where heaven and earth were also parents of many of the gods.

Thus it is indisputably clear that Egyptian religion had a polytheistic aspect, or rather, as Maspero says, was "a well-marked polytheism"; that in this regard

[1] Æschylus, *Agamemnon*, 37, *βοῦς ἐπὶ γλώσσῃ μέγας βέβηκεν*.

[2] Maspero, *Musée de Boulaq*, p. 150; Le Page Renouf, *Hib. Lect.*, pp. 85, 86.

it coincided with other polytheisms, and that this element must be explained in the Egyptian, as it is explained in the Greek or the Aztec, or the Peruvian or the Maori religion.[1] Now an explanation has already been offered in the mythologies previously examined. Some gods have been recognised, like Rangi and Papa, the Maori heaven and earth (Nut and Seb), as representatives of the old personal earth and heaven, which commend themselves to the barbaric fancy. Other gods are the informing and indwelling spirits of other phenomena, of winds or sea or woods. Others, again, whatever their origin, preside over death, over the dead, over the vital functions, such as love, or over the arts of life, such as agriculture; and these last gods of departments of human activity were probably in the beginning culture-heroes, real, or more likely ideal, the first teachers of men. In polytheisms of long standing all these attributes and functions have been combined and reallotted, and the result we see in that confusion which is of the very essence of myth. Each god has many birth-places, one has many sepulchres, all have conflicting genealogies.

If these ideas about other polytheisms be correct, then it is probable that they explain to a great extent the first principles of the polytheism of Egypt. They explain at least the factors in Egyptian religion, which

[1] "It is certainly erroneous to consider Egyptian religion as a polytheistic corruption of a prehistoric monotheism. It is more correct to say that, while polytheistic in principle, the religion developed in two absolutely opposite directions. On one side, the constant introduction of new gods, local or foreign; on the other, a groping after a monotheism never absolutely reached. The learned explained the crowd of gods as so many incarnations of the one hidden uncreated deity."—Tiele, *Manuel de l'Histoire des Religions*, p. 46.

the Greeks recognised as analogous with their own, and which are found among polytheists of every degree of culture, from New Zealand to Hellas. If ever Ptah, or any other name, represented "Our Father" as he is known to the most backward races, he was buried into the background by gods evolved from ghosts, by departmental gods, and by the gods of races amalgamated in the course of conquest and settlement.

Leaving on one side, then, for the moment, the vast system of ancestor-worship and of rites undertaken for the benefit of the dead, and leaving aside the divinity of the king, polytheism was the most remarkable feature of Egyptian religion. The foreign traveller in the time of the pyramid-builders, as in the time of Ramses II., or of the Ptolemies, or of the Roman domination, would have found a crowd of gods in receipt of honour and of sacrifice. He would have learned that one god was most adored in one locality, another in another, that Ammon Ra was predominant in Thebes; Ra, the sun-god, in Heliopolis; Osiris in Abydos, and so forth. He would also have observed that certain animals were sacred to certain gods, and that in places where each beast was revered, his species was not eaten, though it might blamelessly be cooked and devoured in the neighbouring nome or district, where another animal was dominant. Everywhere, in all nomes and towns, the adoration of Osiris, chiefly as the god and redeemer of the dead, was practised.[1]

While these are the general characteristics of

[1] On the different religions of different nomes, and especially the animal worship, see Pietschmann, *Der Ægyptische Fetischdienst und Götterglaube*, *Zeitschrift für Ethnologie*, 1878, p. 163.

Egyptian religion, there were inevitably many modifications in the course of five thousand years. If one might imagine a traveller endowed, like the Wandering Jew, with endless life, and visiting Egypt every thousand, or every five hundred years, we can fancy some of the changes in religion which he would observe. On the whole, from the first dynasty and the earliest monuments to the time when Hor came to wear a dress like that of a Roman centurion, the traveller would find the chief figures of the Pantheon recognisably the same. But there would be novelties in the manner of worshipping and of naming or representing them. "In the oldest tombs, where the oldest writings are found, there are not many gods mentioned—there are Osiris, Horus, Thot, Seb, Nut, Hathor, Anubis, Apheru, and a couple more."[1] Here was a stock of gods who remained in credit till "the dog Anubis" fled from the Star of Bethlehem. Most of these deities bore birth-marks of the sky and of the tomb. If Osiris was "the sun-god of Abydos," he was also the murdered and mutilated culture-hero. If Hor or Horus was the sun at his height, he too had suffered despiteful usage from his enemies. Seb and Nut (named on the coffin of Mycerinus of the fourth dynasty in the British Museum) were our old friends the personal heaven and earth. Anubis, the jackal, was "the lord of the grave," and dead kings are worshipped no less than gods who were thought to have been dead kings. While certain gods, who retained permanent power, appear in the oldest monuments, sacred animals are also present from the first.

[1] Lieblein, *Egyptian Religion*, p. 7.

The gods, in fact, of the earliest monuments were beasts. Here is one of the points in which a great alteration developed itself in the midst of Egyptian religion. Till the twelfth dynasty, when a god is mentioned (and in those very ancient remains gods are not mentioned often), "he is represented by his animal, or with the name spelled out in hieroglyphs, often beside the bird or beast".[1] "The jackal stands for Anup (Anubis), the frog for Hekt, the baboon for Tahuti (Thoth). It is not till after Semitic influence had begun to work in the country that any figures of gods are found." By "figures of gods" are meant the later man-shaped or semi-man-shaped images, the hawk-headed, jackal-headed, and similar representations with which we are familiar in the museums. The change begins with the twelfth dynasty, but becomes most marked under the eighteenth. "During the ancient empire," says M. Maspero, "I only find monuments at four points—at Memphis, at Abydos, in some parts of Middle Egypt, at Sinai, and in the valley of Hammamat. The divine names appear but occasionally, in certain unvaried formulæ. Under the eleventh and twelfth dynasties Lower Egypt comes on the scene. The formulæ are more explicit, but the religious monuments rare. From the eighteenth dynasty onwards, we have *representations* of all the deities, accompanied by legends more or less developed, and we begin to discover books of ritual, hymns, amulets, and other objects."[2] There are also sacred texts in the Pyramids.

[1] Flinders Petrie, *Arts of Ancient Egypt*, p. 8.

[2] *Revue de l'Histoire des Religions*, i. 124.

Other changes, less important than that which turned the beast-god into a divine man or woman, often beast-headed, are traced in the very earliest ages. The ritual of the holy bulls (Hapi, Apis) makes its official appearance under the fourth king of the first, and the first king of the second dynasties.[1] Mr. Le Page Renouf, admitting this, thinks the great development of bull-worship later.[2] In the third dynasty the name of Ra, sun, comes to be added to the royal names of kings, as Nebkara, Noferkara, and so forth.[3] Osiris becomes more important than the jackal-god as the guardian of the dead. Sokar, another god of death, shows a tendency to merge himself in Osiris. With the successes of the eighteenth dynasty in Thebes, the process of *syncretism*, by which various god-names and god-natures are mingled, so as to unite the creeds of different nomes and provinces, and blend all in the worship of the Theban Ammon Ra, is most notable. Now arise schools of theology; pantheism and an approach to monotheism in the Theban god become probable results of religious speculations and imperial success. These tendencies are baffled by the break-up of the Theban supremacy, but the monotheistic idea remains in the esoteric dogmas of priesthoods, and survives into Neo-Platonism. Special changes are introduced—now, as in the case of worship of the solar disk by a heretic king; earlier, as in the prevalence of Set-worship, perhaps by Semitic invaders.[4]

[1] Brugsch, *History of Egypt*, English transl., i. 59, 60.

[2] *Hib. Lect.*, pp. 237, 238.

[3] *Op. cit.*, p. 56.

[4] For Khunaten, and his heresy of the disk in Thebes, see Brugsch, *op. cit.*, i. 442. It had little or no effect on myth. Tiele says (*Hist. Egypt. Rel.*, p. 49), "From the most remote antiquity Set is one of the Osirian circle, and is thus a genuine Egyptian deity".

It is impossible here to do more than indicate the kind of modification which Egyptian religion underwent. Throughout it remained constant in certain features, namely, the *local* character of its gods, their usefulness to the dead (their *Chthonian* aspect), their tendency to be merged into the sun, Ra, the great type and symbol and source of life, and, finally, their inability to shake off the fur and feathers of the beasts, the earliest form of their own development. Thus life, death, sky, sun, bird, beast and man are all blended in the religious conceptions of Egypt. Here follow two hymns to Osiris, hymns of the nineteenth and twentieth dynasties, which illustrate the confusion of lofty and almost savage ideas, the coexistence of notions from every stage of thought, that make the puzzle of Egyptian mythology.

"Hail to thee, Osiris, eldest son of Seb, greatest of the six deities born of Nut, chief favourite of thy father, Ra, the father of fathers; king of time, master of eternity; one in his manifestations, terrible. When he left the womb of his mother he united all the crowns, he fixed the uræus (emblem of sovereignty) on his head. God of many shapes, god of the unknown name, thou who hast many names in many provinces; if Ra rises in the heavens, it is by the will of Osiris; if he sets, it is at the sight of his glory."[1]

In another hymn[2] Osiris is thus addressed: "King of eternity, great god, risen from the waters that were

[1] From Abydos, nineteenth dynasty. Maspero, *Musée de Boulaq*, pp. 49, 50.

[2] Twentieth dynasty. *Op. cit.*, p. 48.

in the beginning, strong hawk, king of gods, master of souls, king of terrors, lord of crowns, thou that art great in Hnes, that dost appear at Mendes in the likeness of a ram, monarch of the circle of gods, king of Amenti (Hades), revered of gods and men. Who so knoweth humility and reckoneth deeds of righteousness, thereby knows he Osiris."[1]

Here the noblest moral sentiments are blended with Oriental salutations in the worship of a god who, for the moment, is recognised as lord of lords, but who is also a ram at Mendes. This apparent confusion of ideas, and this assertion of supremacy for a god who, in the next hymn, is subjected to another god, mark civilised polytheism; but the confusion was increased by the extreme age of the Egyptian faith, and by the doubt that prevailed as to the meaning of tradition. "The seventeenth chapter of the *Book of the Dead*," which seems to contain a statement of the system of the universe as understood at Heliopolis under the first dynasties, "is known to us by several examples of the eleventh and twelfth dynasties. *Each of the verses had already been interpreted in three or four different ways*; so different, that, according to one

[1] "This phase of religious thought," says Mr. Page Renouf, speaking of what he calls *monotheism*, "is chiefly presented to us in a large number of hymns, beginning with the earliest days of the eighteenth dynasty. It is certainly much more ancient, but . . . none of the hymns of that time have come down to us." See a very remarkable pantheistic hymn to Osiris, "lord of holy transformations," in a passage cited, *Hib. Lect.*, p. 218, and the hymns to Ammon Ra, "closely approaching the language of monotheism," pp. 225, 226. Excellent examples of pantheistic litanies of Ra are translated from originals of the nineteenth dynasty, in *Records of the Past*, viii. 105-128. The royal Osiris is identified with Ra. Here, too, it is told how Ra smote Apap, the serpent of evil, the Egyptian Ahi.

school, the Creator, *Râ-Shou*, was the solar fire; according to another school, not the fire, but the waters! The *Book of the Dead*, in fact, is no book, but collections of pamphlets, so to speak, of very different dates. "Plan or unity cannot be expected," and glosses only some four thousand years old have become imbedded in really ancient texts.[1] Fifteen centuries later the number of interpretations had considerably increased.[2]

Where the Egyptians themselves were in helpless doubt, it would be vain to offer complete explanations of their opinions and practices in detail; but it is possible, perhaps, to account for certain large elements of their beliefs, and even to untie some of the knots of the Osirian myth.

The strangest feature in the rites of Egypt was animal-worship, which appeared in various phases. There was the local adoration of a beast, a bird, or fish, to which the neighbours of other districts were indifferent or hostile. There was the presence of the animal in the most sacred *penetralia* of the temple; and there was the god conceived of, on the whole, as anthropomorphic, but often represented in art, after the twelfth dynasty, as a man or woman with the head of a bird or beast.[3]

These points in Egyptian religion have been the

[1] *Cf.* Tiele, *Hist. Egypt. Rel.*, pp. 26-29, and notes.

[2] Maspero, *Musée de Boulaq*, p. 149.

[3] As to the animals which were sacred and might not be eaten in various nomes, an account will be found in Wilkinson's *Ancient Egyptians*, ii. 467. The English reader will find many beast-headed gods in the illustrations to vol. iii. The edition referred to is Birch's, London, 1878. A more scientific authority is Lanzoni, *Dizion. Mit.*

great puzzle both of antiquity and of modern mythology. The common priestly explanations varied. Sometimes it was said that the gods had concealed themselves in the guise of beasts during the revolutionary wars of Set against Horus.[1] Often, again, animal-worship was interpreted as symbolical ; it was not the beast, but the qualities which he personified that were adored.[2] Thus Anubis, really a jackal, is a dog, in the explanations of Plutarch, and is said to be worshipped for his fidelity, or because he can see in the night, or because he is the image of time. "As he brought forth all things out of himself, and contains all things within himself, he gets the title of dog." [3] Once more, and by a nearer approach to what is probably the truth, the beast-gods were said to be survivals of the badges (representing animals) of various tribal companies in the forces of Osiris. Such were the ideas current in Græco-Roman speculation, nor perhaps is there any earlier evidence as to the character of native interpretation of animal-worship. The opinion has also been broached that beast-worship in Egypt is a refraction from the use of hieroglyphs. If the picture of a beast was one of the signs in the writing of a god's name, adoration might be transferred to the beast from the god. It is by no means improbable that this process had its share in producing the results.[4] Some of the explanations of animal-

[1] *De Is. et Os.*, lxxii. [2] *Op. cit.*, xi. [3] *Ibid.*, xliv.

[4] Pietschmann, *op. cit.*, p. 163, contends that the animal-worship is older than these Egyptian modes of writing the divine names, say of Ammon Ra or Hathor. Moreover, the signs were used in writing the names because the gods were conceived of in these animal shapes.

worship which were popular of old are still in some favour. Mr. Le Page Renouf appears to hold that there was something respectably mythical in the worship of the inhabitants of zoological and botanical gardens, something holy apparent at least to the devout.[1] He quotes the opinion attributed to Apollonius of Tyana, that the beasts were symbols of deity, not deities, and this was the view of "a grave opponent". Mr. Le Page Renouf also mentions Porphyry's theory, that "under the semblance of animals the Egyptians worship the universal power which the gods have revealed in the various forms of living nature".[2] It is evident, of course, that all of these theories may have been held by the learned in Egypt, especially after the Christian era, in the times of Apollonius and Porphyry; but that throws little light on the motives and beliefs of the pyramid-builders many thousands of years before, or of the contemporary peasants with their worship of cats and alligators. In short, the systems of symbolism were probably made after the facts, to account for practices whose origin was obscure. Yet another hypothesis is offered by Mr. Le Page Renouf, and in the case of Set and the hippopotamus is shared by M. Maspero. Tiele also remarks that some beasts were promoted to godhead comparatively late, because their names resembled names of gods.[3] The gods, in certain cases, received their animal characteristics by virtue of certain unconscious puns or mistakes in the double senses of words. Seb is the earth. Seb is also the Egyptian name for a

[1] *Hibbert Lectures*, pp. 6, 7. [2] *De Abst.*, iv. c. 9.
[3] *Theolog. Tidjsch.*, 12th year, p. 261.

certain species of goose, and, in accordance with the *homonymous* tendency of the mythological period of all nations, the god and the bird were identified.[1] Seb was called "the Great Cackler".[2] Again, the god Thoth was usually represented with the head of an ibis. A mummied ibis "in the human form is made to represent the god Thoth".[3] This connection between Thoth and the ibis Mr. Le Page Renouf explains at some length as the result of an etymological confusion.[4] Thus metaphorical language reacted upon thought, and, as in other religions, obtained the mastery.

While these are the views of a distinguished modern Egyptologist, another Egyptologist, not less distinguished, is of an entirely opposite opinion as to the question on the whole. "It is possible, nay, certain," writes M. Maspero, "that during the second Theban empire the learned priests may have thought it well to attribute a symbolical sense to certain bestial deities. But whatever they may have worshipped in Thoth-Ibis, it was a bird, and not a hieroglyph, that the first worshippers of the ibis adored."[5] M. Meyer is of the same opinion, and so are Professor Tiele and M. Perrot.[6]

[1] For a statement of the theory of "homonymous tendency," see *Selected Essays*, Max Müller, i. 299, 245. For a criticism of the system, see *Mythology* in *Encyclop. Brit.*, or in *La Mythologie*, A. Lang, Paris, 1886.

[2] *Hibbert Lectures*, 1880, p. 111.

[3] Wilkinson, iii. 325.

[4] *Op. cit.*, pp. 116, 117, 237.

[5] *Revue de l'Histoire des Religions*, vol. i.

[6] Meyer, *Geschichte des Alterthums*, p. 72; Tiele, *Manuel*, p. 45; Perrot and Chipiez, *Egyptian Art*, English transl., i. 54. *Hist. Egypt. Rel.*, pp. 97, 103. Tiele finds the origin of this animal-worship in "animism," and supposes that the original colonists or conquerors from Asia found it prevalent in and adopted it from an African population. Professor Tiele does not appear, when he wrote this chapter, to have observed the world-wide diffusion of animal-worship in totemism, for he says, "Nowhere else does the worship of animals prevail so extensively as among African peoples".

While the learned have advanced at various periods these conflicting theories of the origin of Egyptian animal-worship, a novel view was introduced by Mr. M'Lennan. In his essays on *Plant and Animal Worship*, he regarded Egyptian animal-worship as only a consecrated and elaborate survival of totemism. Mr. Le Page Renouf has ridiculed the "school-boy authorities on which Mr. M'Lennan relied".[1] Nevertheless, Mr. M'Lennan's views are akin to those to which M. Maspero and MM. Perrot and Chipiez are attached, and they have also the support of Professor Sayce.

"These animal forms, in which a later myth saw the shapes assumed by the affrighted gods during the great war between Horus and Typhon, take us back to a remote prehistoric age, when the religious creed of Egypt was still totemism. They are survivals from a long-forgotten past, and prove that Egyptian civilisation was of slow and independent growth, the latest stage only of which is revealed to us by the monuments. Apis of Memphis, Mnevis of Heliopolis, and Pachis of Hermonthis are all links that bind together the Egypt of the Pharaohs and the Egypt of the stone age. These were the sacred animals of the clans which first settled in these localities, and their identification with the deities of the official religion must have been a slow process, never fully carried out, in fact, in the minds of the lower classes."[2]

Thus it appears that, after all, even on philological showing, the religions and myths of a civilised people may be illustrated by the religions and myths of

[1] *Hibbert Lectures*, pp. 6, 30. [2] Herodotus, p. 344.

savages. It is in the study of savage totemism that we too seek a partial explanation of the singular Egyptian practices that puzzled the Greeks and Romans, and the Egyptians themselves. To some extent the Egyptian religious facts were purely totemistic in the strict sense.

Some examples of the local practices and rites which justify this opinion may be offered. It has been shown that the totem of each totem-kindred among the lower races is sacred, and that there is a strict rule against eating, or even making other uses of, the sacred animal or plant.[1] At the same time, one totem-kindred has no scruple about slaying or eating the totem of any other kindred. Now similar rules prevailed in Egypt, and it is not easy for the school which regards the holy beasts as *emblems*, or as the results of misunderstood language, to explain why an emblem was adored in one village and persecuted and eaten in the next. But if these usages be survivals of totemism, the practice at once ceases to be isolated, and becomes part of a familiar, if somewhat obscure, body of customs found all over the world. "The same animal which was revered and forbidden to be slaughtered for the altar or the table in one part of the country was sacrificed and eaten in another."[2] Herodotus bears testimony to this habit in an important passage. He remarks that the people of the Theban nome whose god, Ammon Ra, or Khnum, was ram-headed, abstain from sheep and sacrifice

[1] This must be taken generally. See Spencer and Gillen in the *Natives of Central Australia*, where each kin helps the others to kill its own totem.

[2] Wilkinson, *Ancient Egyptians*, ii. 467.

goats; but the people of Mendes, whose god was goat-headed, abstain from goats, sacrifice sheep, and hold all goats in reverence.[1]

These local rites, at least in Roman times, caused civil brawls, for the customs of one town naturally seemed blasphemous to neighbours with a different sacred animal. Thus when the people of Dog-town were feasting on the fish called oxyrrhyncus, the citizens of the town which revered the oxyrrhyncus began to eat dogs, to which there is no temptation. Hence arose a riot.[2] The most singular detail in Juvenal's famous account of the war between the towns of Ombi and Tentyra does not appear to be a mere invention. They fought "because each place loathes the gods of its neighbours". The turmoil began at a sacred feast, and the victors devoured one of the vanquished. Now if the religion were really totemistic, the worshippers would be of the same blood as the animal they worshipped, and in eating an adorer of the crocodile, his enemies would be avenging the eating of their own sacred beast. When that beast was a crocodile, probably nothing but starvation or religious zeal could induce people to taste his unpalatable flesh. Yet "in the city Apollinopolis it is the custom that every one must by all means eat a bit of crocodile; and on one day they catch and kill as many crocodiles as they can, and lay them out in front of the temple". The mythic reason was that Typhon, in his flight

[1] Herodotus, ii. 42-46. The goat-headed Mendesian god Pan, as Herodotus calls him, is recognised by Dr. Birch as the goat-headed Ba-en-tattu. Wilkinson, ii. 512, note 2.

[2] *De Is. et Os.*, 71, 72.

from Horus, took the shape of a crocodile. Yet he was adored at various places where it was dangerous to bathe on account of the numbers and audacity of the creatures. Mummies of crocodiles are found in various towns where the animal was revered.[1]

It were tedious to draw up a list of the local sacred beasts of Egypt; [2] but it seems manifest that the explanation of their worship as totems at once colligates it with a familiar set of phenomena. The symbolic explanations, on the other hand, are clearly fanciful, mere *jeux d'esprit.* For example, the sacred shrew-mouse was locally adored, was carried to Butis on its death, and its mummy buried with care, but the explanation that it "received divine honours because it is blind, and darkness is more ancient than light," by no means accounts for the mainly *local* respect paid to the little beast.[3]

If this explanation of the *local* worship of sacred beasts be admitted as plausible, the beast-headed gods, or many of them, may be accounted for in the same way. It is always in a town where a certain animal is locally revered that the human-shaped god wearing the head of the same animal finds the centre and chief holy place of his worship. The cat is great in Bubastis,

[1] Wilkinson, iii. 329. Compare Ælian, x. 24, on the enmity between worshippers of crocodiles and hawks (and Strabo, xvii. 558). The hawk-worshippers averred that the hawk was a symbol of fire; the crocodile people said that their beast was an emblem of water; but why one city should be so attached to water-worship and its neighbour to fire-worship does not appear.

[2] A good deal of information will be found in Wilkinson's third volume, but must be accepted with caution.

[3] Wilkinson, iii. 33; Plutarch, *Sympos.*, iv. quæst. 5; Herodot., ii. 67.

and there is Bast, and also the cat-headed Sekhet[1] of Memphis. The sheep was great in Thebes, and there was the sacred city of the ram-headed Khnum or Ammon Ra.[2] If the crocodile was held in supreme regard at Ombos, there, too, was the sacred town of the crocodile-headed god, Sebak.

While Greek writers like Porphyry and Plutarch and Jamblichus repeat the various and inconsistent Egyptian allegorical accounts of the origin of those beast-headed gods, the facts of their worship and chosen residence show that the gods are only semi-anthropomorphic refinements or successors of the animals. It has been said that these representations are later in time, and it is probable that they are later in evolution, than the representations of the deities as mere animals. Nor, perhaps, is it impossible to conjecture how the change in art was made. It is a common ritual custom for the sacrificer to cover himself with the skin and head of the animal sacrificed. In Mexico we know that the Aztec priests wore the flayed skins of their human victims. Herodotus mentions that on the one awful day when a sheep was yearly sacrificed in Thebes, the statue of Zeus, as he calls him, was draped in the hide of the beast. In the same way certain Californian tribes which worship the buzzard sacrifice him, "himself to himself," once a year, and use his skin as a

[1] Wilkinson, iii. 286. But the cat, though Bubastis was her centre and metropolis, was sacred all over the land. Nor was puss only in this proud position. Some animals were *universally* worshipped.

[2] The inconsistencies of statement about this ram-headed deity in Wilkinson are most confusing. Ammon is an adjective = "hidden," and is connected with the ram-headed Khnum, and with the hawk-headed Ra, the sun.

covering in the ritual.[1] Lucian gives an instance in his treatise *De Deâ Syriâ* (55): "When a man means to go on pilgrimage to Hierapolis, he sacrifices a sheep and eats of its flesh. He then kneels down and draws the head over his own head, praying at the same time to the god." Chaldean works of art often represent the priest in the skin of the god, sometimes in that of a fish.[2]

It is a conjecture not unworthy of consideration that the human gods with bestial heads are derived from the aspect of the celebrant clad in the pelt of the beast whom he sacrifices. In Egyptian art the heads of the gods are usually like masks, or flayed skins superimposed on the head of a man.[3] If it be asked *why* the celebrant thus disguises himself in the sacrifice, it is only possible to reply by guess-work. But the hypothesis may be hazarded that this rite was one of the many ways in which the sacred animal has been propitiated in his death by many peoples. It is a kind of legal fiction to persuade him that, like the bear in the Finnish Kalewala and in the Red Indian and Australian legend, "he does not die". His skin is still capering about on other shoulders.[4]

[1] [Robinson, *Life in California*, pp. 241, 303;] Herodotus, ii. 42.

[2] Menant, *Recherches*, ii. 49. See a collection of cases in our *Cupid and Psyche*, pp. lviii., lix.

[3] The idea is Professor Robertson Smith's.

[4] For examples of propitiation of slain animals by this and other arts, see *Prim. Cult.*, i. 467, 469. When the Koriaks slay a bear or wolf, they dress one of their people in his skin, and dance round him, chanting excuses. We must not forget, while offering this hypothesis of the origin of beast-headed gods, that representations of this kind in art may only be a fanciful kind of shorthand. Every one knows the beasts which, in Christian art, accompany the four Evangelists. These do not, of course, signify that St.

While Egyptian myth, religion and ritual is thus connected with the beliefs of the lower races, the animal-worship presents yet another point of contact. Not only were beasts locally adored, but gods were thought of and represented in the shape of various different beasts. How did the evolution work its way? what is the connection between a lofty spiritual conception, as of Ammon Ra, the lord of righteousness, and Osiris, judge of the dead, and bulls, rams, wolves, cranes, hawks, and so forth? Osiris especially had quite a collection of bestial heads, and appeared in divers bestial forms.[1] The bull Hapi "was a fair and beautiful image of the soul of Osiris," in late ritual.[2] We have read a hymn in which he is saluted as a ram. He also "taketh the character of the god Bennu, with the head of a crane," and as Sokar Osiris has the head of a hawk.[3] These phenomena could not but occur, in the long course of time, when political expediency, in Egypt, urged the recognition of the identity of various local deities. In the same way "Ammon Ra, like most of the gods, frequently took the character of other deities, as Khem, Ra and Chnumis, and even the attributes of Osiris".[4] There was a constant come and go of attributes, and gods adopted each other's symbols, as kings and emperors wear the uniform of regiments in each

John was of the eagle totem kin, and St. Mark of the stock of the lion. They are the beasts of Ezekiel and the Apocalypse, regarded as types of the four Gospel writers. Moreover, in mediæval art, the Evangelists are occasionally represented with the heads of their beasts—John with an eagle's head, Mark with a lion's, Luke with that of an ox. See *Bulletin*, *Com. Hist. Archeol.*, iv. 1852. For this note I am indebted to M. H. Gaidoz.

[1] *Cf.* Wilkinson, iii. 86, 87.
[2] *De Is. et Os.*, 29.
[3] Wilkinson, iii. 82.
[4] *Op. cit.*, iii. 9.

other's service. Moreover, it is probable that the process so amply illustrated in Samoan religion had its course in Egypt, and that different holy animals might be recognised as aspects of the same deity. Finally, the intricate connection of gods and beasts is no singular or isolated phenomenon. From Australia upwards, a god, perhaps originally, conceived of as human and moral in character, is also rècognised in a totem, as Pund-jel in the eagle-hawk. Thus the confusion of Egyptian religion is what was inevitable in a land where new and old did not succeed and supersede each other, but coexisted on good terms. Had religion not been thus confused, it would have been a solitary exception among the institutions of the country.[1]

[1] The peculiarity of Egypt, in religion and myth as in every other institution, is the retention of the very rudest and most barbarous things side by side with the last refinements of civilisation (Tiele, *Manuel*, p. 44). The existence of this conservatism (by which we profess to explain the Egyptian myths and worship) is illustrated, in another field, by the arts of everyday life, and by the testimony of the sepulchres of Thebes. M. Passalacqua, in some excavations at Quoarnah (Gurna), struck on the common cemetery of the ancient city of Thebes. Here he found "the mummy of a hunter, with a wooden bow and twelve arrows, the shaft made of reed, the points of hardened wood tipped with edged flints. Hard by lay jewels belonging to the mummy of a young woman, pins with ornamental heads, necklaces of gold and lapis-lazuli, gold earrings, scarabs of gold, bracelets of gold," and so forth (Chabas, *Etudes sur l' Antiquité Historique*, p. 390). The refined art of the gold-worker was contemporary, and this at a late period, with the use of flint-headed arrows, the weapons commonly found all over the world in places where the metals had never penetrated. Again, a razor-shaped knife of flint has been unearthed; it is inscribed in hieroglyphics with the words, "The great Sam, son of Ptah, chief of artists". The "Sams" were members of the priestly class, who fulfilled certain mystic duties at funerals. It is reported by Herodotus that the embalmers opened the bodies of the dead with a knife of stone; and the discovery of such a knife, though it had not belonged to an embalmer, proves that in Egypt the stone age did not disappear, but coexisted throughout with the arts of metal-working. It is alleged that flint chisels and stone hammers were used

The fact is, that the Egyptian mind, when turned to divine matters, was constantly working on, and working over, the primeval stuff of all mythologies and of all religions. First, there is the belief in a moral guardian and father of men; this is expressed in the sacred hymns. Next, there is the belief in "a strange and powerful race, supposed to have been busy on earth before the making, or the evolution, or the emergence of man"; this is expressed in the mythical legends. The Egyptians inherited a number of legends of extra-natural heroes, not unlike the savage Qat, Cagn, Yehl, Pund-jel, Ioskeha and Quahteaht, the Maori Tutenganahau and the South Sea Tangaroa. Some of these were elemental forces, personified in human or bestial guise; some were merely idealised medicine-men. Their "wanderings, rapes and manslaughters and mutilations," as Plutarch says, remained permanently in legend. When these beings, in the advance of thought, had obtained divine attributes, and when the conception of abstract divinity, returning, perhaps, to its first form, had become pure and lofty, the old legends became so many stumbling-blocks to the faithful. They were explained away as allegories (every student having his own allegorical system), or

by the workers of the mines in Sinai, even under Dynasties XII., XIX. The soil of Egypt, when excavated, constantly shows that the Egyptians, who in the remote age of the pyramid-builders were already acquainted with bronze, and even with iron, did not therefore relinquish the use of flint knives and arrow-heads when such implements became cheaper than tools of metal, or when they were associated with religion. Precisely in the same way did the Egyptians, who, in the remotest known times, had imposing religious ideas, decline to relinquish the totems and beast-gods and absurd or blasphemous myths which (like flint axes and arrow-heads) are everywhere characteristic of savages.

the extranatural beings were taken (as by Plutarch) to be "demons, not gods".

A brief and summary account of the chief figures in the Egyptian pantheon will make it sufficiently plain that this is a plausible theory of the gods of Egypt, and a probable interpretation of their adventures.

Accepting the classification proposed by M. Maspero, and remembering the limitations under which it holds good, we find that:—

1. The gods of death and the dead were Sokari, Isis and Osiris, the young Horus and Nephthys.[1]

2. The elemental gods were Seb and Nut, of whom Seb is the earth and Nut the heavens. These two, like heaven and earth in almost all mythologies, are represented as the parents of many of the gods. The other elemental deities are but obscurely known.

3. Among solar deities are at once recognised Ra and others, but there was a strong tendency to identify each of the gods with the sun, especially to identify Osiris with the sun in his nightly absence.[2] Each god, again, was apt to be blended with one or more of the sacred animals. "Ra, in his transformations, assumed the form of the lion, cat and hawk."[3] "The great cat in the alley of persea trees at Heliopolis, which is Ra, crushed the serpent."[4] In different nomes and towns, it either happened that the same gods had different names, or that analogies were recognised

[1] Their special relation to the souls of the departed is matter for a separate discussion.

[2] "The gods of the dead and the elemental gods were almost all identified with the sun, for the purpose of blending them in a theistic unity" (Maspero, *Rev. de l'Hist. des Rel.*, i. 126).

[3] Birch, in Wilkinson, iii. 59.

[4] Le Page Renouf, *op. cit.*, p. 114.

between different local gods; in which case the names were often combined, as in Ammon-Ra, Sabek-Ra, Sokar-Osiris, and so forth.

Athwart all these classes and compounds of gods, and athwart the theological attempt at constructing a monotheism out of contradictory materials, came that ancient idea of dualism which exists in the myths of the most backward peoples. As Pund-jel in Australia had his enemy, the crow, as in America Yehl had his Khanukh, as Ioskeha had his Tawiscara, so the gods of Egypt, and specially Osiris, have their Set or Typhon, the spirit who constantly resists and destroys.

With these premises we approach the great Osirian myth.

The Osirian Myth.

The great Egyptian myth, the myth of Osiris, turns on the antagonism of Osiris and Set, and the persistence of the blood-feud between Set and the kindred of Osiris.[1] To narrate and as far as possible elucidate this myth is the chief task of the student of Egyptian mythology.

Though the Osiris myth, according to Mr. Le Page Renouf, is "as old as Egyptian civilisation," and though M. Maspero finds the Osiris myth in all its details under the first dynasties, our accounts of it are by no means so early.[2] They are mainly allusive,

[1] Herodotus, ii. 144.

[2] The principal native documents are the Magical Harris Papyrus, of the nineteenth or twentieth dynasty, translated by M. Chabas (*Records of the Past*, x. 137); the papyrus of Nebseni (eighteenth dynasty), translated by M. Naville, and in *Records of Past*, x. 159; the hymn to Osiris, on a stele (eighteenth dynasty) translated by M. Chabas (*Rev. Archéol.*, 1857; *Records of Past*, iv. 99); "The Book of Respirations," mythically said to have been

without any connected narrative. Fortunately the narrative, as related by the priests of his own time, is given by the author of *De Iside et Osiride*, and is confirmed both by the Egyptian texts and by the mysterious hints of the pious Herodotus. Here we follow the myth as reported in the Greek tract, and illustrated by the monuments.

The reader must, for the moment, clear his mind of all the many theories of the meaning of the myth, and must forget the lofty, divine and mystical functions attributed by Egyptian theologians and Egyptian sacred usage to Osiris. He must read the story simply as a story, and he will be struck with its amazing resemblances to the legends about their culture-heroes which are current among the lowest races of America and Africa.

Seb and Nut—earth and heaven—were husband and

made by Isis to restore Osiris—a "Book of the Breath of Life" (the papyrus is probably of the time of the Ptolemies—*Records of Past*, iv. 119); "The Lamentations of Isis and Nephthys," translated by M. de Horrack (*Records of Past*, ii. 117). There is also "The Book of the Dead": the version of M. Pierret, (Paris, 1882) is convenient in shape (also Birch, in Bunsen, vol. v.). M. de Naville's new edition is elaborate and costly, and without a translation. Sarcophagi and royal tombs (Champollion) also contain many representations of the incidents in the myth. "The myth of Osiris in its details, the laying out of his body by his wife Isis and his sister Nephthys, the reconstruction of his limbs, his mythical chest, and other incidents connected with his myth are represented in detail in the temple of Philæ" (Birch, ap. Wilkinson, iii. 84). The reverent awe of Herodotus prevents him from describing the mystery-play on the sufferings of Osiris, which he says was acted at Sais, ii. 171, and ii. 61, 67, 86. Probably the clearest and most consecutive modern account of the Osiris myth is given by M. Lefébure in *Les Yeux d'Horus et Osiris*. M. Lefébure's translations are followed in the text; he is not, however, responsible for our treatment of the myth. The Ptolemaic version of the temple of Edfou is published by M. Naville, *Mythe d'Horus* (Geneva, 1870).

wife. In the *De Iside* version, the sun cursed Nut that she should have no child in month or year; but thanks to the cleverness of a new divine co-respondent, five days were added to the calendar. This is clearly a later edition to the fable. On the first of those days Osiris was born, then Typhon or Set, "neither in due time, nor in the right place, but breaking through with a blow, he leaped out from his mother's side".[1] Isis and Nephthys were later-born sisters.

The Greek version of the myth next describes the conduct of Osiris as a "culture-hero". He instituted laws, taught agriculture, instructed the Egyptians in the ritual of worship, and won them from "their destitute and bestial mode of living". After civilising Egypt, he travelled over the world, like the Greek Dionysus, whom he so closely resembles in some

[1] *De Iside et Osiride*, xii. It is a most curious coincidence that the same story is told of Indra in the *Rig-Veda*, iv. 18, 1. "This is the old and well-known path by which all the gods were born: thou mayst not, by other means, bring thy mother unto death." Indra replies, "I will not go out thence, that is a dangerous way: right through the side will I burst". Compare (Leland, *Algonquin Legends*, p. 15) the birth of the Algonquin Typhon, the evil Malsumis, the wolf. "Glooskap said, 'I will be born as others are'." But the evil Malsumis thought himself too great to be brought forth in such a manner, and declared that he would burst through his mother's side. Mr. Leland's note, containing a Buddhist and an Armenian parallel, but referring neither to Indra nor Typhon, shows the *bona fides* of the Algonquin report. The Bodhisattva was born through his mother's right side (Kern., *Der Buddhismus*, 30). The Irish version is that our Lord was born through the crown of the head of the Virgin, like Athene. *Saltair na Rann*, 7529, 7530. See also Liebrecht, *Zur Volkskunde*, p. 490. For the Irish and Buddhist legends (there is an Anglo-Saxon parallel) I am indebted to Mr Whitley Stokes. Probably the feeling that a supernatural child should have no natural birth, and not the borrowing of ideas, accounts for those strange similarities of myth.

portions of his legend that Herodotus supposed the Dionysiac myth to have been imported from Egypt.[1] In the absence of Osiris, his evil brother, Typhon, kept quiet. But, on the hero's return, Typhon laid an ambush against him, like Ægisthus against Agamemnon. He had a decorated coffer (mummy-case?) made of the exact length of Osiris, and offered this as a present to any one whom it would fit. At a banquet all the guests tried it; but when Osiris lay down in it, the lid was closed and fastened with nails and melted lead. The coffer, Osiris and all, was then thrown into the Nile. Isis, arrayed in mourning robes like the wandering Demeter, sought Osiris everywhere lamenting, and found the chest at last in an *erica* tree that entirely covered it. After an adventure like that of Demeter with Triptolemus, Isis obtained the chest. During her absence Typhon lighted on it as he was hunting by moonlight; he tore the corpse of Osiris into fourteen pieces, and scattered them abroad. Isis sought for the mangled remnants, and, whenever she found one, buried it, each tomb being thenceforth recognised as "a grave of Osiris". Precisely the same fable occurs in Central Australian myths of the Alcheringa, or legendary past.[2] The wives "search for the murdered man's mutilated parts". It is a plausible

[1] Osiris is Dionysus in the tongue of Hellas" (Herodotus, ii. 144, ii. 48). "Most of the details of the mystery of Osiris, as practised by the Egyptians, resemble the Dionysus mysteries of Greece. . . . Methinks that Melampus, Amythaon's son, was well seen in this knowledge, for it was Melampus that brought among the Greeks the name and rites and phallic procession of Dionysus." (Compare *De Is. et Os.*, xxxv.) The coincidences are probably not to be explained by borrowing; many of them are found in America.

[2] Spencer and Gillen, p. 399.

suggestion that, if graves of Osiris were once as common in Egypt as cairns of Heitsi Eibib are in Namaqualand to-day, the existence of many tombs of one being might be explained as tombs of his scattered members, and the myth of the dismembering may have no other foundation. On the other hand, it must be noticed that a swine was sacrificed to Osiris, at the full moon, and it was in the form of a black swine that Typhon assailed Horus, the son of Osiris, whose myth is a *doublure* or *replica*, in some respects, of the Osirian myth itself.[1] We may conjecture, then, that the fourteen portions into which the body of Osiris was rent may stand for the fourteen days of the waning moon.[2] It is well known that the phases of the moon and lunar eclipses are almost invariably accounted for in savage science by the attacks of a beast—dog, pig, dragon, or what not—on the heavenly body. Either of these hypothesis (the Egyptians adopted the latter)[3] is consistent with the character of early myth, but both are merely tentative suggestions.[4] The phallus of Osiris was not recovered, and the totemistic habit which made the people of three different districts abstain from three different fish—*lepidotus*, *phagrus* and *oxyrrhyncus*—was accounted for by the legend that these fish had devoured the missing portion of the hero's body.

So far the power of evil, the black swine Typhon,

[1] In the Edfou monuments Set is slain and dismembered in the shape of a red hippopotamus (Naville, *Mythe d'Horus*, p. 7).

[2] The fragments of Osiris were *sixteen*, according to the texts of Denderah, one for each nome.

[3] *De Is. et Os.*, xxxv.

[4] Compare Lefébure, *Les Yeux d'Horus*, pp. 47, 48.

had been triumphant. But the blood-feud was handed on to Horus, son of Isis and Osiris. To spur Horus on to battle, Osiris returned from the dead, like Hamlet's father. But, as is usual with the ghosts of savage myth, Osiris returned, not in human, but in bestial form as a wolf.[1] Horus was victorous in the war which followed, and handed Typhon over bound in chains to Isis. Unluckily Isis let him go free, whereon Horus pushed off her crown and placed a bull's skull on her head.

There the Greek narrator ends, but[2] he expressly declines to tell the more blasphemous parts of the story, such as "the dismemberment of Horus and the beheading of Isis". Why these myths should be considered "more blasphemous" than the rest does not appear.

It will probably be admitted that nothing in this sacred story would seem out of place if we found it in the legends of Pund-jel, or Cagn, or Yehl, among Australians, Bushmen, or Utes, whose own "culture-hero," like the ghost of Osiris, was a wolf. This dismembering of Osiris in particular resembles the dismembering of many other heroes in American myth; for example, of Chokanipok, out of whom were made vines and flint-stones. Objects in the mineral and vegetable world were explained in Egypt as transformed parts or humours of Osiris, Typhon and other heroes.[3]

[1] Wicked squires in Shropshire (Miss Burns, *Shropshire Folk-Lore*) "come" as bulls. Osiris, in the Mendes nome, "came" as a ram (Mariette, *Denderah*, iv. 75).

[2] *De Is. et Os.*, xx.

[3] *Magical Text*, nineteenth dynasty, translated by Dr. Birch *Records of Past*, vi. 115; Lefébure, *Osiris*, pp. 100, 113, 124, 205; *Livre des Morts*, chap. xvii.; *Records of Past*, x. 84.

Once more, though the Egyptian gods are buried here and are immortal in heaven, they have also, like the heroes of Eskimos and Australians and Indians of the Amazon, been transformed into stars, and the priests could tell which star was Osiris, which was Isis, and which was Typhon.[1] Such are the wild inconsistencies which Egyptian religion shares with the fables of the lowest races. In view of these facts it is difficult to agree with Brugsch[2] that "from the root and trunk of a pure conception of deity spring the boughs and twigs of a tree of myth, whose leaves spread into a rank impenetrable luxuriance". Stories like the Osiris myth—stories found all over the whole world—spring from no pure religious source, but embody the delusions and fantastic dreams of the lowest and least developed human fancy and human speculation. And these flourish, like mistletoe on the oak, over the sturdier growth of a religious conception of another root.

The references to the myth in papyri and on the monuments, though obscure and fragmentary, confirm the narrative of the *De Iside*. The coffer in which Osiris foolishly ventured himself seems to be alluded to in the Harris magical papyrus.[3] "Get made for me a shrine of eight cubits. Then it was told to thee, O man of seven cubits, How canst thou enter it? And it had been made for thee, and thou hast reposed in it." Here, too, Isis magically stops the mouths of the Nile, perhaps to prevent the coffer from floating

[1] *Custom and Myth*, "Star Myths"; De Rougé, *Nouv. Not.*, p. 197; Lefébure, *Osiris*, p. 213.

[2] *Religion und Mythologie*, p. 99.

[3] *Records of Past*, x. 154.

out to sea. More to the point is one of the original "Osirian hymns" mentioned by Plutarch.[1] The hymn is on a stele, and is attributed by M. Chabas, the translator, to the seventeenth dynasty.[2] Osiris is addressed as the joy and glory of his parents, Seb and Nut, who overcomes his enemy. His sister, Isis, accords to him due funeral rites after his death and routs his foes. Without ceasing, without resting, she sought his dead body, and wailing did she wander round the world, nor stopped till she found him. Light flashed from her feathers.[3] Horus, her son, is king of the world.

Such is a *précis* of the mythical part of the hymn. The rest regards Osiris in his religious capacity as a sovereign of nature, and as the guide and protector of the dead. The hymn corroborates, as far as it goes, the narrative of the Greek two thousand years later. Similar confirmation is given by "The Lamentations of Isis and Nephthys," a papyrus found within a statue of Osiris in Thebes. The sisters wail for the dead hero, and implore him to "come to his own abode". The theory of the birth of Horus here is that he was formed out of the scattered members of Osiris, an hypothesis, of course, inconsistent with the other myths (especially with the myth that he dived for the members of Osiris in the shape of a crocodile),[4] and, therefore, all the more mythical. The "Book of Respirations," finally, contains the magical songs by which Isis was feigned to have restored breath and

[1] *De Is. et Os.*, 211. [2] *Rev. Archéol.*, May, 1857.

[3] The Greek version says that Isis took the form of a swallow.

[4] Mariette, *Denderah*, iv. 77, 88, 89.

life to Osiris.[1] In the representations of the vengeance and triumph of Horus on the temple walls of Edfou in the Ptolemaic period, Horus, accompanied by Isis, not only chains up and pierces the red hippopotamus (or pig in some designs), who is Set, but, exercising reprisals, cuts him into pieces, as Set cut Osiris. Isis instructs Osiris as to the portion which properly falls to each of nine gods. Isis reserves his head and "saddle"; Osiris gets the thigh; the bones are given to the cats. As each god had his local habitation in a given town, there is doubtless reference to local myths. At Edfou also the animal of Set is sacrificed symbolically in his image made of paste, a common practice in ancient Mexico.[2] Many of these myths, as M. Naville remarks, are doubtless ætiological: the priests, as in the Brahmanas, told them to account for peculiar parts of the ritual, and to explain strange local names. Thus the names of many places are explained by myths setting forth that they commemorate some event in the campaign of Horus against Set. In precisely the same way the local superstitions, originally totemic, about various animals were explained by myths attaching these animals to the legends of the gods.

Explanations of the Osiris myth thus handed down to us were common among the ancient students of religion. Many of them are reported in the familiar tract *De Iside et Osiride.* They are all the interpre-

[1] *Records of Past*, iv. 121.

[2] Herodotus, ii. 47; *De. Is. et Os.*, 90. See also Porphyry's Life of Pythagoras, who sacrificed a bull made of paste. Liebrecht, *Zur Volkskunde*, p. 436.

tations of civilised men, whose method is to ask themselves, "Now, if *I* had told such a tale as this, or invented such a mystery-play of divine misadventures, what meaning could *I* have intended to convey in what is apparently blasphemous nonsense?" There were moral, solar, lunar, cosmical, tellurian, and other methods of accounting for a myth which, in its origin, appears to be one of the world-wide early legends of the strife between a fabulous good being and his brother, a fabulous evil being. Most probably some incidents from a moon-myth have also crept into, or from the first made part of, the tale of Osiris. The enmity of Typhon to the eyes of Horus, which he extinguishes, and which are restored,[1] has much the air of an early mythical attempt to explain the phenomena of eclipses, or even of sunset. We can plainly see how local and tribal superstitions, according to which this or that beast, fish, or tree was held sacred, came to be tagged to the general body of the myth. This or that fish was not eaten; this or that tree was holy; and men who had lost the true explanation of these superstitions explained them by saying that the fish had tasted, or the tree had sheltered, the mutilated Osiris.

This view of the myth, while it does not pretend to account for every detail, refers it to a large class of similar narratives, to the barbarous dualistic legends about the original good and bad extra-natural beings, which are still found current among contemporary savages. These tales are the natural expression of the savage fancy, and we presume that the myth

[1] *Livre des Morts*, pp. 112, 113.

survived in Egypt, just as the use of flint-headed arrows and flint knives survived during millenniums in which bronze and iron were perfectly familiar. The cause assigned is adequate, and the process of survival is verified.

Whether this be the correct theory of the fundamental facts of the myth or not, it is certain that the myth received vast practical and religious developments. Orisis did not remain the mere culture-hero of whom we have read the story, wounded in the house of his friends, dismembered, restored and buried, reappearing as a wolf or bull, or translated to a star. His worship pervaded the whole of Egypt, and his name grew into a kind of hieroglyph for all that is divine.

"The Osirian type, in its long evolution, ended in being the symbol of the whole deified universe—underworld and world of earth, the waters above and the waters below. It is Osiris that floods Egypt in the Nile, and that clothes her with the growing grain. His are the sacred eyes, the sun that is born daily and meets a daily death, the moon that every month is young and waxes old. Osiris is the soul that animates these, the soul that vivifies all things, and all things are but his body. He is, like Ra of the royal tombs, the earth and the sun, the creator and the created."[1]

Such is the splendid sacred vestment which Egyptian theology wove for the mangled and massacred hero of the myth. All forces, all powers, were finally recognised in him; he was sun and moon, and the maker

[1] Lefébure, *Osiris*, p. 248.

of all things; he was the truth and the life; in him all men were justified.

On the origin of the myth philology throws no light. M. Lefébure recognises in the name Osiris the meaning of "the infernal abode," or "the nocturnal residence of the sacred eye," for, in the duel of Set and Horus, he sees a mythical account of the daily setting of the sun.[1] "Osiris himself, the sun at his setting, became a centre round which the other incidents of the war of the gods gradually crystallised." Osiris is also the earth. It would be difficult either to prove or disprove this contention, and the usual divergency of opinion as to the meaning and etymology of the word "Osiris" has always prevailed.[2] The Greek[3] identifies Osiris with Hades. "Both," says M. Lefébure, "originally meant the dwellings—and came to mean the god—of the dead." In the same spirit Anubis, the jackal (a beast still dreaded as a ghost by the Egyptians), is explained as "the circle of the horizon," or "the portals of the land of darkness," the gate kept, as Homer would say, by Hades, the mighty warden. Whether it is more natural that men should represent the circle of the horizon or the twilight at sunset as a jackal, or that a jackal-totem should survive as a god, mythologists will decide for themselves.[4] The jackal, by a myth that cannot be called pious, was said to have eaten his father, Osiris. Mr. Frazer's theory of Osiris as somehow

[1] *Osiris*, p. 129. So Lieblein, *op. cit.*, p. 7.

[2] See the guesses of etymologists (*Osiris*, pp. 132, 133). Horus has even been connected with the Greek Hera, as the atmosphere!

[3] *De Is. et Os.*, 75.

[4] Le Page Renouf, *Hibbert Lectures*, pp. 112-114, 237.

connected with vegetation will be found in his *Golden Bough.* His master, Mannhardt, the great writer on vegetation myths, held that Osiris was the sun.

The conclusions to be drawn from so slight a treatment of so vast a subject are, that in Egypt, as elsewhere, a mythical and a religious, a rational and an irrational stream of thought flowed together, and even to some extent mingled their waters. The rational tendency, declared in prayers and hymns, amplifies the early human belief in a protecting and friendly personal power making for righteousness. The irrational tendency, declared in myth and ritual, retains and elaborates the early human confusions of thought between man and beast and god, things animate and inanimate. On the one hand, we have almost a recognition of supreme divinity; on the other, savage rites and beliefs, shared by Australians and Bushmen. It is not safe or scientific to call one of those tendencies earlier than the other; perhaps we know no race so backward that it is not influenced by forms of both. Nor is it safe or scientific to look on ruder practices as corruptions of the purer beliefs. Perhaps it may never be possible to trace both streams to the same fountain-head; probably they well up from separate springs in the nature of man. We do but recognise and contrast them; the sources of both are lost in the distance, where history can find no record of actual experience. Egyptian religion and myth are thus no isolated things; they are but the common stuff of human thought, decorated or distorted under a hundred influences in the course of unknown centuries of years.

CHAPTER XVII.

GODS OF THE ARYANS OF INDIA.

Difficulties of the study—Development of clan-gods—Departmental gods—Divine patronage of morality—Immorality mythically attributed to gods—Indra—His love of Soma—Scandal about Indra—Attempts to explain Indra as an elemental god—Varuna—Ushas—The Asvins—Their legend and theories about it—Tvashtri—The Maruts—Conclusions arrived at.

NOTHING in all mythology is more difficult than the attempt to get a clear view of the gods of Vedic India. The perplexed nature of the evidence has already been explained, and may be briefly recapitulated. The obscure documents on which we have to rely, the Vedas and the Brahmanas, contain in solution the opinions of many different ages and of many different minds. Old and comparatively modern conceptions of the deities, pious efforts to veil or to explain away what seemed crude or profane, the puerilities of ritual, half-conscious strivings in the direction of monotheism or pantheism, clan or family prejudices, rough etymological guesses, and many other elements of doubt combine to confuse what can never have been clear. Savage legends, philosophic conjectures, individual predilections are all blended into the collection of hymns called the *Rig-Veda.* Who can bring order into such a chaos?

An attempt to unravel the tangled threads of Indian faith must be made. The gods of the Vedas are, on the whole, of the usual polytheistic type, though their forms mix into each other like shadows cast by a flickering fire. The ideas which may be gathered about them from the ancient hymns have, as usual, no consistency and no strict orthodoxy. As each bard of each bardic family celebrates a god, he is apt to make him for the occasion the pre-eminent deity of all.[1] This way of conceiving of the gods leads naturally (as thought advances) in the direction of a pantheistic monotheism, a hospitable theology which accepts each divine being as a form or manifestation of the supreme universal spirit. It is easy, however, to detect certain attributes more or less peculiar to each god. As among races far less forward in civilisation, each of the greater powers has his own special department, however much his worshippers may be inclined to regard him as really supreme sovereign. Thus Indra is mainly concerned with thunder and other atmospheric phenomena : these are his department; but Vayu is the wind or the god of the wind, and Agni as fire or the god of fire is necessarily not unconnected with the lightning. The Maruts, again, are the storm-winds, or gods of the storm-winds ; Mitra and Varuna preside over day and night ; Ushas is the dawn or the goddess of dawn, and Tvashtri is the mechanic among the deities, corresponding more or less closely to the Greek Hephæstus.

[1] Muir, v. 125. Compare Muir, i. 348, on the word *Kusikas*, implying, according to Benfey, that Indra "is designated as the sole or chief deity of this tribe". *Cf.* also Haug, *Ait. Br.*, ii. 384.

Though many of these beings are still in Vedic poetry departmental powers with provinces of their own in external Nature, they are also supposed to be interested not only in the worldly, but in the moral welfare of mankind, and are imagined to "make for righteousness". It is true that the myths by no means always agree in representing the gods as themselves moral. Incest and other hideous offences are imputed to them, and it is common to explain these myths as the result of the forgotten meanings of sayings which originally were only intended to describe processes of nature, especially of the atmosphere. Supposing, for the sake of argument, that this explanation is correct, we can scarcely be expected to think highly of the national taste which preferred to describe pure phenomena like dawn and sunset in language which is appropriate to the worst crimes in the human calendar. It is certain that the Indians, when they came to reflect and philosophise on their own religion (and they had reached this point before the Veda was compiled), were themselves horrified by the immoralities of some of their gods. Yet in Vedic times these gods were already acknowledged as beings endowed with strong moral attributes and interested in the conduct of men. As an example of this high ethical view, we may quote Mr. Max Müller's translation of part of a hymn addressed to Varuna.[1] "Take from me my sin like a fetter, and we shall increase, O Varuna, the spring of thy law. Let not the thread be cut while I weave my song! Let not the form of the workman break before the time. . . . Like as a rope

[1] *Rig-Veda*, ii. 28; *Hibbert Lectures*, p. 284.

from a calf, remove from me my sin, for away from thee I am not master even of the twinkling of an eye. . . . Move far away from me all self-committed guilt, and may I not, O king, suffer for what others have committed. Many dawns have not yet dawned; grant me to live in them, O Varuna." What follows is not on the same level of thought, and the next verse contains an appeal to Varuna to save his worshipper from the effect of magic spells. "Whether it be my companion or a friend who, while I was asleep and trembling, uttered fearful spells against me, whether it be a thief or a wolf who wishes to hurt me, protect us against them, O Varuna."[1] Agni, again, the god of fire, seems to have no original connection with righteousness. Yet even Agni[2] is prayed to forgive whatever sin the worshipper may have committed through folly, and to make him guiltless towards Aditi.[3] The goddess Aditi once more, whether her name (rendered the "boundless") be or be not "one of the oldest names of the dawn,"[4] is repeatedly called on by her worshippers to "make them sinless". In the same way sun, dawn, heaven, soma, and earth are implored to pardon sin.

Though the subject might be dwelt on at very great length, it is perhaps already apparent that the gods of the Vedic poetry are not only potent over regions of the natural world, but are also conceived of, at times, as being powers with ethical tendencies and punishers

[1] An opposite view is expressed in Weber's *Hist. of Sansk. Literature.*

[2] *Rig-Veda*, iv. 12, 4; viii. 93, 7.

[3] For divergent opinions about Aditi, compare *Revue de l'Histoire des Religions*, xii. 1, pp. 40-42; Muir, v. 218.

[4] Max Müller, *Hibbert Lectures*, p. 228.

of mortal guilt. It would be difficult to overstate the ethical nobility of certain Vedic hymns, which even now affect us with a sense of the "hunger and thirst after righteousness" so passionately felt by the Hebrew psalmists. How this emotion, which seems naturally directed to a single god, came to be distributed among a score, it is hard to conjecture. But all this aspect of the Vedic deities is essentially the province of the science of religion rather than of mythology. Man's consciousness of sin, his sense of being imperfect in the sight of "larger other eyes than ours," is a topic of the deepest interest, but it comes but by accident into the realm of mythological science. That science asks, not with what feelings of awe and gratitude the worshipper approaches his gods, but what myths, what stories, are told to or told by the worshipper concerning the origin, personal characteristics and personal adventures of his deities. As a rule, these stories are a mere *chronique scandaleuse*, full of the most absurd and offensive anecdotes, and of the crudest fictions. The deities of the Vedic poems, so imposing when regarded as vast natural forces, or as the spiritual beings that master vast natural forces, so sympathetic when looked on as merciful gods conscious of, yet lenient towards, the sins of perishing mortals, have also their mythological aspect and their *chronique scandaleuse*.[1]

It is, of course, in their anthropomorphic aspect that

[1] Here we must remind the reader that the Vedas do not offer us all these tales, nor the worst of them. As M. Barth says, "Le sentiment religieux a écarté la plupart de ces mythes ainsi que beaucoup d'autres qui le choquaient, mais il ne les a pas écartés tous" (*Religions de l'Inde*, p. 14).

the Vedic deities share or exceed the infirmities of mortals. The gods are not by any means always regarded as practically equal in supremacy. There were great and small, young and old gods,[1] though this statement, with the habitual inconsistency of a religion without creeds and articles, is elsewhere controverted. "None of you, O gods, is small or young; you are all great."[2] As to the immortality and the origin of the gods, opinions are equally divided among the Vedic poets and in the traditions collected in the Brahmanas. Several myths of the origin of the gods have already been discussed in the chapter on "Aryan Myths of the Creation of the World and of Man". It was there demonstrated that many of the Aryan myths were on a level with those current among contemporary savages all over the world, and it was inferred that they originally sprang from the same source, the savage imagination.

In this place, while examining the wilder divine myths, we need only repeat that, in one legend, heaven and earth, conceived of as two sentient living beings of human parts and passions, produced the Aryan gods, as they did the gods of the New Zealanders and of other races. Again, the gods were represented in the children of Aditi, and this might be taken either in a high and refined sense, as if Aditi were the infinite region from which the solar deities rise,[3] or we may hold that Aditi is the eternal which sustains and is sustained by the gods,[4] or the Indian imagination could sink to the vulgar and half-magical conception of Aditi

[1] *Rig-Veda,* i. 27, 13. [2] *Ibid.*, viii. 30; Muir, v. 12.
[3] Max Müller, *Hibbert Lectures,* p. 230. [4] Roth, in Muir, iv. 56.

as a female, who, being desirous of sons, cooked a Brahmandana oblation for the gods, the Sadhyas.[1] Various other gods and supernatural beings are credited with having created or generated the gods. Indra's father and mother are constantly spoken of, and both he and other gods are often said to have been originally mortal, and to have reached the heavens by dint of that "austere fervour," that magical asceticism, which could do much more than move mountains. The gods are thus by no means always credited in Aryan mythology with inherent immortality. Like most of the other deities whose history we have been studying, they had struggles for pre-eminence with powers of a titanic character, the Asuras. "Asura, 'living,' was originally an epithet of certain powers of Nature, particularly of the sky," says Mr. Max Müller.[2] As the gods also are recognised as powers of Nature, particularly of the sky, there does not seem to be much original difference between Devas and Asuras.[3] The opposition between them may be "secondary," as Mr. Max Müller says, but in any case it too strongly resembles the other wars in heaven of other mythologies to be quite omitted. Unluckily, the most consecutive account of the strife is to be found, not in the hymns of the Vedas, but in the collected body of mythical and other traditions called the Brahmanas.[4] The story in the Brahmana begins by saying that

[1] *Taittirya Brahmana*, i. 1, 9, 1; Muir, v. 55, 1, 27.

[2] *Hibbert Lectures*, p. 318.

[3] In the *Atharva Veda* it is said that a female Asura once drew Indra from among the gods (Muir, v. 82). Thus gods and Asuras are capable of amorous relations.

[4] *Satapatha Br.* throughout. See the Oxford translation.

Prajapati (the producer of things, whose acquaintance we have made in the chapter on cosmogonic myths) was half mortal and half immortal. After creating things endowed with life, he created Death, the devourer. With that part of him which was mortal he was afraid of Death, and the gods were also "afraid of this ender, Death". The gods in this tradition are regarded as mortals. Compare the *Black Yajur Veda*:[1] "*The gods were formerly just like men.* They desired to overcome want, misery, death, and to go to the divine assembly. They saw, took and sacrificed with this Chaturvimsatiratra, and in consequence overcame want, misery and death, and reached the divine assembly." In the same Veda we are told that the gods and Asuras contended together; the gods were less numerous, but, as politicians make men peers, they added to their number by placing some bricks in the proper position to receive the sacrificial fire. They then used incantations: "Thou art a multiplier"; and so the bricks became animated, and joined the party of the gods, and made numbers more equal.[2] To return to the gods in the *Satapatha Brahmana* and their

[1] *Taittirya Sanhita;* Muir, v. 15, note 22.

[2] According to a later legend, or a legend which we have received in a later form, the gods derived immortality from drinking of the churned ocean of milk. They churned it with Mount Mandara for a staff and the serpent Hasuki for a cord. The *Ramayana* and *Mahabharata* ascribe this churning to the desire of the gods to become immortal. According to the *Mahabharata*, a Daitya named Rahu insinuated himself among the gods, and drank some of the draught of immortality. Vishnu beheaded him before the draught reached lower than his throat; his *head* was thus immortal, and is now a constellation. He pursues the sun and moon, who had spied him among the gods, and causes their eclipses by his ferocity. All this is on a level with Australian mythology.

dread of death. They overcame him by certain sacrifices suggested by Prajapati. Death resented this, and complained that men would now become immortal and his occupation would be gone. To console him the gods promised that no man in future should become immortal with his body, but only through knowledge after parting with his body. This legend, at least in its present form, is necessarily later than the establishment of minute sacrificial rules. It is only quoted here as an example of the opinion that the gods were once mortal and "just like men". It may be urged, and probably with truth, that this belief is the figment of religious decadence. As to the victory of the gods over the Asuras, that is ascribed by the *Satapatha Brahmana*[1] to the fact that, at a time when neither gods nor Asuras were scrupulously veracious, the gods invented the idea of speaking the truth. The Asuras stuck to lying. The first results not unnaturally were that the gods became weak and poor, the Asuras mighty and rich. The gods at last overcame the Asuras, not by veracity, but by the success of a magical sacrifice. Earlier dynasties of gods, to which the generation of Indra succeeded, are not unfrequently mentioned in the *Rig-Veda*.[2] On the whole, the accounts of the gods and of their nature present in Aryan mythology the inconsistent anthropomorphism, and the mixture of incongruous and often magical and childish ideas, which mark all other mythological systems. This will become still more manifest when we examine the legends of the various gods separately, as they have been disentangled by

[1] Muir, iv. 60. [2] *Ibid.*, v. 16,

Dr. Muir and M. Bergaigne from the Vedas, and from the later documents which contain traditions of different dates.

The Vedas contain no such orderly statements of the divine genealogies as we find in Hesoid and Homer. All is confusion, all is contradiction.[1] In many passages heaven and earth, Dyaus and Prithivi, are spoken of as parents of the other gods. Dyaus is commonly identified, as is well known, with Zeus by the philologists, but his legend has none of the fulness and richness which makes that of Zeus so remarkable. Before the story of Dyaus could become that of Zeus, the old Aryan sky or heaven god had to attract into his cycle that vast collection of miscellaneous adventures from a thousand sources which fill the legend of the chief Hellenic deity. In the Veda, Dyaus appears now, as with Prithivi,[2] the parent of all, both men and gods, now as a created thing or being fashioned by Indra or by Tvashtri.[3] He is "essentially beneficent, but has no marked individuality, and can only have become the Greek Zeus by inheriting attributes from other deities".[4]

Another very early divine person is Aditi, the mother of the great and popular gods called Adityas. "Nothing is less certain than the derivation of the name of Aditi," says M. Paul Regnaud.[5] M. Regnaud finds the root of Aditi in *ad*, to shine. Mr. Max Müller looks for the origin of the word in *a*, privative, and *da*, to

[1] Certain myths of the beginnings of things will be found in the chapter on cosmogonic traditions.

[2] Muir, v. 21-24.

[3] *Ibid.*, v. 30.

[4] Bergaigne, iii. 112.

[5] *Revue de l'Histoire des Religions*, xii. 1, 40.

bind; thus Aditi will mean "the boundless," the "infinite," a theory rejected by M. Regnaud. The expansion of this idea, with all its important consequences, is worked out by Mr. Max Müller in his *Hibbert Lectures.* "The dawn came and went, but there remained always behind the dawn that heaving sea of light or fire from which she springs. Was not this the invisible infinite? And what better name could be given than that which the Vedic poets gave to it, Aditi, the boundless, the yonder, the beyond all and everything." This very abstract idea "may have been one of the earliest intuitions and creations of the Hindu mind" (p. 229). M. Darmesteter and Mr. Whitney, on the other hand, explain Aditi just as Welcker and Mr. Max Müller explain Cronion. There was no such thing as a goddess named Aditi till men asked themselves the meaning of the title of their own gods, "the Adityas". That name might be interpreted "children of Aditi," and so a goddess called Aditi was invented to fit the name, thus philologically extracted from Adityas.[1]

M. Bergaigne[2] finds that Aditi means "free," "untrammelled," and is used both as an adjective and as a name. This vague and floating term was well suited to convey the pantheistic ideas natural to the Indian mind, and already notable in the Vedic hymns. "Aditi," cries a poet, "is heaven; Aditi is air; Aditi is the father, the mother and the son; Aditi is all the gods; Aditi is that which is born and which awaits

[1] The Brahmanic legend of the birth of the Adityas (*Aitareya Brahmana* iii. 33) is too disgusting to be quoted.

[2] *Religion Vedique*, iii. 88.

the birth."[1] Nothing can be more advanced and metaphysical. Meanwhile, though Aditi is a personage so floating and nebulous, she figures in fairly definite form in a certain myth. The *Rig-Veda* (x. 72, 8) tells us the tale of the birth of her sons, the Adityas. "Eight sons were there of Aditi, born of her womb. To the gods went she with seven; Martanda threw she away." The *Satapatha Brahmana* throws a good deal of light on her conduct. Aditi had eight sons; but there are only seven gods whom men call Adityas. The eighth she bore a shapeless lump, of the dimensions of a man, as broad as long, say some. The Adityas then trimmed this ugly duckling of the family into human shape, and an elephant sprang from the waste pieces which they threw away; therefore an elephant partakes of the nature of man. The shapen eighth son was called Vivasvat, the sun.[2] It is not to be expected that many, if any, remains of a theriomorphic character should cling to a goddess so abstract as Aditi. When, therefore, we find her spoken of as a cow, it is at least as likely that this is only part of "the pleasant unconscious poetry" of the Veda, as that it is a survival of some earlier zoomorphic belief. Gubernatis offers the following lucid account of the metamorphosis of the infinite (for so he understands Aditi) into the humble domestic animal: "The inexhaustible soon comes to mean that which can be milked without end" (it would be more plausible to say that what can be milked without end soon comes to mean the inexhaustible), "and hence also a celestial cow, an inoffensive

[1] *Rig-Veda*, i. 89, 10. [2] Muir, iv. 15.

cow, which we must not offend. . . . The whole heavens being thus represented as an infinite cow, it was natural that the principal and most visible phenomena of the sky should become, in their turn, children of the cow." Aditi then is "the great spotted cow". Thus did the Vedic poets (according to Gubernatis) descend from the unconditioned to the byre.

From Aditi, however she is to be interpreted, we turn to her famous children, the Adityas, the high gods.

There is no kind of consistency, as we have so often said, in Vedic mythical opinion. The Adityas, for example, are now represented as three, now as seven; for three and seven are sacred numbers. To the triad a fourth is sometimes added, to the seven an eighth Aditya. The Adityas are a brotherhood or college of gods, but some of the members of the fraternity have more individual character than, for example, the Maruts, who are simply a company with a tendency to become confused with the Adityas. Considered as a triad, the Adityas are Varuna, Mitra, Aryaman. The name of Varuna is commonly derived from *vri* (or Var),[1] to cover, according to the commentator Sayana, because "he envelops the wicked in his snares," the nets which he carries to capture the guilty. As god of the midnight sky, Varuna is also "the covering" deity, with his universal pall of darkness. Varuna's name has frequently been compared to that of Uranus (*Οὐρανὸς*), the Greek god of heaven, who was mutilated by his son Cronos.

[1] Max Müller, *Select Essays*, i. 371.

Supposing Varuna to mean the heaven, we are not much advanced, for *dyu* also has the same meaning; yet Dyaus and Varuna have little in common. The interpreters of the Vedas attempted to distinguish Mitra from Varuna by making the former the god of the daylight, the latter the god of the midnight vault of heaven. The distinction, like other Vedic attempts at drawing a line among the floating phantasms of belief, is not kept up with much persistency.

Of all Vedic deities, Varuna has the most spiritual and ethical character. "The grandest cosmical functions are ascribed to Varuna." "His ordinances are fixed and unassailable." "He who should flee far beyond the sky would not escape Varuna the king." He is "gracious even to him who has committed sin". To be brief, the moral sentiments, which we have shown to be often present in a pure form, even in the religion of savages, find a lofty and passionate expression in the Vedic psalms to Varuna.[1] But even Varuna has not shaken off all remains of the ruder mythopœic fancy. A tale of the grossest and most material obscenity is told of Mitra and Varuna in the *Rig-Veda* itself—the tale of the birth of Vasistha.[2]

In the *Aitareya Brahmana* (ii. 460) Varuna takes a sufficiently personal form. He has somehow fallen heir to a *rôle* familiar to us from the Russian tale of *Tsar Morskoi*, the Gaelic "Battle of the Birds," and the Scotch "Nicht, Nought, nothing".[3] Varuna, in short, becomes the giant or demon who demands from

[1] Muir, v. 66. [2] *Rig-Veda*, vii. 33, 2.

[3] See *Custom and Myth*, "A Far-Travelled Tale," and our chapter *postea*, on "Romantic Myths".

the king the gift of his yet unborn son. Harischandra is childless, and is instructed to pray to Varuna, promising to offer the babe as a human sacrifice. When the boy is born, Harischandra tries to evade the fulfilment of his promise. Finally a young Brahman is purchased, and is to be sacrificed to Varuna as a substitute for the king's son. The young Brahman is supernaturally released.

Thus even in Vedic, still more in Brahmanic myth, the vague and spiritual form of Varuna is brought to shame, or confused with some demon of lower earlier legends.

There are believed on somewhat shadowy evidence to be traces of a conflict between Varuna and Indra (the fourth Aditya sometimes added to the triad), a conflict analogous to that between Uranus and Cronos.[1] The hymn, as M. Bergaigne holds, proves that Indra was victorious over Varuna, and thereby obtained possession of fire and of the soma juice. But these births and battles of gods, who sometimes are progenitors of their own fathers, and who seem to change shapes with demons, are no more to be fixed and scientifically examined than the torn plumes and standards of the mist as they roll up a pass among the mountain pines.[2]

We next approach a somewhat better defined and more personal figure, that of the famous god Indra, who is the nearest Vedic analogue of the Greek Zeus. Before dealing with the subject more systematically, it may be interesting to give one singular example of the parallelisms between Aryan and savage mythology.

[1] *Rig-Veda*, x. 124. [2] Bergaigne, iii. 147.

In his disquisition on the Indian gods, Dr. Muir has been observing[1] that some passages of the *Rig-Veda* imply that the reigning deities were successors of others who had previously existed. He quotes, in proof of this, a passage from *Rig-Veda*, iv. 18, 12: "Who, O Indra, made thy mother a widow? Who sought to kill thee, lying or moving? What god was present in the fray when thou didst slay thy father, seizing him by the foot?" According to M. Bergaigne,[2] Indra slew his father, Tvashtri, for the purpose of stealing and drinking the soma, to which he was very partial. This is rather a damaging passage, as it appears that the Vedic poet looked on Indra as a parricide and a drunkard. To explain this hint, however, Sayana the ancient commentator, quotes a passage from the *Black Yajur Veda* which is no explanation at all. But it has some interest for us, as showing how the myths of Aryans and Hottentots coincide, even in very strange details. Yajna (sacrifice) desired Dakshina (largesse). He consorted with her. Indra was apprehensive of this. He reflected, "Whoever is born of her will be this". He entered into her. Indra himself was born of her. He reflected, "Whoever is born of her besides me will be this". Having considered, he cut open her womb. She produced a cow. Here we have a high Aryan god passing into and being born from the womb of a being who also bore a cow. The Hottentot legend of the birth of their god, Heitsi Eibib, is scarcely so repulsive.[3] "There was grass growing, and a cow

[1] *Sanskrit Texts*, v. 16, 17. [2] *Religion Vedique*, iii. 99.
[3] *Tsuni Goam*, Hahn, p. 68.

came and ate of that grass, and she became pregnant" (as Hera of Ares in Greek myth), "and she brought forth a young bull. And this bull became a very large bull." And the people came together one day in order to slaughter him. But he ran away down hill, and they followed him to turn him back and catch him. But when they came to the spot where he had disappeared, they found a man making milk tubs. They asked this man, "Where is the bull that passed down here?" He said, "I do not know; has he then passed here?" And all the while it was he himself, who had again become Heitsi Eibib. Thus the birth of Heitsi Eibib resembled that of Indra as described in *Rig-Veda*, iv. 18, 10. "His mother, a cow, bore Indra, an unlicked calf."[1] Whatever view we may take of this myth, and of the explanation in the Brahmana, which has rather the air of being an invention to account for the Vedic cow-mother of Indra, it is certain that the god is not regarded as an uncreated being.[2]

[1] Ludwig, *Die färse hat den groszen, starken, nicht zu verwundenden stier, den tosenden Indra, geboren.*

[2] As to the etymological derivation and original significance of the name of Indra, the greatest differences exist among philologists. Yaska gives thirteen guesses of old, and there are nearly as many modern conjectures. In 1846 Roth described Indra as the god of "the bright clear vault of heaven" (Zeller's *Theologisches Jahrbuch*, 1846, p. 352). Compare for this and the following conjectures, E. D. Perry, *Journal of American Oriental Society*, vol. i. p. 118. Roth derived the "radiance" from *idh*, *indh*, to kindle. Roth afterwards changed his mind, and selected *in* or *inv*, to have power over. Lassen (*Indische Alterthumskunde*, 2nd ed., i. p. 893) adopted a different derivation. Benfey (*Or. und Occ.*, 1862, p. 48) made Indra God, not of the *radiant*, but of the *rainy* sky. Mr. Max Müller (*Lectures on Science of Language*, ii. 470) made Indra "another conception of the bright blue sky," but (p. 473, note 35) he derives Indra from

It seems incontestable that in Vedic mythology Tvashtri is regarded as the father of Indra.[1] Thus (ii. 17, 6) Indra's thunderbolts are said to have been fashioned by his father. Other proofs are found in the account of the combat between father and son. Thus (iii. 48, 4) we read, "Powerful, victorious, *he gives his body what shape he pleases.* Thus Indra, having vanquished Tvashtri even at his birth, stole and drank the soma."[2] These anecdotes do not quite correspond with the version of Indra's guilt given in the Brahmanas. There it is stated[3] that Tvashtri had a three-headed son akin to the Asuras, named Vairupa. This Vairupa was suspected of betraying to the Asuras the secret of soma. Indra therefore cut off his three heads. Now Vairupa was a Brahman, and Indra was only purified of his awful guilt, Brahmanicide, when earth, trees and women accepted each their share of the iniquity. Tvashtri, the father of Vairupa, still excluded Indra from a share of the soma, which, however, Indra seized by force. Tvashtri threw what remained of Indra's share into the fire with

the same root as in Sanskrit gives *indu*, drop or sap, that is, apparently, rainy sky, the reverse of blue. It means originally "the giver of rain," and Benfey is quoted *ut supra*. In *Chips*, ii. 91, Indra becomes "the chief solar deity of India". Muir (*Texts*, v. 77) identifies the character of Indra with that of Jupiter Pluvius, the Rainy Jove of Rome. Grassman (*Dictionary*, *s. v.*) calls Indra "the god of the bright firmament." Mr. Perry takes a distinction, and regards Indra as a god, not of sky, but of air, a *midgarth* between earth and sky, who inherited the skyey functions of Dyu. In the Veda Mr. Perry finds him "the personification of the thunderstorm". And so on!

[1] On the parentage of Indra, Bergaigne writes, iii. 58.

[2] iii. 61. Bergaigne identifies Tvashtri and Vritra. Cf. *Aitareya Brahmana*, ii. 483, note 5.

[3] *Aitareya Brahmana*, ii. 483, note 5.

imprecations, and from the fire sprang Vritra, the enemy of Indra. Indra is represented at various times and in various texts as having sprung from the mouth of Purusha, or as being a child of heaven and earth, whom he thrust asunder, as Tutenganahau thrust asunder Rangi and Papa in the New Zealand myth. In a passage of the *Black Yajur Veda,* once already quoted, Indra, sheep and the Kshattriya caste were said to have sprung from the breast and arms of Prajapati.[1] In yet another hymn in the *Rig-Veda* he is said to have conquered heaven by magical austerity.

Leaving the Brahmanas aside, Mr. Perry[2] distinguishes four sorts of Vedic texts on the origin of Indra:—

1. Purely physical.
2. Anthropomorphic.
3. Vague references to Indra's parents.
4. Philosophical speculations.

Of the first class,[3] it does not appear to us that the purely physical element is so very pure after all. Heaven, earth, Indra, "the cow," are all thought of as *personal* entities, however gigantic and vague.

In the second or anthropomorphic myths we have[4] the dialogue already referred to, in which Indra, like Set in Egypt and Malsumis or Chokanipok in America, insists on breaking his way through his mother's side.[5] In verse 5 his mother exposes Indra, as Maui and the youngest son of Aditi were exposed. Indra soon after,

[1] Muir, i. 16.
[2] *Op. cit.*, p. 124.
[3] *Rig-Veda,* iv. 17, 4, 2, 12; iv. 22, 4; i. 63, 1; viii. 59, 4; viii. 6, 28-30.
[4] *Ibid.*, iv. 18, 1.
[5] *Cf.* "Egyptian Divine Myths".

as precocious as Heitsi Eibib, immediately on his birth kills his father.[1] He also kills Vritra, as Apollo when new-born slew the Python. In iii. 48, 2, 3, he takes early to soma-drinking. In x. 153, 1, women cradle him as the nymphs nursed Zeus in the Cretan cave.

In the third class we have the odd myth,[2] "while an immature boy, he mounted the new waggon and roasted for father and mother a fierce bull".

In the fourth class a speculative person tries to account for the statement that Indra was born from a horse, "or the verse means that Agni was a horse's son". Finally, Sayana[4] explains nothing, but happens to mention that the goddess Aditi *swallowed* her rival Nisti, a very primitive performance, and much like the feat of Cronos when he dined on his family, or of Zeus when he swallowed his wife. Thus a fixed tradition of Indra's birth is lacking in the Veda, and the fluctuating traditions are not very creditable to the purity of the Aryan fancy. In personal appearance Indra was handsome and ruddy as the sun, but, like Odin and Heitsi Eibib and other gods and wizards, he could assume any shape at will. He was a great charioteer, and wielded the thunderbolt forged for him by Tvashtri, the Indian Hephæstus. His love of

[1] Why do Indra and his family behave in this bloodthirsty way? Hillebrandt says that the father is the heaven which Indra "kills" by covering it with clouds. But, again, Indra kills his father by concealing the sun. He is abandoned by his mother when the clear sky, from which he is born, disappears behind the veil of cloud. Is the father sun or heaven? is the mother clear sky, or, as elsewhere, the imperishability of the daylight? (Perry, *op. cit.*, p. 149).

[2] *Rig-Veda*, viii. 58, 15.

[3] *Ibid.*, x. 73, 10.

[4] *Ibid.*, x. 101, 12. For Sayana, see Mr. Perry's Essay, *Journal A. O. S.* 1882, p. 130.

the intoxicating soma juice was notorious, and with sacrifices of this liquor his adorers were accustomed to inspire and invigorate him. He is even said to have drunk at one draught thirty bowls of soma. Dr. Haug has tasted it, but could only manage one teaspoonful. Indra's belly is compared by his admirers to a lake, and there seems to be no doubt that they believed the god really drank their soma, as Heitsi Eibib really enjoys the honey left by the Hottentots on his grave. "I have verily resolved to bestow cows and horses. I have quaffed the soma. The draughts which I have drunk impel me as violent blasts. I have quaffed the soma. I surpass in greatness the heaven and the vast earth. I have quaffed the soma. I am majestic, elevated to the heavens. I have quaffed the soma."[1] So sings the drunken and bemused Indra, in the manner of the Cyclops in Euripides, after receiving the wine, the treacherous gift of Odysseus.

According to the old commentator Sayana, Indra got at the soma which inspired him with his drinking-song by assuming the shape of a quail.

The great feats of Indra, which are constantly referred to, are his slaughter of the serpent Vritra, who had taken possession of all the waters, and his recovery of the sun, which had also been stolen.[2] These myths are usually regarded as allegorical ways of stating that the lightning opens the dark thunder-cloud, and makes it disgorge the rain and reveal the sun. Whether this theory be correct or not, it is important for our purpose to show that the feats thus attributed to Indra are really identical in idea with,

[1] *Rig-Veda*, x. 119. [2] *Ibid.*, 139, 4; iii. 39, 5; viii. 85, 7.

though more elevated in conception and style, than certain Australian, Iroquois and Thlinkeet legends. In the Iroquois myth, as in the Australian,[1] a great frog swallowed all the waters, and was destroyed by Ioskeha or some other animal. In Thlinkeet legends, Yehl, the raven-god, carried off to men the hidden sun and the waters. Among these lower races the water-stealer was thought of as a real reptile of some sort, and it is probable that a similar theory once prevailed among the ancestors of the Aryans. Vritra and Ahi, the mysterious foes whom Indra slays when he recovers the sun and the waters, were probably once as real to the early fancy as the Australian or Iroquois frog. The extraordinary myth of the origin of Vritra, only found in the Brahmanas, indicates the wild imagination of an earlier period. Indra murdered a Brahman, a three-headed one, it is true, but still a Brahman. For this he was excluded from the banquet and was deprived of his favourite soma. He stole a cup of it, and the dregs, thrown into the fire with a magical imprecation, became Vritra, whom Indra had such difficulty in killing. Before attacking Vritra, Indra supplied himself with Dutch courage. "A copious draught of soma provided him with the necessary courage and strength." The terror of the other gods was abject.[2] After slaying him, he so lost self-possession that in his flight he behaved like Odin when he flew off in terror with the head of Suttung.[3] If our opinion be correct, the

[1] Brinton, *Myths of New World*, pp. 184, 185. See also chapter i.

[2] Perry, *op. cit.*, p. 137 ; *Rig-Veda*, v. 29, 3, 7 ; iii. 43, 7 ; iv. 18, 11 ; viii. 85, 7.

[3] *Rig-Veda*, i. 32, 14, tells of a flight as headlong as that of Apollo after killing the Python. Mr. Perry explains the flight as the rapid journey of the thunderstorm.

elemental myths which abound in the Veda are not myths "in the making," as is usually held, but rather myths gradually dissolving into poetry and metaphor. As an example of the persistence in civilised myth of the old direct savage theory that animals of a semi-supernatural sort really cause the heavenly phenomena, we may quote Mr. Darmesteter's remark, in the introduction to the *Zendavesta:* "The storm floods that cleanse the sky of the dark fiends in it were described in a class of myths as the urine of a gigantic animal in the heavens".[1] A more savage and theriomorphic hypothesis it would be hard to discover among Bushmen or Nootkas.[2] Probably the serpent Vritra is another beast out of the same menagerie.

If our theory of the evolution of gods is correct, we may expect to find in the myths of Indra traces of a theriomorphic character. As the point in the ear of man is thought or fabled to be a relic of his arboreal ancestry, so in the shape of Indra there should, if gods were developed out of divine beasts, be traces of fur and feather. They are not very numerous nor very distinct, but we give them for what they may be worth.

The myth of Yehl, the Thlinkeet raven-god, will not have been forgotten. In his raven gear Yehl stole the sacred water, as Odin, also in bird form, stole the mead of Suttung. We find a similar feat connected with Indra. Gubernatis says:[3] "In the *Rig-Veda* Indra often appears as a hawk. While the

[1] *Sacred Books of the East*, vol. iv. p. lxxxviii.

[2] The etymology of Vritra is usually derived from *vri*, to "cover," "hinder," "restrain," then "what is to be hindered," then "enemy," "fiend".

[3] *Zoological Mythology*, ii. 182.

hawk carries the ambrosia through the air, he trembles for fear of the archer Kriçanus, who, in fact, shot off one of his claws, of which the hedgehog was born, according to the *Aitareya Brahmana*, and according to the Vedic hymn, one of his feathers, which, falling on the earth, afterwards became a tree."[1] Indra's very peculiar relations with rams are also referred to by Gubernatis.[2] They resemble a certain repulsive myth of Zeus, Demeter and the ram referred to by the early Christian fathers. In the *Satapatha Brahmana*[3] Indra is called "ram of Medhâtithi," wife of Vrishanasva. Indra, like Loki, had taken the part of a woman.[4] In the shape of a ram he carried off Medhâtithi, an exploit like that of Zeus with Ganymede.[5]

In the Vedas, however, all the passages which connect Indra with animals will doubtless be explained away as metaphorical, though it is admitted that, like Zeus, he could assume whatever form he pleased.[6] Vedic poets, probably of a late period, made Indra as anthropomorphic as the Homeric Zeus. His domestic life in the society of his consort Indrani is described.[7] When he is starting for the war, Indrani calls him back, and gives him a stirrup-cup of soma. He and she quarrel very naturally about his pet monkey.[8]

In this brief sketch, which is not even a summary, we have shown how much of the irrational element, how much, too, of the humorous element, there is in the myths about Indra. He is a drunkard, who gulps down cask, spigot and all.[9] He is an adulterer and

[1] Compare *Rig-Veda*, iv. 271. [2] *Zool. Myth.*, i. 414. [3] ii. 81.
[4] *Rig-Veda*, i. 51, 13. [5] *Ibid.*, viii. 2, 40. [6] *Ibid.*, iii. 48, 4.
[7] *Ibid.*, 53, 4-6; vii. 18, 2. [8] *Ibid.*, x. 86. [9] *Ibid.*, 116.

a "shape-shifter," like all medicine-men and savage sorcerers. He is born along with the sheep from the breast of a vast non-natural being, like Ymir in Scandinavian myth; he metamorphoses himself into a ram or a woman; he rends asunder his father and mother, heaven and earth; he kills his father immediately after his birth, or he is mortal, but has attained heaven by dint of magic, by "austere fervour". Now our argument is that these and such as these incongruous and irrational parts of Indra's legend have no necessary or natural connection with the worship of him as a nature-god, an elemental deity, a power of sky and storm, as civilised men conceive storm and sky. On the other hand, these legends, of which plenty of savage parallels have been adduced, are obviously enough survivals from the savage intellectual myths, in which sorcerers, with their absurd powers, are almost on a level with gods. And our theory is, that the irrational part of Indra's legend became attached to the figure of an elemental divinity, a nature-god, at the period when savage men mythically attributed to their gods the qualities which were claimed by the most illustrious among themselves, by their sorcerers and chiefs. In the Vedas the nature-god has not quite disengaged himself from these old savage attributes, which to civilised men seem so irrational. "Trailing clouds of" anything but "glory" does Indra come "from heaven, which is his home." If the irrational element in the legend of Indra was neither a survival of, nor a loan from, savage fancy, why does it tally with the myths of savages?

The other Adityas, strictly so called (for most gods

are styled Adityas now and then by way of compliment), need not detain us. We go on to consider the celebrated soma.

Soma is one of the most singular deities of the Indo-Aryans. Originally Soma is the intoxicating juice of a certain plant.[1] The wonderful personifying power of the early imagination can hardly be better illustrated than by the deification of the soma juice. We are accustomed to hear in the *märchen* or peasant myths of Scotch, Russian, Zulu and other races, of drops of blood or spittle which possess human faculties and intelligence, and which can reply, for example, to questions. The personification of the soma juice is an instance of the same exercise of fancy on a much grander scale. All the hymns in the ninth book of the *Rig-Veda*, and many others in other places, are addressed to the milk-like juice of this plant, which, when personified, holds a place almost as high as that of Indra in the Indo-Aryan Olympus. The sacred plant was brought to men from the sky or from a mountain by a hawk, or by Indra in guise of a hawk, just as fire was brought to other races by a benevolent bird, a raven or a cow. According to the *Aitareya Brahmana* (ii. 59), the gods bought some from the Gandharvas in exchange for one of their own number, who was metamorphosed into a woman, "a big naked woman" of easy virtue. In the *Satapatha Brahmana*,[2] the gods, while still they lived on earth, desired to obtain soma, which was then in the sky. A Gandharva

[1] As to the true nature and home of the soma plant, see a discussion in the *Academy*, 1885.

[2] Muir, v. 263.

robbed the divine being who had flown up and seized the soma, and, as in the *Aitareya Brahmana*, the gods won the plant back by the aid of Vach, a woman-envoy to the amorous Gandharvas. The *Black Yajur Veda* has some ridiculous legends about Soma (personified) and his thirty-three wives, their jealousies, and so forth. Soma, in the *Rig-Veda*, is not only the beverage that inspires Indra, but is also an anthropomorphic god who created and lighted up the sun,[1] and who drives about in a chariot. He is sometimes addressed as a kind of Atlas, who keeps heaven and earth asunder.[2] He is prayed to forgive the violations of his law.[3] Soma, in short, as a personified power, wants little of the attributes of a supreme deity.[4]

Another, and to modern ideas much more poetical personified power, often mentioned in the Vedas, is Ushas, or the dawn. As among the Australians, the dawn is a woman, but a very different being from the immodest girl dressed in red kangaroo-skins of the Murri myth. She is an active maiden, who[5] "advances, cherishing all things; she hastens on, arousing footed creatures, and makes the birds fly aloft. . . . The flying birds no longer rest after thy dawning, O bringer of food (?). She has yoked her horses from the remote rising-place of the sun. . . . Resplendent on thy massive car, hear our invocations." Ushas is "like a fair girl adorned by her mother. . . . She has been beheld like the bosom of a bright maiden. . . .

[1] *Rig-Veda*, vi. 44, 23. [2] *Ibid.*, 44, 24. [3] *Ibid.*, viii. 48, 9.

[4] Bergaigne, i. 216. To me it seems that the Rishis when hymning Soma simply gave him all the predicates of God that came into their heads. *Cf.* Bergaigne, i. 223.

[5] *Rig-Veda*, i. 48.

Born again and again though ancient, shining with an ever uniform hue, she wasteth away the life of mortals." She is the sister of Night, and the bright sun is her child. There is no more pure poetry in the Vedic collections than that which celebrates the dawn, though even here the Rishis are not oblivious of the rewards paid to the sacrificial priests.[1] Dawn is somewhat akin to the Homeric Eos, the goddess of the golden throne,[2] she who loved a mortal and bore him away, for his beauty's sake, to dwell with the immortals. Once Indra, acting with the brutality of the Homeric Ares, charged against the car of Ushas and overthrew it.[3] In her legend, however, we find little but pure poetry, and we do not know that Ushas, like Eos, ever chose a mortal lover. Such is the Vedic Ushas, but the Brahmanas, as usual, manage either to retain or to revive and introduce the old crude element of myth. We have seen that the Australians account to themselves for the ruddy glow of the morning sky by the hypothesis that dawn is a girl of easy virtue, dressed in the red opossum-skins she has received from her lovers. In a similar spirit the *Aitareya Brahmana* (iv. 9) offers brief and childish ætiological myths to account for a number of natural phenomena. Thus it explains the sterility of mules by saying that the gods once competed in a race; that Agni (fire) drove in a chariot drawn by mules and scorched them, so that they do not conceive. But in this race Ushas was drawn by red cows; "hence after the coming of dawn there is a reddish colour". The red cows of the

[1] *Rig-Veda*, i. 48, 4. [2] *Ibid.*, i. 48, 10.
[3] *Ibid.*, iv. 30, 8; *Ait. Br.*, iv. 9.

Brahmana may pair off with the red opossums of the Australian imagination.

We now approach a couple of deities whose character, as far as such shadowy things can be said to have any character at all, is pleasing and friendly. The Asvins correspond in Vedic mythology to the Dioscuri, the Castor and Polydeuces of Greece. They, like the Dioscuri, are twins, are horsemen, and their legend represents them as kindly and helpful to men in distress. But while the Dioscuri stand forth in Greek legend as clearly and fairly fashioned as two young knights of the Panathenaic procession, the Asvins show as bright and formless as melting wreaths of mist.

The origin of their name has been investigated by the commentator Yaska, who "quotes sundry verses to prove that the two Asvins belong together" (*sic*).[1] The etymology of the name is the subject, as usual, of various conjectures. It has been derived from *Asva*, a horse, from the root *as*, "to pervade," and explained as a patronymic from Asva, the sun. The nature of the Asvins puzzled the Indian commentators no less than their name. Who, then, are these Asvins? "Heaven and earth," say some.[2] The "some" who held this opinion relied on an etymological guess, the derivation from *as* "to pervade". Others inclined to explain the Asvins as day and night, others as the sun and moon, others—Indian euhemerists—as two real kings, now dead and gone. Professor Roth thinks the Asvins contain an historical element, and are "the

[1] Max Müller, *Lectures on Language*, ii. 536.

[2] Yaska in the *Nirukta*, xii. 1. See Muir, v. 234.

earliest bringers of light in the morning sky". Mr. Max Müller seems in favour of the two twilights. As to these and allied modes of explaining the two gods in connection with physical phenomena, Muir writes thus: "This allegorical method of interpretation seems unlikely to be correct, as it is difficult to suppose that the phenomena in question should have been alluded to under such a variety of names and circumstances. It appears, therefore, to be more probable that the Rishis merely refer to certain legends which were popularly current of interventions of the Asvins in behalf of the persons whose names are mentioned." In the Veda[1] the Asvins are represented as living in fraternal polyandry, with but one wife, Sûryâ, the daughter of the sun, between them. They are thought to have won her as the prize in a chariot-race, according to the commentator Sayana. "The time of their appearance is properly the early dawn," when they receive the offerings of their votaries.[2] "When the dark (night) stands among the tawny cows, I invoke you, Asvins, sons of the sky."[3] They are addressed as young, beautiful, fleet, and the foes of evil spirits.

There can be no doubt that, when the Vedas were composed, the Asvins shone and wavered and were eclipsed among the bright and cloudy throng of gods, then contemplated by the Rishis or sacred singers. Whether they had from the beginning an elemental origin, and what that origin exactly was, or whether they were merely endowed by the fancy of poets with

[1] *Rig-Veda*, i. 119, 2; i. 119, 5; x. 39, 11 (?).
[2] Muir, v. 238. [3] *Rig-Veda*, x. 61, 4.

various elemental and solar attributes and functions, it may be impossible to ascertain. Their legend, meanwhile, is replete with features familiar in other mythologies. As to their birth, the *Rig-Veda* has the following singular anecdote, which reminds one of the cloud-bride of Ixion, and of the woman of clouds and shadows that was substituted for Helen of Troy: "Tvashtri makes a wedding for his daughter. Hearing this, the whole world assembled. The mother of Yama, the wedded wife of the great Vivasvat, disappeared. They concealed the immortal bride from mortals. Making another of like appearance, they gave her to Vivasvat. Saranyu bore the two Asvins, and when she had done so, deserted the twins."[1] The old commentators explain by a legend in which the daughter of Tvashtri, Saranyu, took on the shape of a mare. Vivasvat followed her in the form of a horse, and she became the mother of the Asvins, "sons of the horse," who more or less correspond to Castor and Pollux, sons of the swan. The Greeks were well acquainted with local myths of the same sort, according to which, Poseidon, in the form of a horse, had become the parent of a horse by Demeter Erinnys (Saranyu ?), then in the shape of a mare. The Phigaleians, among whom this tale was current, worshipped a statue of Demeter in a woman's shape with a mare's head. The same tale was told of Cronus and Philyra.[2] This myth of the birth of gods, who "are lauded as Asvins" sprung from a horse,[3] may be the result of a

[1] *Rig-Veda*, x. 17, 1-2; Bergaigne, ii. 306, 318.

[2] Pausanias, viii. 25; Virgil, *Georgics*, iii. 91; Muir, v. 128. See chapter on "Greek Divine Myths," Demeter.

[3] Muir, v. 228.

mere *volks etymologie.* Some one may have asked himself what the word Asvins meant; may have rendered it "sprung from a horse," and may either have invented, by way of explanation, a story like that of Cronus and Philyra, or may have adapted such a story, already current in folk-lore, to his purpose; or the myth may be early, and a mere example of the prevalent mythical fashion which draws no line between gods and beasts and men. It will probably be admitted that this and similar tales prove the existence of the savage element of mythology among the Aryans of India, whether it be borrowed, or a survival, or an imitative revival.

The Asvins were usually benefactors of men in every sort of strait and trouble. A quail even invoked them (Mr. Max Müller thinks this quail was the dawn, but the Asvins were something like the dawn already), and they rescued her from the jaws of a wolf. In this respect, and in their beauty and youth, they answer to Castor and Pollux as described by Theocritus. "Succourers are they of men in the very thick of peril, and of horses maddened in the bloody press of battle, and of ships that, defying the setting and the rising of the stars in heaven, have encountered the perilous breath of storms."[1] A few examples of the friendliness of the Asvins may be selected from the long list given by Muir. They renewed the youth of Kali. After the leg of Vispala had been cut off in battle, the Asvins substituted an iron leg! They restored sight to Rijrasva, whom his father had blinded because, in an access of altruism, he had given

[1] Theoc., *Idyll,* xxii. i. 17.

one hundred and one sheep to a hungry she-wolf. The she-wolf herself prayed to the Asvins to succour her benefactor.[1] They drew the Rishi Rebha out of a well. They made wine and liquors flow from the hoof of their own horse.[2] Most of the persons rescued, quail and all, are interpreted, of course, as semblances of the dawn and the twilight. Goldstücker says they are among "the deities forced by Professor Müller to support his dawn-theory". M. Bergaigne also leans to the theory of physical phenomena. When the Asvins restore sight to the blind Kanva, he sees no reason to doubt that the blind Kanva is the sun during the night, or Agni or Soma is concealment". A proof of this he finds in the statement that Kanva is "dark"; to which we might reply that "dark" is still a synonym for "blind" among the poor.[3]

M. Bergaigne's final hypothesis is that the Asvins "may be assimilated to the" two celebrants "who in the beginning seemed to represent the terrestrial and celestial fires". But this origin, he says, even if correctly conjectured, had long been forgotten.

Beyond the certainty that the Asvins represent the element of kindly and healing powers, as commonly conceived of in popular mythology—for example, in the legends of the saints—there is really nothing certain or definite about their original meaning.

A god with a better defined and more recognisable department is Tvashtri, who is in a vague kind of way the counterpart of the Greek Hephæstus. He sharpens the axe of Brahmanaspiti, and forges the

[1] *Rig-Veda*, i. 116, 16. [2] *Ibid.*, i. 116, 7.
[3] Bergaigne, *Rel. Ved.*, ii. 460, 465.

bolts of Indra. He also bestows offspring, is a kind of male Aphrodite, and is the shaper of all forms human and animal. Saranyu is his daughter. Professor Kuhn connects her with the storm-cloud, Mr. Max Müller with the dawn.[1] Her wedding in the form of a mare to Vivasvat in the guise of a horse has already been spoken of and discussed. Tvashtri's relations with Indra, as we have shown, are occasionally hostile; there is a blood-feud between them, as Indra slew Tvashtri's three-headed son, from whose blood sprang two partridges and a sparrow.[2]

The Maruts are said to be gods of the tempest, of lightning, of wind and of rain. Their names, as usual, are tortured on various by the etymologists. Mr. Max Müller connects *Maruts* with the roots *mar*, "to pound," and with the Roman war-god Mars. Others think the root is *mar*, "to shine". Benfey[3] says "that the Maruts (their name being derived from *mar*, 'to die') are personfications of the souls of the departed". Their numbers are variously estimated. They are the sons of Rudra and Prisni. Rudra as a bull, according to a tale told by Sayana, begat the Maruts on the earth, which took the shape of a cow. As in similar cases, we may suppose this either to be a survival or revival of a savage myth or a merely symbolical statement. There are traces of rivalry between Indra and the Maruts. It is beyond question that the Rishis regard them as elementary and mainly as storm-gods. Whether they were originally ghosts (like the Australian Mrarts, where the name tempts

[1] Max Müller, *Lectures on Language*, ii. 530.
[2] Muir, v. 224, 233. [3] *Ibid.*, v. 147.

the wilder kind of etymologists), or whether they are personified winds, or, again, winds conceived as persons (which is not quite the same thing), it is difficult, and perhaps impossible, to determine.

Though divers of the Vedic gods have acquired solar characteristics, there is a regular special sun-deity in the Veda, named Surya or Savitri. He answers to the Helios of the Homeric hymn to the sun, conceived as a personal being, a form which he still retains in the fancy of the Greek islanders.[1] Surya is sometimes spoken of as a child of Aditi's or of Dyaus and Ushas is his wife, though she also lives in Spartan polyandry with the Asvin twins.[2] Like Helios Hyperion, he beholds all things, the good and evil deeds of mortals. He is often involved in language of religious fervour.[3] The English reader is apt to confuse Surya with the female being Sûryâ. Surya is regarded by Grassmann and Roth as a feminine personification of the sun.[4] M. Bergaigne looks on Sûryâ as the daughter of the sun or daughter of Savitri, and thus as the dawn. Savitri is the sun, golden-haired and golden-handed. From the *Satapatha Brahmana*[5] it appears that people were apt to identify Savitri with Prajapati.[6] These blendings of various conceptions and of philosophic systems with early traditions have now been illustrated as far as our space will permit. The natural conclusion, after a rapid view of Vedic deities, seems to be that they

[1] Bent's *Cyclades*. [2] *Rig-Veda*, vii. 75, 5.

[3] Muir, v. 155-162. [4] Bergaigne, ii. 486. [5] xiii. 3, 5, 1.

[6] The very strange and important personage of Prajapati is discussed in the chapter on "Indian Cosmogonic Myths".

are extremely composite characters, visible only in the shifting rays of the Indian fancy, at a period when the peculiar qualities of Indian thought were already sufficiently declared. The lights of ritualistic dogma and of pantheistic and mystic and poetic emotion fall in turn, like the changeful hues of sunset, on figures as melting and shifting as the clouds of evening. Yet even to these vague shapes of the divine there clings, as we think has been shown, somewhat of their oldest raiment, something of the early fancy from which we suppose them to have floated up ages before the Vedas were compiled in their present form. If this view be correct, Vedic mythology does by no means represent what is primitive and early, but what, in order of development, is late, is peculiar, and is marked with the mark of a religious tendency as strongly national and characteristic as the purest Semitic monotheism. Thus the Veda is not a fair starting-point for a science of religion, but is rather, in spite of its antiquity, a temporary though advanced resting-place in the development of Indian religious speculation and devotional sentiment.[1]

[1] In the chapters on India the translation of the *Veda* used is Herr Ludwig's (Prag, 1876). Much is owed to Mr. Perry's essay on Indra, quoted above.

CHAPTER XVIII.

GREEK DIVINE MYTHS.

Gods in myth, and God in religion—The society of the gods like that of men in Homer—Borrowed elements in Greek belief—Zeus—His name —Development of his legend—His bestial shapes explained—Zeus in religion—Apollo—Artemis—Dionysus—Athene—Aphrodite—Hermes —Demeter—Their names, natures, rituals and legends—Conclusions.

In the gods of Greece, when represented in ideal art and in the best religious sentiment, as revealed by poets and philosophers, from Homer to Plato, from Plato to Porphyry, there is something truly human and truly divine. It cannot be doubted that the religion of Apollo, Athene, Artemis and Hermes was, in many respects, an adoration directed to the moral and physical qualities that are best and noblest. Again, even in the oldest Greek literature, in Homer and in all that follows, the name of the chief god, Zeus, might in many places be translated by our word "God".[1] It is God that takes from man half his virtue on the day of slavery; it is God that gives to each his lot in life, and ensures that as his day is so shall his strength be. This spiritual conception of deity, undifferentiated by shape or attributes, or even by name, declares itself in the Homeric terms *τὸ δαιμόνιον* and in the *τὸ θεῖον* of Herodotus. These are spiritual forces or tendencies

[1] *Postea*, "Zeus".

ruling the world, and these conceptions are present to the mind even of Homer, whose pictures of the gods are so essentially anthropomorphic; even of Herodotus, in all things so cautiously reverent in his acceptation of the popular creeds and rituals. When Socrates, therefore, was doomed to death for his theories of religion, he was not condemned so much for holding a pure belief in a spiritual divinity, as for bringing that opinion (itself no new thing) into the market-place, and thereby shocking the popular religion, on which depended the rites that were believed to preserve the fortune of the state.

It is difficult or impossible quite to unravel the tangled threads of mythical legend, of sacerdotal ritual, of local religion, and of refined religious sentiment in Greece. Even in the earliest documents, the Homeric poems, religious sentiment deserts, in moments of deep and serious thought, the brilliant assembly of the Olympians, and takes refuge in that fatherhood of the divine "after which all men yearn".[1] Yet, even in Pausanias, in the second century of the Christian era, and still more in Plutarch and Porphyry, there remains an awful acquiescence in such wild dogmas and sacred traditions as antiquity handed down. We can hardly determine whether even Homer actually believed in his own turbulent cowardly Ares, in his own amorous and capricious Zeus. Did Homer, did any educated Greek, turn in his thoughts, when pain, or sorrow, or fear fell on him, to a hope in the help of Hermes or Athene? He was ready to perform all their rites and offer all the sacrifices due, but it

[1] *Odyssey*, iii. 48.

may be questioned whether, even in such a god-fearing man as Nicias, this ritualism meant more than a desire to "fulfil all righteousness," and to gratify a religious sentiment in the old traditional forms.

In examining Greek myths, then, it must be remembered that, like all myths, they have far less concern with religion in its true guise—with the yearning after the divine which "is not far from any one of us," after the God "in whom we live, and move, and have our being"—than with the *religio*, which is a tissue of old barbarous fears, misgivings, misapprehensions. The religion which retained most of the myths was that ancient superstition which is afraid of "changing the luck," and which, therefore, keeps up acts of ritual that have lost their significance in their passage from a dark and dateless past. It was the local priesthoods of demes and remote rural places that maintained the old usages of the ancient tribes and kindreds—usages out of keeping with the mental condition of the splendid city state, or with the national sentiment of Hellenism. But many of the old tales connected with, and explanatory of, these ritual practices, after "winning their way to the mythical," as Thucydides says, won their way into literature, and meet us in the odes of Pindar, the plays of Æschylus and Sophocles, the notes of commentators, and the apologetic efforts of Plutarch and Porphyry. It is with these antique stories that the mythologist is concerned. But even here he need not loose his reverence for the nobler aspects of the gods of Greece. Like the archæologist and excavator, he must touch with careful hand these—

Strange clouded fragments of the ancient glory,
Late lingerers of the company divine;
For even in ruin of their marble limbs
They breathe of that far world wherefrom they came,
Of liquid light and harmonies serene,
Lost halls of heaven and far Olympian air.[1]

'Homer and Hesiod named the gods for the Greeks;" so Herodotus thought, and constructed the divine genealogies. Though the gods were infinitely older than Homer, though a few of them probably date from before the separation of the Indo-Aryan and Hellenic stocks, it is certain that Homer and Hesiod stereotyped, to some extent, the opinions about the deities which were current in their time.[2] Hesiod codified certain priestly and Delphian theories about their origin and genealogies. Homer minutely described their politics and society. His description, however, must inevitably have tended to develop a

[1] Ernest Myers, Hermes, in *The Judgment of Prometheus.*

[2] As a proof of the Pre-Homeric antiquity of Zeus, it has often been noticed that Homer makes Achilles pray to Zeus of Dodona (the Zeus, according to Thrasybulus, who aided Deucalion after the deluge) as the "Pelasgian" Zeus (*Iliad*, xvi. 233). "Pelasgian" may be regarded as equivalent to "pre-historic Greek". Sophocles (*Trach.*, 65; see Scholiast) still speaks of the Selli, the priests of Dodonean Zeus, as "mountain-dwelling and couching on the earth". They retained, it seems, very primitive habits. Be it observed that Achilles has been praying for confusion and ruin to the Achæans, and so invokes the deity of an older, perhaps hostile, race. Probably the oak-oracle at Dodona, the message given by "the sound of a going in the tree-tops" or by the doves, was even more ancient than Zeus, who, on that theory, fell heir to the rites of a peasant oracle connected with tree-worship. Zeus, according to Hesiod, "dwelt in the trunk of the oak tree" (cited by Preller, i. 98), much as an Indian forest-god dwells in the peepul or any other tree. It is rather curious that, according to Eustathius (*Iliad*, xvi. 233), "Pelargicus," "connected with storks," was sometimes written for Pelasgicus; that there was a Dodona in Thessaly, and that storks were sacred to the Thessalians.

later scepticism. While men lived in city states under heroic kings, acknowledging more or less the common sway of one king at Argos or Mycenæ, it was natural that the gods (whether in the dark backward of time Greece knew a Moral Creative Being or not) should be conceived as dwelling in a similar society, with Zeus for their Agamemnon, a ruler supreme but not absolute, not safe from attempts at resistance and rebellion. But when Greek politics and society developed into a crowd of republics, with nothing answering to a certain imperial sway, then men must have perceived that the old divine order was a mere survival from the time when human society was similarly ordained. Thus Xenophanes very early proclaimed that men had made the gods in their own likeness, as a horse, could he draw, would design his deity in equine semblance. But the detection by Xenophanes of the anthropomorphic tendency in religion could not account for the instinct which made Greeks, like other peoples, as Aristotle noticed, figure their gods not only in human shape, but in the guise of the lower animals. For that zoomorphic element in myth an explanation, as before, will be sought in the early mental condition which takes no great distinction between man and the beasts. The same method will explain, in many cases, the other peculiarly un-Hellenic elements in Greek divine myth. Yet here, too, allowance must be made for the actual borrowing of rites and legends from contiguous peoples.

The Greeks were an assimilative race. The alphabet of their art they obtained, as they obtained their written alphabet, from the kingdoms of the East.[1] Like the Romans, they readily recognised their own gods, even under the barbarous and brutal disguises of Egyptian popular religion; and, while recognising their god under an alien shape, they may have taken over legends alien to their own national character.[2] Again, we must allow, as in India, for myths which are really late, the inventions, perhaps, of priests or oracle-mongers. But in making these deductions, we must remember that the later myths would be moulded, in many cases, on the ancient models. These ancient models, there is reason to suppose, were often themselves of the irrational and savage character which has so frequently been illustrated from the traditions of the lower races.

The elder dynasties of Greek gods, Uranus and Cronos, with their adventures and their fall, have already been examined.[3] Uranus may have been an ancient sky-god, like the Samoyed Num, deposed by Cronus, originally, perhaps, one of the deputy-gods, active where their chief is otiose, whom we find in barbaric theology. But this is mere guess-work. We may now turn to the deity who was the acknowledged sovereign of the Greek Olympus during all the classical period from the date of Homer and Hesiod to the establishment of Christianity. We have to consider the legend of *Zeus*.

[1] Helbig, *Homerische Epos aus dem Denkmälern*. Perrot and Chipiez, on Mycenæan art, represent a later view.

[2] On the probable amount of borrowing in Greek religion see Maury, *Religions de la Greece*, iii. 70-75; Newton, *Nineteenth Century*, 1878, p. 305. Gruppe, *Griech. Culte u. Mythen.*, pp. 153-163.

[3] "Greek Cosmogonic Myths," *antea*.

It is necessary first to remind the reader that all the legends in the epic poems date after the time when an official and national Olympus had been arranged. Probably many tribal gods, who had originally no connection with gods of other tribes, had, by Homer's age, thus accepted places and relationships in the Olympic family. Even rude low-born Pelasgian deities may have been adopted into the highest circles, and fitted out with a divine pedigree in perfect order.

To return to Zeus, his birth (whether as the eldest or the youngest of the children of Cronus) has already been studied; now we have to deal with his exploits and his character.

About the meaning of the name of Zeus the philologists seem more than commonly harmonious. They regard the Greek Zeus as the equivalent of the Sanskrit Dyaus, "the bright one," a term for the sky.[1] He was especially worshipped on hill-tops (like the Aztec rain-god); for example, on Ithome, Parnes, Cithæron, and the Lycæan hill of Arcadia. On the Arcadian mountain, a centre of the strangest and oldest rites, the priest of Zeus acted as what the African races call a "rainmaker". There was on the hill the sacred well of the nymph Hagno, one of the nurses of the child Zeus. In time of drought the priest of Zeus offered sacrifice and prayer to the water according to ritual law, and it would be interesting to know what it was that he sacrificed. He then gently stirred the well with a bough from the oak, the holy tree of the god, and when the water was stirred, a

[1] Max Müller, *Selected Essays*, ii. 419; Preller, *Gr. Myth.*, i. 92.

cloud arose like mist, which attracted other clouds and caused rain. As the priest on a mountain practically occupied a meteorological observatory, he probably did not perform these rites till he knew that a "depression" might be expected from one quarter or another.[1] Wonderful feats of rain-prophecy are done by Australian seers, according to Mrs. Langloh Parker and others. As soon as we meet Zeus in Homer, we find that he is looked on, not as the sky, but as the deity who "dwells in the heights of air," and who exercises supreme sway over all things, including storm and wind and cloud. He casts the lightning forth (τερπικέραυνος), he thunders on high (ὑψιβρεμέτης), he has dark clouds for his covering (κελαινεφής). Under all these imposing aspects he is *religiously* regarded by people who approach him in prayer. These aspects would be readily explained by the theory that Zeus, after having been the personal sky, came to be thought a powerful being who dwelt in the sky, if we did not find such beings worshipped where the sky is not yet adored, as in Australia. Much the same occurred if, as M. Maspero points out, in Egypt the animals were worshipped first, and then later the gods supposed to be present in the animals. So the sky, a personal sky, was first adored, later a god dwelling in the sky. But it is less easy to show how this important change in opinion took place, if it really occurred. A philological theory of the causes which produced the change is set forth by Mr. Keary in his book *Primitive Belief.* In his opinion the sky was first worshipped as a vast

[1] See similar examples of popular magic in Gervase of Tilbury, *Otia Imperialia;* Liebrecht, ii. 146. The citation is due to Preller, i. 102.

non-personal phenomenon, "the bright thing" (*Dyaus*). But, to adopt the language of Mr. Max Müller, who appears to hold the same views, "Dyaus ceased to be an expressive predicate; it became a traditional name";[1] it "lost its radical meaning". Thus where a man had originally said, "It thunders," or rather "He thunders," he came to say, "Dyaus" (that is, the sky) "thunders". Next Dyaus, or rather the Greek form Zeus, almost lost its meaning of the sky, and the true sense being partially obscured, became a name supposed to indicate a person. Lastly the expression became "Zeus thunders," Zeus being regarded as a person, because the old meaning of his name, "the sky," was forgotten, or almost forgotten. The *nomen* (name) has become a *numen* (god). As Mr. Keary puts it, "The god stands out as clear and thinkable in virtue of this name as any living friend can be". The whole doctrine resolves itself into this, a phenomenon originally (according to the theory) considered impersonal, came to be looked on as personal, because a word survived in colloquial expressions after it had lost, or all but lost, its original meaning. As a result, all the changes and processes of the impersonal sky came to be spoken of as personal actions performed by a personal being, Zeus. The record of these atmospheric processes on this theory is the legend of Zeus. Whatever is irrational and abominable in the conduct of the god is explained as originally a simple statement of meteorological phenomena. "Zeus weds his mother;" that must mean the rain descends on the earth, from which it previously arose in vapour. "Zeus

[1] *Select Essays*, ii. 419.

weds his daughter," that is, the rain falls on the crop, which grew up from the rainy embrace of sky and earth.

Here then we have the philological theory of the personality and conduct of Zeus. To ourselves and those who have followed us the system will appear to reverse the known conditions of the working of the human mind among early peoples. On the philological theory, man first regards phenomena in our modern way as impersonal; he then gives them personality as the result of a disease of language, of a forgetfulness of the sense of words. Thus Mr. Keary writes: "The idea of personality as apart from matter must have been growing more distinct when men could attribute personality to such an abstract phenomenon as the sky". Where is the distinctness in a conception which produces such confusion? We have seen that as the idea of personality becomes more distinct the range of its application becomes narrower, not wider. The savage, it has been thought, attributes personality to everything without exception. As the idea of personality grows more distinct it necessarily becomes less extensive, till we withdraw it from all but intelligent human beings. Thus we must look for some other explanation of the personality of Zeus, supposing his name to mean the sky. This explanation we find in a survival of the savage mental habit of regarding all phenomena, even the most abstract, as persons. Our theory will receive confirmation from the character of the personality of Zeus in his myth. Not only is he a person, but in myth, as distinct from religion, he is a very savage person, with all the powers of the medicine-man and all the passions of the barbarian. Why should this be so on the philological theory? When we examine the legend of Zeus, we shall see which explanation best meets the difficulties of the problem. But the reader must again be reminded that the Zeus of myth, in Homer and elsewhere, is a very different being from the Zeus of religion of Achilles's prayer, from the Zeus whom the Athenians implored to rain on their fields, and from the Zeus who was the supreme being of the tragedians, of the philosophers, and of later Greece.

The early career, *la jeunesse orageuse*, of Zeus has been studied already. The child of Cronus and Rhea, countless places asserted their claim to be the scene of his birth, though the Cretan claim was most popular.[1] In Crete too was the grave of Zeus: a scandal to pious heathendom. The euhemerists made this tomb a proof that Zeus was a deified man. Preller takes it for an allegory of winter and the death of the god of storm, who in winter is especially active. Zeus narrowly escaped being swallowed by his father, and, after expelling and mediatising that deity, he changed his own wife, Metis, into a fly, swallowed her, and was delivered out of his own head of Athene, of whom his wife had been pregnant. He now became ruler of the world, with his brother Poseidon for viceroy, so to speak, of the waters, and his brother Hades for lord of the world of the dead. Like the earlier years of Louis XIV., the earlier centuries of the existence of Zeus were given up to a series of amours, by which he, like Charles II., became the father of many noble

[1] Hesiod, *Theog.*, 468; Paus., iv. 33, 2.

families. His legitimate wife was his sister Hera, whom he seduced before wedlock "without the knowledge of their dear parents," says Homer,[1] who neglects the myth that one of the "dear parents" ate his own progeny, "like him who makes his generation messes to gorge his appetite". Hera was a jealous wife, and with good cause.[2] The Christian fathers calculated that he sowed his wild oats and persecuted mortal women with his affections through seventeen generations of men. His amours with his mother and daughters, with Deo and Persephone, are the great scandals of Clemens Alexandrinus and Arnobius.[3] Zeus seldom made love *in propria persona*, in all his meteorological pomp. When he thus gratified Semele she was burned to a cinder.[4] The amour with Danaë,

[1] It is probable that this myth of the seduction of Hera is of Samian origin, and was circulated to account for and justify the Samian custom by which men seduced their loves first and celebrated the marriage afterwards (Scholia on *Iliad*, xiv. 201). "Others say that Samos was the place where Zeus betrayed Hera, whence it comes that the Samians, when they go a-wooing, anticipate the wedding first in secret, and then celebrate it openly." Yet another myth (*Iliad*, xiv. 295, Scholiast) accounts for the hatred which Zeus displayed to Prometheus by the fable that, before her wedding with Zeus, Hera became the mother of Prometheus by the giant Eurymedon. Euphorion was the authority for this tale. Yet another version occurs in the legend of Hephæstus. See also Schol., *Theoc.*, xv. 64.

[2] *Iliad*, xiv. 307, 340.

[3] Arnobius, *Adv. Nat.*, v. 9, where the abominations described defy repetition. The myth of a rock which became the mother of the offspring of Zeus may recall the maternal flint of Aztec legend and the vagaries of Iroquois tradition. Compare *Clemens Alex.*, Oxford, 1719, i. 13, for the amours of Zeus, Deo and Persephone, with their representations in the mysteries; also Arnob., *Adv. Cent.*, v. 20. Zeus adopted the shape of a serpent in his amour with his daughter. An ancient Tarentine sacred ditty is quoted as evidence, *Taurus draconem genuit, et taurum draco*, and certain repulsive performances with serpents in the mysteries are additional testimony.

[4] Apollodorus, iii. 4, 3.

when Zeus became a shower of gold, might be interpreted as a myth of the yellow sunshine. The amours of Zeus under the disguise of various animal forms were much more usual, and are familiar to all.[1] As Cronus when in love metamorphosed himself into a stallion, as Prajapati pursued his own daughter in the shape of a roebuck, so Zeus became a serpent, a bull, a swan, an eagle, a dove,[2] and, to woo the daughter of Cletor, an ant. Similar disguises are adopted by the sorcerers among the Algonkins for similar purposes. When Pund-jel, in the Australian myth of the Pleiades, was in love with a native girl, he changed himself into one of those grubs in the bark of trees which the Blacks think edible, and succeeded as well as Zeus did when he became an ant.[3] It is not improbable that the metamorphosis of Zeus into an ant is the result of a *volks-etymologie* which derived "Myrmidons" from μύρμηξ, an ant. Even in that case the conversion of the ant into an avatar of Zeus would be an example of the process of gravitation or attraction, whereby a great mythical name and

[1] The mythologists, as a rule, like the heathen opponents of Arnobius, Clemens and Eusebius, explain the amours of Zeus as allegories of the fruitful union of heaven and earth, of rain and grain. Preller also allows for the effects of human vanity, noble families insisting on tracing themselves to gods. On the whole, says Preller, "Zeugung in der Natur-religion und Mythologie, dasselbe ist was Schopfüng inden deistischen Religionen" (i. 110). Doubtless all these elements come into the legend; the unions of Zeus with Deo and Persephone especially have much the air of a nature-myth told in an exceedingly primitive and repulsive manner. The amours in animal shape are explained in the text as in many cases survivals of the totemistic belief in descent from beasts, *sans phrase*.

[2] Ælian., *Hist. Var.*, i. 15.

[3] Dawson, *Australian Aborigines; Custom and Myth*, p. 126.

personality attracts to itself floating fables.[1] The remark of Clemens on this last extraordinary intrigue is suggestive. The Thessalians, he says, are reputed to worship ants because Zeus took the semblance of an ant when he made the daughter of Cletor mother of Myrmidon. Where people worship any animal from whom they claim descent (in this case through Myrmidon, the ancestor of the famed Myrmidons), we have an example of straightforward totemism. To account for the adoration of the animal on the hypothesis that it was the incarnation of a god, is the device which has been observed in Egyptian as in Samoan religion, and in that of aboriginal Indian tribes, whose animal gods become saints "when the Brahmans get a turn at them".[2]

The most natural way of explaining such tales about the amours and animal metamorphoses of so great a god, is to suggest that Zeus inherited,[3] as it were, legends of a lower character long current among separate families and in different localities. In the same way, where a stone had been worshipped, the stone was, in at least one instance, dubbed with the name of Zeus.[4] The tradition of descent from this or that beast or plant has been shown to be most widely prevalent. On the general establishment of a higher faith in a national deity, these traditions, it is

[1] Clemens, p. 34.

[2] See Mr. H. H. Risley on "Primitive Marriage in Bengal," in *Asiatic Quarterly Review*, June, 1886.

[3] In Pausanias's opinion Cecrops first introduced the belief in Zeus, the most highest.

[4] Paus., iii. 21, 1; but the reading is doubtful.

presumed, would not wholly disappear, but would be absorbed into the local legend of the god. The various beasts would become sacred to him, as the sheep was sacred to Hera in Samos, according to Mandrobulus,[1] and images of the animals would congregate in his temple. The amours of Zeus, then, are probably traceable to the common habit of deriving noble descents from a god, and in the genealogical narrative older totemistic and other local myths found a place.[2] Apart from his intrigues, the youth of Zeus was like that of some masquerading and wandering king, such as James V. in Scotland. Though Plato, in the *Republic*, is unwilling that the young should be taught how the gods go about disguised as strangers, this was their conduct in the myths. Thus we read of

> Lycaon and his fifty sons, whom Zeus
> In their own house spied on, and unawares
> Watching at hand, from his disguise arose,
> And overset the table where they sat
> Around their impious feast, and slew them all.[3]

Clemens of Alexandria[4] contrasts the "human festival" of Zeus among the Ethiopians with the inhuman banquet offered to him by Lycaon in Arcadia.[5] The permanence of Arcadian human sacrifice has already been alluded to, and it is confirmed by the superstition that whoever tasted the human portion in the mess sacrificed to Zeus became a were-wolf, resuming his

[1] *Ap.* Clem. Alex., i. 36.
[2] Compare Heyne, *Observ.* in *Apollodor.*, i. 3, 1.
[3] Bridges, *Prometheus the Firegiver.*
[4] Clem. Alex., i. 31. [5] Paus., viii. 2, 1.

original shape if for ten years he abstained from the flesh of men.[1]

A very quaint story of the domestic troubles of Zeus was current in Platæa, where it was related at the festival named *Dædala*. It was said that Hera, indignant at the amours of her lord, retired to Eubœa Zeus, wishing to be reconciled to her, sought the advice of Cithæron, at that time king of Platæa. By his counsel the god celebrated a sham marriage with a wooden image, dressed up to personate Platæa, daughter of Asopus. Hera flew to the scene and tore the bridal veil, when, discovering the trick, she laughed, and was reconciled to her husband.[2] Probably this legend was told to explain some incident of ritual or custom in the feast of the *Dædala*, and it is certainly a more innocent myth than most that were commemorated in local mystery-plays.

It was not only when he was *en bonne fortune* that Zeus adopted the guise of a bird or beast. In the

[1] The wolves connected with the worship of Zeus, like his rams, goats, and other animals, are commonly explained as mythical names for elemental phenomena, clouds and storms. Thus the ram's fleece, Δίος κώδων, used in certain expiatory rites (Hesych., *s. v.*, Lobeck, p. 183), is presumed by Preller to be a symbol of the cloud. In the same way his ægis or goat-skin is the storm-wind or the thunder-cloud. The opposite view will be found in Professor Robertson Smith's article on "Sacrifice" in *Encyc. Brit.*, where the similar totemistic rites of the lower races are adduced. The elemental theory is set forth by Decharme, *Mythologie de la Grece Antique* (Paris, 1879), p. 16. For the "storm-wolf," see Preller, i. 101. It seems a little curious that the wolf, which, on the solar hypothesis, was a brilliant beast connected with the worship of the sun-god, Apollo Lycæus, becomes a cloud or storm-wolf when connected with Zeus. On the whole subject of the use of the skins of animals as clothing of the god or the ministrant, see Lobeck, *Aglaoph.*, pp. 183-186, and Robertson Smith, *op. cit.*

[2] Paus., ix. 3, 1.

very ancient temple of Hera near Mycenæ there was a great statue of the goddess, of gold and ivory, the work of Polycletus, and therefore comparatively modern. In one hand the goddess held a pomegranate, in the other a sceptre, on which was perched a cuckoo, like the Latin woodpecker Picus on his wooden post. About the pomegranate there was a myth which Pausanias declines to tell, but he does record the myth of the cuckoo. "They say that when Zeus loved the yet virgin Hera, he changed himself into a cuckoo, which she pursued and caught to be her playmate." Pausanias admits that he did not believe this legend. Probably it was invented to account for the companionship of the cuckoo, which, like the cow, was one of the sacred animals of Hera. Myths of this class are probably later than the period in which we presume the divine relationships of gods and animals to have passed out of the totemistic into the Samoan condition of belief. The more general explanation is, that the cuckoo, as a symbol of the vernal season, represents the heaven in its wooing of the earth. On the whole, as we have tried to show, the symbolic element in myth is late, and was meant to be explanatory of rites and usages whose original significance was forgotten. It would be unfair to assume that a god was disrespectfully viewed by his earliest worshippers because ætiological, genealogical, and other myths, crystallised into his legend.

An extremely wild legend of Zeus was current among the Galatæ, where Pausanias expressly calls it a "local myth," differing from the Lydian variant. Zeus in his sleep became, by the earth, father of Attes, a being both male and female in his nature Agdistis was the local name of this enigmatic character, whom the gods feared and mutilated. From the blood grew up, as in so many myths, an almond tree. The daughter of Sangarius, Nana, placed some of the fruit in her bosom, and thereby became pregnant, like the girl in the Kalewala by the berry, or the mother of Huitzilopochtli, in Mexico, by the floating feather. The same set of ideas recurs in Grimm's *Märchen Machandelboom*,[1] if we may suppose that in an older form the juniper tree and its berries aided the miraculous birth.[2] It is customary to see in these wild myths a reflection of the Phrygian religious tradition, which leads up to the birth of Atys, who again is identified with Adonis as a hero of the spring and the reviving year. But the story has been introduced in this place as an example of the manner in which floating myths from all sources gravitate towards one great name and personality, like that of Zeus. It would probably be erroneous to interpret these and many other myths in the vast legend of Zeus, as if they had originally and intentionally described the phenomena of the heavens. They are, more probably, mere accretions round the figure of Zeus conceived as a personal god, a "magnified non-natural man".[3]

[1] Mrs. Hunt's translation, i. 187.

[2] For parallels to this myth in Chinese, Aztec, Indian, Phrygian and other languages, see *Le Fils de la Vierge*, by M. H. de Charency, Havre, 1879. See also "Les Deux Frères" in M. Maspero's *Contes Egyptiens.*

[3] As to the Agdistis myth, M. de Charency writes (after quoting forms of the tale from all parts of the world), "This resemblance between different shapes of the same legend, among nations separated by such expanses of land and sea, may be brought forward as an important proof of the antiquity of the myth, as well as of the distant date at which it began to be diffused".

Another example of local accretion is the fable that Zeus, after carrying off Ganymede to be his cupbearer, made atonement to the royal family of Troy by the present of a vine of gold fashioned by Hephæstus.[1] The whole of the myth of Callisto, again, whom Zeus loved, and who bore Arcas, and later was changed into a bear, and again into a star, is clearly of local Arcadian origin. If the Arcadians, in very remote times, traced their descent from a she-bear, and if they also, like other races, recognised a bear in the constellation, they would naturally mix up those fables later with the legend of the all-powerful Zeus.[2]

So far we have studied some of the details in the legend of Zeus which did not conspicuously win their way into the national literature. The object has been to notice a few of the myths which appear the most ancient, and the most truly native and original. These are the traditions preserved in mystery-plays, tribal genealogies, and temple legends, the traditions surviving from the far off period of the village Greeks. It has already been argued, in conformity with the opinion of C. O. Müller, that these myths are most antique and thoroughly local. "Any attempt to explain these myths in order, such, for instance, as we now find them in the collection of Apollodorus, as a system of thought and knowledge, must prove a fruitless task." Equally useless is it to account for them all as stories originally told to describe,

[1] Scholia on *Odyssey*, xi. 521; *Iliad*, xx. 234; Eurip., *Orestes*, 1392, and Scholiast quoting the *Little Iliad*.

[2] Compare C. O. Muller, *Introduction to a Scientific System of Mythology*, London, 1884, pp. 16, 17; Pausanias, i. 25, 1, viii. 35, 7.

consciously or unconsciously, or to explain any atmospheric and meteorological phenomena. Zeus is the bright sky; granted, but the men who told how he became an ant, or a cuckoo, or celebrated a sham wedding with a wooden image, or offered Troy a golden vine, "the work of Hephæstus," like other articles of jewellery, were not thinking of the bright sky when they repeated the story. They were merely strengthening some ancient family or tribal tradition by attaching it to the name of a great, powerful, personal being, an immortal. This being, not the elemental force that was Zeus, not the power "making for righteousness" that is Zeus, not the pure spiritual ruler of the world, the Zeus of philosophy, is the hero of the myths that have been investigated.

In the tales that actually won their way into national literature, beginning with Homer, there is observable the singular tendency to combine, in one figure, the highest religious ideas with the fables of a capricious, and often unjust and lustful supernatural being. Taking the myths first, their contrast with the religious conception of Zeus will be the more remarkable.

Zeus is the king of all gods and father of some, but he cannot keep his subjects and family always in order. In the first book of the *Iliad*, Achilles reminds his mother, the sea-nymph Thetis, how she once "rescued the son of Cronus, lord of the storm-clouds, from shameful wreck, when all other Olympians would have bound him, even Hera, and Poseidon, and Pallas Athene". Thetis brought the hundred-handed Briareus to the help of the outnumbered and over-mastered

Zeus. Then Zeus, according to the Scholiast, hung Hera out of heaven in chains, and gave Apollo and Poseidon for slaves to Laomedon, king of Troy. So lively was the recollection of this *coup d'état* in Olympus, that Hephæstus implores Hera (his mother in Homer) not to anger Zeus, "lest I behold thee, that art so dear, chastised before mine eyes, and then shall I not be able to save thee for all my sorrow".[1] He then reminds Hera how Zeus once tossed him out of heaven (as the Master of Life tossed Ataentsic in the Iroquois myth), and how he fell in Lemnos, "and little life was left in me". The passage is often interpreted as if the fall of Hephæstus, the fire-god, were a myth of lightning; but in Homer assuredly the incident has become thoroughly personal, and is told with much humour. The offence of Hera was the raising of a magic storm (which she could do as well as any Lapland witch) and the wrecking of Heracles on Cos. For this she was chained and hung out of heaven, as on the occasion already described.[2] The constant bickerings between Hera and Zeus in the *Iliad* are merely the reflection in the upper Olympian world of the wars and jealousies of men below. Ilios is at war with Argos and Mycenæ, therefore the chief protecting gods of each city take part in the strife. This conception is connected with the heroic genealogies. Noble and royal families, as in most countries, feigned a descent from the gods. It followed that Zeus was a partisan of his "children," that is, of the

[1] *Iliad*, i. 587.

[2] *Ibid.*, 590; *Scholia*, xiv. 255. The myth is derived from Pherecydes.

royal houses in the towns where he was the most favoured deity. Thus Hera when she sided with Mycenæ had a double cause of anger, and there is an easy answer to the question, *quo numine læso?* She had her own townsmen's quarrel to abet, and she had her jealousy to incite her the more; for to become father of the human families Zeus must have been faithless to her. Indeed, in a passage (possibly interpolated) of the fourteenth *Iliad* he acts as his own Leporello, and recites the list of his conquests. The Perseidæ, the Heraclidæ, the Pirithoidæ, with Dionysus, Apollo and Artemis spring from the amours there recounted.[1] Moved by such passions, Hera urges on the ruin of Troy, and Zeus accuses her of a cannibal hatred. "Perchance wert thou to enter within the gates and long walls, and devour Priam raw, and Priam's sons, and all the Trojans, then mightest thou assuage thine anger."[2] That great stumbling-block of Greek piety, the battle in which the gods take part,[3] was explained as a physical allegory by the Neo-Platonists.[4] It is in reality only a refraction of the wars of men, a battle produced among the heavenly folk by men's battles, as the earthly imitations of rain in the Vedic ritual beget rain from the firmament. The favouritism which Zeus throughout shows to Athene[5] is explained by that rude and ancient myth of her birth from his brain after he had swallowed her pregnant mother.[6]

[1] Pherecydes is the authority for the treble night, in which Zeus persuaded the sun not to rise when he wooed Alcmena.

[2] See the whole passage, *Iliad*, iv. 160. [3] *Ibid.*, v. 385.

[4] *Scholia*, ed. Dindorf, vol iii.; *Ibid.*, v. 385. [5] *Ibid.*, v. 875.

[6] *Cf.* "Hymn to Apollo Pythius," 136.

But Zeus cannot allow the wars of the gods to go on unreproved, and[1] he asserts his power, and threatens to cast the offenders into Tartarus, "as far beneath Hades as heaven is high above earth". Here the supremacy of Zeus is attested, and he proposes to prove it by the sport called "the tug of war". He says, "Fasten ye a chain of gold from heaven, and all ye gods lay hold thereof, and all goddesses, yet could ye not drag from heaven to earth Zeus, the supreme counsellor, not though ye strove sore. But if once I were minded to drag with all my heart, then I could hang gods and earth and sea to a pinnacle of Olympus."[2] The supremacy claimed here on the score of strength, "by so much I am beyond gods and men," is elsewhere based on primogeniture,[3] though in Hesiod Zeus is the youngest of the sons of Cronos. But there is, as usual in myth, no consistent view, and Zeus cannot be called omnipotent. Not only is he subject to fate, but his son Heracles would have perished when he went to seek the hound of hell but for the aid of Athene.[4] Gratitude for his relief does not prevent Zeus from threatening Athene as well as Hera with Tartarus, when they would thwart him in the interest of the Achæans. Hera is therefore obliged to subdue him by the aid of love and sleep, in that famous and beautiful passage,[5] which is so frankly anthropomorphic, and was such a scandal to religious minds.[5]

[1] *Iliad*, viii. *ad init.*

[2] M. Decharme regards this challenge to the tug of war as a very noble and sublime assertion of supreme sovereignty. *Myth. de la Greece*, p. 19.

[3] *Iliad*, xv. 166. [4] *Ibid.*, viii. 369. [5] *Ibid.*, xiv. 150-350.

[5] *Schol. Iliad*, xiv. 346; Dindorf, vol. iv. In the Scholiast's explanation the scene is an allegorical description of spring; the wrath of Hera is the

Not to analyse the whole divine plot of the *Iliad*, such is Zeus in the mythical portions of the epic. He is the father and master of gods and men, and the strongest; but he may be opposed, he may be deceived and cajoled; he is hot-tempered, amorous, luxurious, by no means omnipotent or omniscient. He cannot avert even from his children the doom that Fate span into the threads at their birth; he is no more omniscient than omnipotent, and if he can affect the weather, and bring storm and cloud, so at will can the other deities, and so can any sorcerer, or Jossakeed, or Biraark of the lower races.

In Homeric religion, as considered apart from myth, in the religious thoughts of men at solemn moments of need, or dread, or prayer, Zeus holds a far other place. All power over mortals is in his hands, and is acknowledged with almost the fatalism of Islam. "So meseems it pleaseth mighty Zeus, who hath laid low the head of many a city, yea, and shall lay low, for his is the highest power."[1] It is Zeus who gives sorrows to men,[2] and he has, in a mythical picture, two jars by him full of evil and good, which he deals to his children on earth. In prayer[3] he is addressed as Zeus, most glorious, most great, veiled in the storm-cloud, that dwelleth in the heaven. He gives his sanction to the oath:[4] "Father Zeus, that rulest from Ida, most glorious, most great, and thou sun, that seest all

remains of winter weather; her bath represents the April showers; when she busks her hair, the new leaves on the boughs, "the high leafy tresses of the trees," are intended, and so forth.

[1] *Iliad*, ii. 177.
[2] *Ibid.*, 378.
[3] *Ibid.*, 408.
[4] *Ibid.*, iii. 277.

things, and hearest all things, and ye rivers, and thou earth, and ye that in the underworld punish men forsworn, whosoever sweareth falsely, be ye witnesses, and watch over the faithful oath ". Again it is said: "Even if the Olympian bring not forth the fulfilment" (of the oath) "at once, yet doth he fulfil at the last, and men make dear amends, even with their own heads, and their wives and little ones".[1] Again, "Father Zeus will be no helper of liars".[2]

As to the religious sentiment towards Zeus of a truly devout man in that remote age, Homer has left us no doubt. In Eumæus the swineherd of Odysseus, a man of noble birth stolen into slavery when a child, Homer has left a picture of true religion and undefiled. Eumæus attributes everything that occurs to the will of the gods, with the resignation of a child of Islam or a Scot of the Solemn League and Covenant.[3] "From Zeus are all strangers and beggars," he says, and believes that hospitality and charity are well pleasing in the sight of the Olympian. When he flourishes, "it is God that increaseth this work of mine whereat I abide". He neither says "Zeus" nor "the gods," but in this passage simply "god". "Verily the blessed gods love not froward deeds, but they reverence justice and the righteous acts of men;" yet it is "Zeus that granteth a prey to the sea-robbers". It is the gods that rear Telemachus like a young sapling, yet is it the gods who "mar his wits within him" when he sets forth on a perilous adventure. It is to Zeus Cronion that the swineherd chiefly prays,[4] but he does not exclude

[1] *Iliad*, iv. 160.
[2] *Ibid.*, iv. 235.
[3] *Odyssey*, xiv. *passim*.
[4] *Ibid.*, 406.

the others from his supplication.[1] Being a man of scrupulous piety, when he slays a swine for supper, he only sets aside a seventh portion "for Hermes and the nymphs" who haunt the lonely uplands.[2] Yet his offering has no magical intent of constraining the immortals. "One thing God will give, and another withhold, even as he will, for with him all things are possible." [3]

Such is a Homeric ideal of piety, and it would only gain force from contrast with the blasphemy of Aias, "who said that in the god's despite he had escaped the great deep of the sea".[4]

The epics sufficiently prove that a noble religion may coexist with a wild and lawless mythology. That ancient sentiment of the human heart which makes men listen to a human voice in the thunder and yearn for immortal friends and helpers, lives its life little disturbed by the other impulse which inspires men when they come to tell stories and romances about the same transcendent beings.

As to the actual original form of the faith in Zeus, we can only make guesses. To some it will appear that Zeus was originally the clear bright expanse which was taken for an image or symbol of the infinite. Others will regard Zeus as the bright sky, but the bright sky conceived of in savage fashion, as a being with human parts and passions, a being with all the magical accomplishments of metamorphosis, rain-making and the rest, with which the medicine-man is credited. A third set of mythologists, remembering

[1] *Odyssey*, iv. 423.
[2] *Ibid.*, xiv. 435.
[3] *Ibid.*, 444, 445.
[4] *Ibid.*, iv. 504.

how gods and medicine-men have often interchangeable names, and how, for example, the Australian Biraark, who is thought to command the west wind, is himself styled "West Wind," will derive Zeus from the ghost of some ancestral sorcerer named "Sky". This euhemerism seems an exceedingly inadequate explanation of the origin of Zeus. In his moral aspect Zeus again inherits the quality of that supernatural and moral watcher of man's deeds who is recognised (as we have seen) even by the most backward races, and who, for all we can tell, is older than any beast-god or god of the natural elements. Thus, whatever Zeus was in his earliest origin, he had become, by the time we can study him in ritual, poem or sacred chapter, a complex of qualities and attributes, spiritual, moral, elemental, animal and human.

It is curious that, on our theory, the mythical Zeus must have morally degenerated at a certain period as the Zeus of religion more and more approached the rank of a pure and almost supreme deity. On our hypothesis, it was while Greece was reaching a general national consciousness, and becoming more than an aggregate of small local tribes, that Zeus attracted the worst elements of his myth. In deposing or relegating to a lower rank a crowd of totems and fetishes and ancestral ghosts, he inherited the legends of their exploits. These were attached to him still more by the love of genealogies derived from the gods. For each such pedigree an amour was inevitably invented, and, where totems had existed, the god in this amour borrowed the old bestial form. For example, if a Thessalian stock had believed in descent from an ant, and wished to trace their pedigree to Zeus, they had merely to say, "Zeus was that ant". Once more, as Zeus became supreme among the other deities of men in the patriarchal family condition, those gods were grouped round him as members of his family, his father, mother, brothers, sisters, wife, mistresses and children. Here was a noble field in which the mythical fancy might run riot ; hence came stories of usurpations, rebellions, conjugal skirmishes and jealousies, a whole world of incidents in which humour had free play. Nor would foreign influences be wanting. A wandering Greek, recognising his Zeus in a deity of Phœnicia or Babylon, might bring home some alien myth which would take its place in the general legend, with other myths imported along with foreign objects of art, silver bowls and inlaid swords. Thus in all probability grew the legend of the Zeus of myth, certainly a deplorable legend, while all the time the Greek intellect was purifying itself and approaching the poetical, moral and philosophical conception of the Zeus of religion. At last, in the minds of the philosophically religious, Zeus became pure deity, and the details of the legend were explained away by this or that system of allegory; while in the minds of the sceptical Zeus yielded his throne to the "vortex" of the Aristophanic comedy. Thus Zeus may have begun as a kindly supreme being; then ætiological and totemistic myths may have accrued to his legend, and, finally, philosophic and pious thought introduced a rational conception of his nature. But myth lived on, ritual lived on, and human victims were slain on the altars of Zeus till Christianity was the established religion. "So let it be," says Pausanias, "as it hath been from the beginning."

The gods who fill the court of Zeus and surround his throne are so numerous that a complete account of each would exceed the limits of our space. The legend of Zeus is typical, on the whole, of the manner in which the several mythical chapters grew about the figures of each of the deities. Some of these were originally, it is probable, natural forces or elemental phenomena, conceived of at first as personal beings; while, later, the personal earth or sun shaded off into the informing genius of the sun or earth, and still later was almost freed from all connection with the primal elemental phenomenon or force. In these processes of evolution it seems to have happened occasionally that the god shed, like a shell or chrysalis, his original form, which continued to exist, however, as a deity of older family and inferior power. By such processes, at least, it would not be difficult to explain the obvious fact that several gods have "under-studies" of their parts in the divine comedy. It may be well to begin a review of the gods by examining those who were, or may be supposed to have been, originally forces or phenomena of Nature.

APOLLO.

This claim has been made for almost all the Olympians, but in some cases appears more plausible than in others. For example, Apollo is regarded as a solar divinity, and the modes in which he attained his detached and independent position as a brilliant anthropomorphic deity, patron of art, the lover of the nymphs, the inspirer of prophecy, may have been something in this fashion. First the sun may have been regarded (in the manner familiar to savage races) as a personal being. In Homer he is still the god "who sees and hears all things,"[1] and who beholds and reveals the loves of Ares and Aphrodite. This personal character of the sun is well illustrated in the Homeric hymn to Hyperion, the sun that dwells on high, where, as Mr. Max Müller says, "the words would seem to imply that the poet looked upon Helios as a half-god, almost as a hero, who had once lived upon earth".[2] It has already been shown that this mythical theory of the origin of the sun is met with among the Aztecs and the Bushmen.[3] In Homer, the sun, Helios Hyperion, though he sees and hears all things,[4] needs to be informed by one of the nymphs that the companions of Odysseus have devoured his sacred cattle. In the same way the supreme Baiame of Australia needs to ask questions of mortals. Apollo then speaks in the Olympian assembly, and threatens that if he is not avenged he will "go down to Hades and shine among the dead". The sun is capable of marriage, as in the Bulgarian *Volkslied*, where he marries a peasant girl,[5] and, by Perse, he is the father of Circe and Æetes.[6] According to the early lyric poet Stesichorus, the sun sails over ocean in a golden cup or bowl. "Then Helios Hyperionides went down into his golden cup to cross Ocean-stream, and come to the deeps of dark and sacred Night, to his mother, and his wedded wife, and his children dear." This belief, in more

[1] *Odyssey*, viii. 270.
[2] *Selected Essays*, i. 605, note 1.
[3] "Nature Myths," *antea*.
[4] *Iliad*, iii. 277.
[5] Dozon, *Chansons Bulgares*.
[6] *Odyssey*, x. 139.

barbaric shape, still survives in the Greek islands.[1] "The sun is still to them a giant, like Hyperion, bloodthirsty when tinged with gold. The common saying is that the sun 'when he seeks his kingdom' expects to find forty loaves prepared for him by his mother. . . . Woe to her if the loaves be not ready! The sun eats his brothers, sisters, father and mother in his wrath."[2] A well-known amour of Helios was his intrigue with Rhode by whom he had Phaethon and his sisters. The tragedians told how Phaethon drove the chariot of the sun, and upset it, while his sisters were turned into poplar trees, and their tears became amber.[3]

Such were the myths about the personal sun, the hero or demigod, Helios Hyperion. If we are to believe that Apollo also is a solar deity, it appears probable that he is a more advanced conception, not of the sun as a person, but of a being who represents the sun in the spiritual world, and who exercises, by an act of will, the same influence as the actual sun possesses by virtue of his rays. Thus he brings pestilence on the Achæans in the first book of the *Iliad*, and his viewless shafts slay men suddenly, as sunstroke does. It is a pretty coincidence that a German scholar, Otfried Müller, who had always opposed Apollo's claim to be a sun-god, was killed by a sunstroke at Delphi. The god avenged himself in his ancient home. But if this deity was once merely the sun, it may be said, in the

[1] Bent's *Cyclades*, p. 57.

[2] Stesichorus, *Poetæ Lyrici Græci*, Pomtow, vol. i. p. 148; *cf.* also Mimnermus, *op. cit.*, i. 78.

[3] *Odyssey*, xvii. 208; Scholiast. The story is ridiculed by Lucian, *De Electro*.

beautiful phrase of Paul de St. Victor, "Pareil à une statue qui surgit des flammes de son moule, Apollo se dégage vite du soleil".[1] He becomes a god of manifold functions and attributes, and it is necessary to exercise extreme caution in explaining any one myth of his legend as originally a myth of the sun.[2] *Phoibos* certainly means "the brilliant" or "shining". It is, however, unnecessary to hold that such epithets as *Lyceius, Lycius, Lycegenes* indicate "light," and are not connected, as the ancients, except Macrobius, believed, with the worship of the wolf.[3] The character of Apollo as originally a sun-god is asserted on the strength not only of his names, but of many of his attributes and his festivals. It is pointed out that he is the deity who superintends the measurement of time.[4] "The chief days in the year's reckoning, the new and full moons and the seventh and twentieth days of the month, also the beginning of the solar year, are reckoned Apolline." That curious ritual of the Daphnephoria, familiar to many English people from Sir Frederick Leighton's picture, is believed to have symbolised the year. Proclus says that a staff of olive wood decorated with flowers supported a central ball of brass beneath which was a smaller ball, and thence little globes were hung.[5] The greater ball means the

[1] *Hommes et Dieux*, p. 11.

[2] There is no agreement nor certainty about the etymology and original meaning of the name Apollo. See Preller, *Gr. Myth.*, i. 189. "Comparative philologists have not yet succeeded in finding the true etymology of Apollo" (Max Müller, *Selected Essays*, i. 467).

[3] Compare Zeus Lyceius and his wolf-myths; compare also Roscher, *Ausführliches Lexikon*, p. 423.

[4] *Sonnengott als Zeitordner*, Roscher, *op. cit.*, p. 423.

[5] *Cf.* Photius, *Bibl.*, 321.

sun, the smaller the moon, the tiny globes the stars and the 365 laurel garlands used in the feast are understood to symbolise the days. Pausanias[1] says that the ceremony was of extreme antiquity. Heracles had once been the youth who led the procession, and the tripod which Amphitryon dedicated for him was still to be seen at Thebes in the second century of our era. Another proof of Apollo's connection with the sun is derived from the cessation of his rites at Delphi during the three winter months which were devoted to Dionysus.[2] The sacred birthday feasts of the god are also connected with the year's renewal.[3] Once more, his conflict with the great dragon, the Pytho, is understood as a symbol of the victory of light and warmth over the darkness and cold of winter.

The discomfiture of a dragon by a god is familiar in the myth of the defeat of Ahi or Vritra by Indra, and it is a curious coincidence that Apollo, like Indra, fled in terror after slaying his opponent. Apollo, according to the myth, was purified of the guilt of the slaying (a ceremony unknown to Homer) at Tempe.[4] According to the myth, the Python was a snake which forbade access to the chasm whence rose the mysterious fumes of divination. Apollo slew the snake and usurped the oracle. His murder of the serpent was more or less resented by the Delphians of the time.[5] The snake, like the other animals, frogs and lizards,

[1] ix. 10, 4. [2] Plutarch, *De pa Ei. Delph.*, 9.

[3] Roscher, *op. cit.*, p. 427.

[4] Proclus, *Chrest.*, ed. Gaisford, p. 387; Homer, *Hymn to Apollo*, 122, 178; Apollod., i. 4, 3; Plutarch, *Quæst. Græc.*, 12.

[5] Apollod., Heyne, *Observationes*, p. 19. Compare the Scholiast on the argument to Pindar's Pythian odes.

in Andaman, Australian and Iroquois myth, had swallowed the waters before its murder.[1] Whether the legend of the slaying of the Python was or was not originally an allegory of the defeat of winter by sunlight, it certainly at a very early period became mixed up with ancient legal ideas and local traditions. It is almost as necessary for a young god or hero to slay monsters as for a young lady to be presented at court; and we may hesitate to explain all these legends of an useful feat of courage as nature-myths. In the Homeric Hymn to Apollo Pythius, the monster is called *Dracœna*, the female form of *drakon*. The Drakos and his wife are still popular bogies in modern Greek superstition and folk-song.[2] The monster is the fosterling of Hera in the Homeric hymn, and the bane of flocks and herds. She is somehow connected with the fable of the birth of the monster Typhœus, son of Hera without a father. The Homeric hymn derives *Pythius*, the name of the god, from πύθω, "rot," the disdainful speech of Apollo to the dead monster, "for there the pest rotted away beneath the beams of the sun". The derivation is a *volks-etymologie*. It is not clear whether the poet connected in his mind the sun and the god. The local legend of the dragon-slaying was kept alive in men's minds at Delphi by a mystery-play, in which the encounter was represented in action. In one version of the myth the slavery of Apollo in the house of Admetus was an expiation of the dragon's

[1] Preller, i. 194.

[2] Forchhammer takes the *Dracœna* to be a violent winter torrent, dried up by the sun's rays. *Cf.* Decharme, *Myth. Grec.*, p. 100. It is also conjectured that the snake is only the sacred serpent of the older oracle of the earth on the same site. Æschylus, *Eumenides*, 2.

death.[1] Through many of the versions runs the idea that the slaying of the serpent was a deed which required purification and almost apology. If the serpent was really the deity of an elder faith, this would be intelligible, or, if he had kinsfolk, a serpent-tribe in the district, we could understand it. Apollo's next act was to open a new spring of water, as the local nymph was hostile and grudged him her own. This was an inexplicable deed in a sun god, whose business it is to dry up rather than to open water-springs. He gave oracles out of the laurel of Delphi, as Zeus out of the oaks of Dodona.[2] Presently Apollo changed himself into a huge dolphin, and in this guise approached a ship of the Cretan mariners.[3] He guided, in his dolphin shape, the vessel to Crisa, the port of Delphi, and then emerged splendid from the waters, and filled his fane with light, a sun-god indeed. Next, assuming the shape of a man, he revealed himself to the Cretans, and bade them worship him in his *Delphic* seat as Apollo Delphinios, the Dolphin-Apollo.

Such is the ancient tale of the founding of the Delphic oracle, in which gods, and beasts, and men are mixed in archaic fashion. It is open to students to regard the dolphin as only one of the many animals whose earlier worship is concentrated in Apollo, or to take the creature for the symbol of spring, when seafaring becomes easier to mortals, or to interpret the dolphin as the result of a *volks-etymologie*, in which the name Delphi (meaning originally a

[1] Eurip., *Alcestis*, Schol., line 1.
[2] Hymn, 215. [3] *Op. cit.*, 220-225.

hollow in the hills) was connected with *delphis*, the dolphin.[1]

On the whole, it seems impossible to get a clear view of Apollo as a sun-god from a legend built out of so many varied materials of different dates as the myth of the slaying of the Python and the founding of the Delphic oracle. Nor does the tale of the birth of the god—*les enfances Apollon*—yield much more certain information. The most accessible and the oldest form of the birth-myth is preserved in the Homeric hymn to the Delian Apollo, a hymn intended for recital at the Delian festival of the Ionian people.

The hymn begins without any account of the amours of Zeus and Leto; it is merely said that many lands refused to allow Leto a place wherein to bring forth her offspring. But barren Delos listened to her prayer, and for nine days Leto was in labour, surrounded by all the goddesses, save jealous Hera and Eilithyia, who presides over child-birth. To her Iris went with the promise of a golden necklet set with amber studs, and Eilithyia came down to the isle, and Leto, grasping the trunk of a palm tree, brought forth Apollo and Artemis.[2]

Such is the narrative of the hymn, in which some interpreters, such as M. Decharme, find a rich allegory of the birth of Light. Leto is regarded as Night or Darkness, though it is now admitted that this meaning cannot be found in the etymology of her name.[3] M. Decharme presumes that the palm tree (φοῖνιξ) origin-

[1] Roscher, *Lexikon;* Preller, i. 208; Schol. ad *Lycophr.*, v. 208.

[2] Compare Theognis, 5-10.

[3] Preller, i. 190, note 4; Curtius, *Gr. Et.*, 120.

ally meant the morning red, by aid of which night gives birth to the sun, and if the poet says the young god loves the mountain tops, why, so does the star of day. The moon, however, does not usually arise simultaneously with the dawn, as Artemis was born with Apollo. It is vain, in fact, to look for minute touches of solar myth in the tale, which rests on the womanly jealousy of Hera, and explains the existence of a great fane and feast of Apollo, not in one of the rich countries that refused his mother sanctuary, but in a small barren and remote island.[1]

Among the wilder myths which grouped themselves round the figure of Apollo was the fable that his mother Leto was changed into a wolf. The fable ran that Leto, in the shape of a wolf, came in twelve days from the Hyperboreans to Delos.[2] This may be explained as a *volks-etymologie* from the god's name, "Lycegenes," which is generally held to mean "born of light". But the presence of very many animals in the Apollo legend and in his temples, corresponding as it does to similar facts already observed in the religion of the lower races, can scarcely be due to popular etymologies alone. The Dolphin-Apollo has already been remarked. There are many traces of connection between Apollo and the wolf. In Athens there was the Lyceum of *Apollo Lukios*, Wolf-Apollo, which tradition connected with the primeval strife wherein Ægeus (goat-man) defeated Lukios (wolf-

[1] The French excavators in Delos found the original unhewn stone on which, in later days, the statue of the anthropomorphic god was based.

[2] Aristotle, *Hist. An.*, vi. 35; Ælian., *N. A.*, iv. 4: Schol. on Apol. Rhod., ii. 123.

man). The Lukian Apollo was the deity of the defeated side, as Athene of the ægis (goat-skin) was the deity of the victors.[1] The Argives had an Apollo of the same kind, and the wolf was stamped on their coins.[2] According to Pausanias, when Danaus came seeking the kingship of Argos, the people hesitated between him and Gelanor. While they were in doubt, a wolf attacked a bull, and the Argives determined that the bull should stand for Gelanor, the wolf for Danaus. The wolf won; Danaus was made king, and in gratitude raised an altar to *Apollo Lukios*, Wolf-Apollo. That is (as friends of the totemic system would argue), a man of the wolf-stock dedicated a shrine to the wolf-god.[3] In Delphi the presence of a bronze image of a wolf was explained by the story that a wolf once revealed the place where stolen temple treasures were concealed. The god's beast looked after the god's interest.[4] In many myths the children of Apollo by mortal girls were exposed, but fostered by wolves.[5] In direct contradiction with Pausanias, but in accordance with a common rule of mythical interpretation, Sophocles[6] calls Apollo "the wolf-slayer". It has very frequently happened that when animals were found closely connected with a god, the ancients explained the fact indifferently by calling the deity the protector or the destroyer of the beasts in question. Thus, in the case of Apollo, mice were held sacred and were fed in his temples in the Troad and elsewhere, the people of Hamaxitus especi-

[1] Paus., i. 19, 4. [2] Preller, i. 202, note 3; Paus., ii. 19, 3.
[3] *Encyc. Brit.*, *s. v.* "Sacrifice". [4] Paus., x. 14, 4.
[5] *Ant. Lib.*, 30. [6] *Electra*, 6.

ally worshipping mice.[1] The god's name, Smintheus, was understood to mean "Apollo of the Mouse," or "Mouse-Apollo".[2] But while Apollo was thus at some places regarded as the patron of mice, other narratives declared that he was adored as Sminthian because from mice he had freed the country. This would be a perfectly natural explanation if the vermin which had once been sacred became a pest in the eyes of later generations.[3]

Flies were in this manner connected with the services of Apollo. It has already been remarked that an ox was sacrificed to flies near the temple of Apollo in Leucas. The sacrifice was explained as a device for inducing flies to settle in one spot, and leave the rest of the coast clear. This was an expensive, and would prove a futile arrangement. There was a statue of the Locust-Apollo (Parnopios) in Athens. The story ran that it was dedicated after the god had banished a plague of locusts.[4] A most interesting view of the way in which pious heathens of a late age regarded Apollo's menagerie may be got from Plutarch's essay on the Delphic responses. It is the description of a visit to Delphi. In the hall of the Corinthians the writer and his friends examine the sacred palm tree of bronze, and "the snakes and frogs in relief round the root of the tree". "Why," said they, "the palm tree is not a marsh plant, and frogs are not a Corinthian crest." And indeed one would think ravens and swans, and hawks and wolves, and anything else than these

[1] Ælian, *H. A.*, xii. 5. [2] Strabo, xiii. 604.

[3] It is the explanation Preller gives of the Mouse-Apollo, i. 202.

[4] Paus., i. 24, 8; Strabo, xiii. 912.

reptiles would be agreeable to the god. Then one of the visitors, Serapion, very learnedly showed that Apollo was the sun, and that the sun arises from water. "Still slipping into the story your lightings up and your exhalations," cried Plutarch, and chaffed him, as one might chaff Kuhn, or Schwartz, or Decharme, about his elemental interpretations. In fact, the classical writers knew rather less than we do about the origin of many of their religious peculiarities.

In connection with sheep, again, Apollo was worshipped as the ram Apollo.[1] At the festival of the Carneia a ram was his victim.[2] These facts are commonly interpreted as significant of the god's care for shepherds and the pastoral life, a memory of the days when Apollo kept a mortal's sheep and was the hind of Admetus of Thessaly. He had animal names derived from sheep and goats, such as *Malœis Tragios*.[3] The tale which made Apollo the serf and shepherd of mortal men is as old as the *Iliad*,[4] and is not easy to interpret, whether as a nature-myth or a local legend. Laomedon, one of Apollo's masters, not only refused him his wage, but threatened to put him in chains and sell him to foreign folk across the sea, and to crop his ears with the blade of bronze. These legends may have brought some consolation to the hearts of free men enslaved. A god had borne like calamities, and could feel for their affliction.

To return to the beasts of Apollo, in addition to dolphins, mice, rams and wolves, he was constantly

[1] Karneios, from κάρνος (Heyschius, *s.v.*), a ram.
[2] Theocritus, *Idyll*, v. 82.
[3] Preller, i. 215, note 1. [4] ii. 766. xxi. 448.

associated with lizards (powerful totems in Australia), cicalas, hawks, swans, ravens, crows, vultures, all of which are, by mythologists, regarded as symbols of the sun-god, in one or other capacity or function. In the *Iliad*,[1] Apollo puts on the gear of a hawk, and flits on hawk's wings down Ida, as the Thlinkeet Yehl does on the feathers of a crane or a raven.

The loves of Apollo make up a long and romantic chapter in his legend. They cannot all be so readily explained, as are many of the loves of Zeus, by the desire to trace genealogical pedigrees to a god. It is on this principle, however, that the birth of Ion, for example, is to be interpreted. The ideal eponymous hero of the Ionian race was naturally feigned to be the son of the deity by whose fatherhood all Ionians became "brethren in Apollo". Once more, when a profession like that of medicine was in the hands of a clan conceiving themselves to be of one blood, and when their common business was under the protection of Apollo, they inevitably traced their genealogy to the god. Thus the medical clan of the Asclepiadæ, of which Aristotle was a member, derived their origin from Asclepius or (as the Romans called him) Æsculapius.

So far everything in this myth appears natural and rational, granting the belief in the amours of an anthropomorphic god. But the details of the story are full of that *irrational* element which is said to "make mythology mythological". In the third Pythian ode Pindar sings how Apollo was the lover of Coronis; how she was faithless to him with a stranger. Pindar does not tell how the crow or the raven flew to Apollo with

[1] xv. 237.

the news, and how the god cursed the crow, which had previously been white, that it should for ever be black. Then he called his sister, Artemis, to slay the false nymph, but snatched from her funeral pyre the babe Asclepius, his own begotten. This myth, which explains the colour of the crow as the result of an event and a divine curse, is an example of the stage of thought already illustrated in the Namaqua myth of Heitsi Eibib, and the peculiarities which his curse attached to various animals. There is also a Bushman myth according to which certain blackbirds have white breasts, because some women once tied pieces of white fat round their necks.[1] It is instructive to observe, as the Scholiast on Pindar quotes Artemon, that Pindar omits the incident of the crow as foolish and unworthy. Apollo, according to the ode, was himself aware, in his omniscience, of the frailty of Coronis. But Hesiod, a much earlier poet, tells the story in the usual way, with the curse of the crow, and his consequent change of colour.[2] The whole story, in its most ancient shape, and with the omissions suggested by the piety of a later age, is an excellent example of the irrational element in Greek myth, of its resemblance to savage myth, and of the tendency of more advanced thought to veil or leave out features revolting to pure religion.[3]

[1] Bleek, *Bushman Folk-Lore*; Pindar, *Pyth.*, iii., with notes of the Scholiast.

[2] Pindar, Estienne, Geneva, 1599, p. 219.

[3] For the various genealogies of Asclepius and a discussion of the authenticity of the Hesiodic fragments, see Roscher, *Lexikon*, pp. 615, 616. The connection of Asclepius with the serpent was so close that he was received into Roman religion in the form of a living snake, while dogs were so intimately connected with his worship that Panofka believed him to have been originally a dog-god (Roscher, p. 629, *Revue Archeologique*).

In another myth Apollo succeeds to the paternal honours of a totem. The Telmissians in Lycia claimed descent from Telmessus, who was the child of an amour in which Apollo assumed the form of a dog. "In this guise he lay with a daughter of Antenor." Probably the Lycians of Telmissus originally derived their pedigree from a dog, *sans phrase*, and, later, made out that the dog was Apollo metamorphosed. This process of veiling a totem, and explaining him away as a saint of the same name, is common in modern India.[1]

The other loves of Apollo are numerous, but it may be sufficient to have examined one such story in detail. Where the tale of the amour was not a necessary consequence of the genealogical tendency to connect clans with gods, it was probably, as Roscher observes in the case of Daphne, an ætiological myth. Many flowers and trees, for example, were nearly connected with the worship and ritual of Apollo; among these were notably the laurel, cypress and hyacinth. It is no longer possible to do more than conjecture why each of these plants was thus favoured, though it is a plausible guess that the god attracted into his service various local tree-worships and plant-worships. People would ask why the deity was associated with the flowers and boughs, and the answer would be readily developed on the familiar lines of nature-myth. The laurel is dear to the god because the laurel was once a girl whom he pursued with his love, and who, to escape his embraces, became a tree. The hyacinth

[1] Suidas, *s. v.* τελμισσεῖς. His authority is Dionysius of Chalcis 200 B.C. See "Primitive Marriage in Bengal," *Asiatic Quarterly*, June, 1886.

and cypress were beautiful youths, dear to Apollo, and accidentally slain by him in sport. After their death they became flowers. Such myths of metamorphoses, as has been shown, are an universal growth of savage fancy, and spring from the want of a sense of difference between men and things.[1]

The legend of Apollo has only been slightly sketched, but it is obvious that many elements from many quarters enter into the sum of his myths and rites.[2] If Apollo was originally the sun-god, it is certain that his influence on human life and society was as wide and beneficent as that of the sun itself. He presides over health and medicine, and over purity of body and soul. He is the god of song, and the hexameter, which first resounded in his temples, uttered its latest word in the melancholy music of the last oracle from Delphi:—

Say to the king that the beautiful fane hath fallen asunder,
  Phœbus no more hath a sheltering roof nor a sacred cell,
And the holy laurels are broken and wasted, and hushed is the wonder
  Of water that spake as it flowed from the deeps of the Delphian well.

In his oracle he appears as the counsellor of men, between men and Zeus he is a kind of mediator (like the son of Baiame in Australia, or of Puluga in the Andaman isles), tempering the austerity of justice with a yearning and kind compassion. He

[1] See "Nature-Myths," *antea*. Schwartz, as usual, takes Daphne to be connected, not with the dawn, but with lightning. "Es ist der Gewitterbaum." *Der Ursprung der Mythologie*, Berlin, 1860, pp. 160-162.

[2] For the influence of Apollo-worship on Greek civilisation, see Curtius's *History of Greece*, English transl., vol. i. For a theory that Apollo answers to Mitra among "the Arians of Iran," see Duncker's *History of Greece*, vol. i. 173.

sanctifies the pastoral life by his example, and, as one who had known bondage to a mortal, his sympathy lightens the burden of the slave. He is the guide of colonists, he knows all the paths of earth and all the ways of the sea, and leads wanderers far from Greece into secure havens, and settles them on fertile shores. But he is also the god before whom the Athenians first flogged and then burned their human scapegoats.[1] His example consecrated the abnormal post-Homeric vices of Greece. He is capable of metamorphosis into various beasts, and his temple courts are thronged with images of frogs, and mice, and wolves, and dogs, and ravens, over whose elder worship he throws his protection. He is the god of sudden death; he is amorous and revengeful. The fair humanities of old religion boast no figure more beautiful; yet he, too, bears the birth-marks of ancient creeds, and there is a shadow that stains his legend and darkens the radiance of his glory.

Artemis.

If Apollo soon disengages himself from the sun, and appears as a deity chiefly remarkable for his moral and prophetic attributes, Artemis retains as few traces of any connection with the moon. "In the development of Artemis may most clearly be distinguished," says Claus, "the progress of the human intellect from the early, rude, and, as it were, natural ideas, to the fair and brilliant fancies of poets and sculptors."[2] There is no goddess more beautiful,

[1] At the Thergelia. See Meursius, *Græcia Feriata.*

[2] *De Dianæ Antiquissima apud Græcos Natura*, Vratislaviæ, 1881.

pure and maidenly in the poetry of Greece. There she shines as the sister of Apollo; her chapels are in the wild wood; she is the abbess of the forest nymphs, "chaste and fair," the maiden of the precise life, the friend of the virginal Hippolytus; always present, even if unseen, with the pure of heart.[1] She is like Milton's lady in the revel route of the *Comus*, and among the riot of Olympian lovers she alone, with Athene, satisfies the ascetic longing for a proud remoteness and reserve. But though it is thus that the poets dream of her, from the author of the *Odyssey* to Euripides, yet the local traditions and cults of Artemis, in many widely separated districts, combine her worship and her legend with hideous cruelties, with almost cannibal rites, with relics of the wild worship of the beasts whom, in her character as the goddess of the chase, she "preserves," rather than protects. To her human victims are sacrificed; for her bears, deer, doves, wolves, all the tameless herds of the hills and forests are driven through the fire in Achæa. She is adored with bear-dances by the Attic girls; there is a gloomy Chthonian or sepulchral element in her worship, and she is even blended in ritual with a monstrous many-breasted divinity of Oriental religion. Perhaps it is scarcely possible to separate now all the tangled skeins in the mixed conception of Artemis, or to lay the finger on the germinal conception of her nature. "Dark," says Schreiber, "is the original conception, obscure the meaning of the name of Artemis."[2] It is certain that

[1] *Hippolytus*, Eurip., 73-87.

[2] Roscher's *Lexikon*, *s. v.*

many tribal worships are blended in her legend and each of two or three widely different notions of her nature may be plausibly regarded as the most primitive.

In the attempt to reach the original notion of Artemis, philology offers her distracting aid and her competing etymologies. What is the radical meaning of her name? On this point Claus[1] has a long dissertation. In his opinion Artemis was originally (as Dione) the wife, not the daughter, of Zeus, and he examines the names Dione, Diana, concluding that Artemis, Dione and Diana are essentially one, and that Diana is the feminine of Janus (Djanus), corresponding to the Greek *Ζάν* or *Ζήν*. As to the etymology of Artemis, Curtis wisely professes himself uncertain.[2] A crowd of hypotheses have been framed by more sanguine and less cautious etymologists. Artemis has been derived from ἀρτεμής, "safe," "unharmed," "the stainless maiden". Goebel,[3] suggests the root στρατ or ῥατ, "to shake," and makes Artemis mean the thrower of the dart or the shooter. But this is confessedly conjectural. The Persian language has also been searched for the root of Artemis, which is compared with the first syllables in Artaphernes, Artaxerxes, Artaxata, and so forth. It is concluded that Artemis would simply mean "the great goddess". Claus again, returning to his theory of Artemis as originally the wife of Zeus, inclines to regard her as originally the earth, the "mighty mother".[4] As Schreiber observes,

[1] Roscher's *Lexikon*, *s. v.*, p. 7. [2] *Etym. Gr.*, 5th ed., p. 556.

[3] *Lexilogus*, i. 554.

[4] For many other etymologies of Artemis, see Roscher's *Lexikon*, p. 558. Among these is ἀερότεμις, "she who cuts the air". Even Ἄρκτεμις connected with ἄρκτος, the bear, has occurred to inventive men.

the philological guesses really throw no light on the nature of Artemis. Welcker, Preller and Lauer take her for the goddess of the midnight sky, and "the light of the night".[1] Claus, as we have seen, is all for night, not light; for "Night is identical in conception with the earth"—night being the shadow of earth, a fact probably not known to the very early Greeks. Claus, however, seems well inspired when he refuses to deduce all the many properties, myths and attributes of Artemis from lunar aspects and attributes. The smallest grain of ingenuity will always suffice as the essential element in this mythological alchemy, this "transmutation" of the facts of legend into so many presumed statements about any given natural force or phenomenon.

From all these general theories and vague hypotheses it is time to descend to facts, and to the various local or tribal cults and myths of Artemis. Her place in the artistic poetry, which wrought on and purified those tales, will then be considered. This process is the converse of the method, for example, of M. Decharme. He first accepts the "queen and huntress, chaste and fair," of poetry, and then explains her local myths and rituals as accidental corruptions of and foreign additions to that ideal.

The Attic and Arcadian legends of Artemis are confessedly among the oldest.[2] Both in Arcadia and Attica, the goddess is strangely connected with that animal worship, and those tales of bestial metamor-

[1] Welcker, *Griechische Götterlehre*, i. 561, Göttingen, 1857; Preller, i. 239.

[2] Roscher, *Lexikon*, 580.

phosis, which are the characteristic elements of myths and beliefs among the most backward races.

The Arcadian myth of Artemis and the she-bear is variously narrated. According to Pausanias, Lycaon, king of Arcadia, had a daughter, Callisto, who was loved by Zeus. Hera, in jealous wrath, changed Callisto into a she-bear; and Artemis, to please Hera, shot the beast. At this time the she-bear was pregnant with a child by Zeus, who sent Hermes to save the babe, Arcas, just as Dionysus was saved at the burning of Semele and Asclepius at the death of his mother, whom Apollo slew. Zeus then transformed Callisto into a constellation, the bear.[1] No more straightforward myth of descent from a beast (for the Arcadians claimed descent from Arcas, the she-bear's son) and of starry or bestial metamorphosis was ever told by Cahrocs or Kamilaroi. Another story ran that Artemis herself, in anger at the unchastity of Callisto, caused her to become a bear. So the legend ran in a Hesiodic poem, according to the extract in Eratosthenes.[2]

Such is the ancient myth, which Otfried Müller endeavours to explain by the light of his lucid common sense, without the assistance which we can now derive from anthropological research. The nymph Callisto, in his opinion, is a mere refraction from Artemis herself, under her Arcadian and poetic name of Calliste, "the most beautiful". Hard by the tumulus known as the grave of Callisto was a shrine, Pausanias tells us, of

[1] Paus., viii. 3, 5.

[2] O. Müller, Engl. transl., p. 15; *Catast.*, i.; Apollodor., iii. 82; Hyginus, 176, 177. A number of less important references are given in Bachofen's *Der Bär in den Religionen des Alterthums.*

Artemis *Calliste*.[1] Pamphos, he adds, was the first poet known to him who praised Artemis by this title, and *he* learned it from the Arcadians. Müller next remarks on the attributes of Artemis in Athens, the Artemis known as Brauronia. "Now," says he, "we set out from this, that the circumstance of the goddess *who is served at Brauron by she-bears* having a friend and companion changed into a bear, cannot possibly be a freak of chance, but that this metamorphosis has its foundation in the fact that the animal was sacred to the goddess."

It will become probable that the animal actually *was* mythically identified with the goddess at an extremely remote period, or, at all events, that the goddess succeeded to, and threw her protection over, an ancient worship of the animal.

Passing then from Arcadia, where the friend of the goddess becomes a she-bear, to Brauron and Munychia in Attica, we find that the local Artemis there, an Artemis connected by legend with the fierce Taurian goddess, is served by young girls, who imitate, in dances, the gait of bears, who are called little bears, ἄρκτοι, and whose ministry is named ἀρκτεία, that is, "a playing the bear". Some have held that the girls once wore bear-skins.[2] Familiar examples in

[1] Paus., viii. 3.

[2] Claus, *op. cit.*, p. 76. [Suchier, *De Dian Brauron*, p. 33.] The bear-skin seems later to have been exchanged for a saffron raiment, κροκωτός. Compare Harpokration, ἀρκτεῦσαι, Aristophanes, *Lysistrata*, 646. The Scholiast on that passage collects legendary explanations, setting forth that the rites were meant to appease the goddess for the slaying of a tame bear (*cf.* Apostolius, vii. 10). Mr. Parnell has collected all the lore in his work on the Cults of the Greek States.

ancient and classical times of this religious service by men in bestial guise are the wolf-dances of the Hirpi or "wolves," and the use of the ram-skin (*Δίος κώδων*) in Egypt and Greece.[1] These Brauronian rites point to a period when the goddess was herself a bear, or when a bear-myth accrued to her legend, and this inference is confirmed by the singular tradition that she was not only a bear, but a bear who craved for human blood.[2]

The connection between the Arcadian Artemis, the Artemis of Brauron, and the common rituals and creeds of totemistic worship is now, perhaps, undeniably apparent. Perhaps in all the legend and all the cult of the goddess there is no more archaic element than this. The speech of the women in the *Lysistrata*, recalling the days of their childhood when they "were bears," takes us back to a remote past when the tribes settled at Brauron were bear-worshippers, and, in all probability, claimed to be of the bear stock or kindred. Their distant descendants still imitated the creature's movements in a sacred dance; and the girls of Periclean Athens acted at that moment like the young men of the Mandans or Nootkas in their wolf-dance or buffalo-dance. Two questions remain

[1] Servius, *Æn.*, xi. 785. For a singular parallel in modern French folk-lore to the dance of the Hirpi, see Mannhardt, *Wald und Feld Cultus*, ii. 324, 325. For the ram, see Herodotus, ii. 42. In Thebes the ram's skin was in the yearly festival flayed, and placed on the statue of the god. Compare, in the case of the buzzard, Bancroft, iii. 168. Great care is taken in preserving the skin of the sacrificed totem, the buzzard, as it makes part of a sacred dress.

[2] Apostolius, viii. 19, vii. 10, quoted by O. Müller (*cf.* Welcker, i. 573).

unanswered: how did a goddess of the name of Artemis, and with her wide and beneficent functions, succeed to a cult so barbarous? or how, on the other hand, did the cult of a ravening she-bear develop into the humane and pure religion of Artemis?

Here is a moment in mythical and religious evolution which almost escapes our inquiry. We find, in actual historical processes, nothing more akin to it than the relation borne by the Samoan gods to the various animals in which they are supposed to be manifest. How did the complex theory of the nature of Artemis arise? what was its growth? at what precise hour did it emancipate itself on the whole from the lower savage creeds? or how was it developed out of their unpromising materials? The science of mythology may perhaps never find a key to these obscure problems.[1]

The goddess of Brauron, succeeding probably to the cult of a she-bear, called for human blood. With human blood the Artemis Orthia of Sparta was propitiated. Of this goddess and her rights Pausanias tells a very remarkable story. The image of the goddess, he declares, is barbarous; which probably means that even among the archaic wooden idols of Greece it seemed peculiarly savage in style. Astrabacus and Alopecus (the ass and the fox), sons of Agis, are said to have found the idol in a bush, and to have been struck mad at the sight of it. Those who sacri-

[1] The symbolic explanation of Bachofen, Claus and others is to the effect that the she-bear (to take that case) is a beast in which the maternal instinct is very strong, and apparently that the she-bear, deprived of her whelps, is a fit symbol of a goddess notoriously virginal, and without offspring.

ficed to the goddess fell to blows and slew each other; a pestilence followed, and it became clear that the goddess demanded human victims. "Her altar must be drenched in the blood of men," the victim being chosen by lot. Lycurgus got the credit of substituting the rite in which boys were flogged before the goddess to the effusion of blood for the older human sacrifices.[1] The Taurian Artemis, adored with human sacrifice, and her priestess, Iphigenia, perhaps a form of the goddess, are familiar examples of this sanguinary ritual.[2] Suchier is probably correct in denying that these sacrifices are of foreign origin. They are closely interwoven with the oldest idols and oldest myths of the districts least open to foreign influence. An Achæan example is given by Pausanias.[3] Artemis was adored with the offering of a beautiful girl and boy. Not far from Brauron, at Halæ, was a very ancient temple of Artemis Tauropolos, in which blood was drawn from a man's throat by the edge of the sword, clearly a modified survival of human sacrifice. The whole connection of Artemis with Taurian rites has been examined by Müller,[4] in his *Orchomenos*.[5] Horns grow from the shoulders of Artemis Tauropolos, on the coins of Amphipolis, and on Macedonian coins she rides on a bull. According to Decharme,[6] the

[1] Paus., iii. 8, 16. *Cf.* Müller, *Dorians*, book ii. chap. 9, 6. Pausanias, viii. 23, 1, mentions a similar custom, ordained by the Delphian oracle, the flogging of women at the feast of Dionysus in Alea of Arcadia.

[2] *Cf.* Müller, *Dorians*, ii. 9, 6, and Claus, *op. cit.*, cap. v.

[3] Paus., vii. 19.

[4] *Op. cit.*, ii. 9, 6.

[5] *Ibid.*, p. 311. *Cf.* Euripides, *Iph.* Taur., 1424, and Roscher, *Lexikon*, p. 568.

[6] *Mythol. de la Grece*, p. 137.

Taurian Artemis, with her hideous rites, was confused, by an accidental resemblance of names, with this Artemis Tauropolos, whose "symbol" was a bull, and who (whatever we may think of the symbolic hypothesis) used bulls as her "vehicle" and wore bull's horns. Müller, on the other hand,[1] believes the Greeks found in Tauria (*i.e.*, Lemnos) a goddess with bloody "rites, whom they identified by reason of those very human sacrifices, with their own Artemis Iphigenia". Their own worship of that deity bore so many marks of ancient barbarism that they were willing to consider the northern barbarians as its authors. Yet it is possible that the Tauric Artemis was no more derived from the Taurians than Artemis Æthiopia from the Æthiopians.

The nature of the famous Diana of the Ephesians, or Artemis of Ephesus, is probably quite distinct in origin from either the Artemis of Arcadia and Attica or the deity of literary creeds. As late as the time of Tacitus[2] the Ephesians maintained that Leto's twins had been born in their territory. "The first which showed themselves in the senate were the Ephesians, declaring that Diana and Apollo were not born in the island Delos, as the common people did believe; and there was in their country a river called Cenchrius, and a wood called Ortegia, where Latona, being great with child, and leaning against an olive tree which is yet in that place, brought forth these two gods, and that by the commandment of the gods the wood was made sacred."[3] This was a mere

[1] *Mythol. de la Grece*, ii. 9, 7. [2] *Annals*, iii. 61.
[3] Greenwey's *Tacitus*, 1622.

adaptation of the Delian legend, the olive (in Athens sacred to Athene) taking the place of the Delian palm-tree. The real Artemis of Ephesus, "the image that fell from heaven," was an Oriental survival. Nothing can be less Greek in taste than her many-breasted idol, which may be compared with the many-breasted goddess of the beer-producing maguey plant in Mexico.[1]

The wilder elements in the local rites and myths of Diana are little if at all concerned with the goddess in her Olympian aspect as the daughter of Leto and sister of Apollo. It is from this lofty rank that she descends in the national epic to combat on the Ilian plain among warring gods and men. Claus has attempted, from a comparison of the epithets applied to Artemis, to show that the poets of the *Iliad* and the *Odyssey* take different views of her character. In the *Iliad* she is a goddess of tumult and passion; in the *Odyssey*, a holy maiden with the "gentle darts" that deal sudden and painless death. But in both poems she is a huntress, and the death-dealing shafts are hers both in *Iliad* and *Odyssey*. Perhaps the apparent difference is due to nothing but the necessity for allotting her a part in that battle of the Olympians which rages in the *Iliad*. Thus Hera in the *Iliad* addresses her thus:[2] "How now! art thou mad, bold vixen, to match thyself against me? Hard were it for thee to match my might, bow-bearer though thou art, since against women Zeus made thee a lion, and giveth thee to slay whomso of them thou wilt. Truly

[1] For an alabaster statuette of the goddess, see Roscher's *Lexikon*, p. 588

[2] *Iliad*, xxi. 481.

it is better on the mountains to slay wild beasts and deer than to fight with one that is mightier than thou."

These taunts of Hera, who always detests the illegitimate children of Zeus, doubtless refer to the character of Artemis as the goddess of childbirth. Here she becomes confused with Ilithyia and with Hecate; but it is unnecessary to pursue the inquiry into these details.[1]

Like most of the Olympians, Artemis was connected not only with beast-worship, but with plant-worship. She was known by the names Daphnæa and Cedreatis; at Ephesus not only the olive but the oak was sacred to her; at Delos she had her palm tree. Her idol was placed in or hung from the branches of these trees, and it is not improbable that she succeeded to the honours either of a tree worshipped in itself and for itself, or of the spirit or genius which was presumed to dwell in and inform it. Similar examples of one creed inheriting the holy things of its predecessor are common enough where either missionaries, as in Mexico and China, or the early preachers of the gospel in Brittany or Scandinavia, appropriated to Christ the holy days of pagan deities and consecrated fetish stones with the mark of the cross. Unluckily, we have no historical evidence as to the moment in which the ancient tribal totems and fetishes and sacrifices were placed under the protection of the various

[1] *Cf.* Preller, i. 256, 257. Bacchylides make Hecate the daughter of "deep-bosomed Night". (40). The Scholiast on the second idyll of Theocritus, in which the sorceress appeals to the magic of the moon, makes her a daughter of Zeus and Demeter, and identified with Artemis. Here, more clearly than elsewhere, the Artemis appears *sub luce maligna*, under the wan uncertain light of the moon.

Olympians, in whose cult they survive, like flies in amber. But that this process did take place is the most obvious explanation of the rude factors in the religion of Artemis, as of Apollo, Zeus or Dionysus.

It was ever the tendency of Greek thought to turn from the contemplation of dark and inscrutable things in the character of the gods and to endow them with the fairest attributes. The primitive formless *Zoana* give place to the ideal statues of gold and ivory. The Artemis to whom a fawn in a maiden's dress is sacrificed does not haunt the memory of Euripides; his Artemis is fair and honourable, pure and maidenly, a goddess wandering in lonely places unbeholden of man. It is thus, if one may rhyme the speech of Hippolytus, that her votary addresses her :—

For thee soft crowns in thine untrampled mead
  I weave, my lady, and to thee I bear;
Thither no shepherd drives his flocks to feed,
  Nor scythe of steel has ever laboured there;
  Nay, through the spring among the blossoms fair
The brown bee comes and goes, and with good heed
Thy maiden, Reverence, sweet streams doth lead
  About the grassy close that is her care!

Souls only that are gracious and serene
  By gift of God, in human lore unread,
May pluck these holy blooms and grasses green
  That now I wreathe for thine immortal head,
I who may walk with thee, thyself unseen,
  And by thy whispered voice am comforted.[1]

In passages like this we find the truly *natural* religion, the religion to which man's nature tends, "groaning and travailing" till the goal is won. But

[1] Hippol., 73-87.

it is long in the winning; the paths are rough; humanity is "led by a way that it knew not".

Dionysus.

Among deities whose origin has been sought in the personification, if not of the phenomena, at least of the forces of Nature, Dionysus is prominent.[1] He is regarded by many mythologists[2] as the "spiritual form" of the new vernal life, the sap and pulse of vegetation and of the new-born year, especially as manifest in the vine and the juice of the grape. Thus Preller[3] looks on his mother, Semele, as a personification of the pregnant soil in spring.[4] The name of Semele is explained with the familiar diversity of conjecture. Whether the human intellect, at the time of the first development of myth, was capable of such abstract thought as is employed in the recognition of a deity presiding over "the revival of earth-life" or not and whether, having attained to this abstraction, men would go on to clothe it in all manner of animal and other symbolisms, are questions which mythologists seem to take for granted. The popular story of the birth of Dionysus is well known. His mother, Semele, desired to see Zeus in all his glory, as he appeared when he made love to Hera. Having promised to grant all the nymph's requests, Zeus was

[1] It is needless to occupy space with the etymological guesses at the sense of the name "Dionysus". Greek, Sanskrit and Assyrian have been tortured by the philologists, but refuse to give up their secret, and Curtis does not even offer a conjecture (*Gr. Etym.*, 609).

[2] Preller, i. 544. [3] i. 546.

[4] The birth of Dionysus is recorded (*Iliad*, xiv. 323; Hesiod, *Theog.*, 940) without the story of the death of Semele, which occurs in Æschylus, *Frg.*, 217-218; Eurip., *Bacchæ*, i. 3.

constrained to approach her in thunder and lightning. She was burned to death, but the god rescued her unborn child and sowed him up in his own thigh. In this wild narrative Preller finds the wedlock of heaven and earth, "the first day that it thunders in March". The thigh of Zeus is to be interpreted as "the cool moist clouds". If, on the other hand, we may take Dionysus himself to be the rain, as Kuhn does, and explain the thigh of Zeus by comparison with certain details in the soma sacrifice and the right thigh of Indra, as described in one of the Brahmanas, why then, of course, Preller's explanation cannot be admitted.[1]

These examples show the difficulty, or rather indicate the error, of attempting to interpret all the details in any myth as so many statements about natural phenomena and natural forces. Such interpretations are necessarily conjectural. Certainly Dionysus, the god of orgies, of wine, of poetry, became in later Greek thought something very like the "spiritual form" of the vine, and the patron of Nature's moods of revelry. But that he was originally conceived of thus, or that this conception may be minutely traced through each incident of his legend, cannot be scientifically established. Each mythologist, as has been said before, is, in fact, asking himself, "What meaning would I have had if I told this or that story of the god of the vine or the god of the year's renewal?" The imaginations in which the tale of the double birth of Dionysus arose were so unlike the imagination of an erudite

[1] Kuhn, *Herabkunft*, pp. 166, 167, where it appears that the gods buy soma and place it on the right thigh of Indra.

modern German that these guesses are absolutely baseless. Nay, when we are told that the child was sheltered in his father's body, and was actually brought to birth by the father, we may be reminded, like Bachofen, of that widespread savage custom, the *couvade.* From Brazil to the Basque country it has been common for the father to pretend to lie-in while the mother is in childbed; the husband undergoes medical treatment, in many cases being put to bed for days.[1] This custom, "world-wide," as Mr. Tylor calls it, has been used by Bachofen as the source of the myth of the double birth of Dionysus. Though other explanations of the *couvade* have been given, the most plausible theory represents it as a recognition of paternity by the father. Bachofen compares the ceremony by which, when Hera became reconciled to Herakles, she adopted him as her own through the legal fiction of his second birth. The custom by which, in old French marriage rites, illegitimate children were legitimised by being brought to the altar under the veil of the bride is also in point.[2] Diodorus says that barbarians still practise the rite of adoption by a fictitious birth. Men who returned home safely after they were believed to be dead had to undergo a similar ceremony.[3] Bachofen therefore explains the names and myths of the "double-mothered Dionysus" as relics of the custom of the *couvade,* and of the legal recognition of children by the father, after a period of kinship through women only. This theory is put by

[1] Tylor, *Prim. Cult.*, i. 94; *Early History of Mankind*, p. 293.
[2] Bachofen, *Das Mutterrecht*, Stuttgart, 1861, p. 254.
[3] Plutarch, *Quæst. Rom.*, 5.

Lucian in his usual bantering manner. Poseidon wishes to enter the chamber of Zeus, but is refused admission by Hermes.

"Is Zeus *en bonne fortune?*" he asks.

"No, the reverse. Zeus has just had a baby."

"A baby! why there was nothing in his figure . . . ! Perhaps the child was born from his head, like Athene?"

"Not at all—his *thigh;* the child is Semele's."

"Wonderful God! what varied accomplishments! But who is Semele?"

"A Theban girl, a daughter of Cadmus, much noticed by Zeus."

"And so he kindly was confined for her?"

"Exactly!"

"So Zeus is both father and mother of the child?"

"Naturally! And now I must go and make him comfortable."[1]

We need not necessarily accept Bachofen's view. This learned author employed indeed a widely comparative method, but he saw everything through certain mystic speculations of his own. It may be deemed, however, that the authors of the myth of the double birth of Dionysus were rather in the condition of men who practise the *couvade* than capable of such vast abstract ideas and such complicated symbolism as are required in the system of Preller. It is probable enough that the struggle between the two systems of kindred—maternal and paternal—has left its mark in Greek mythology. Undeniably it is present in the *Eumenides* of Æschylus, and perhaps it

[1] *Dial. Deor.*, xi.

inspires the tales which represent Hera and Zeus as emulously producing offspring (Athene and Hephæstus) without the aid of the opposite sex.[1]

In any case, Dionysus, Semele's son, the patron of the vine, the conqueror of India, is an enigmatic figure of dubious origin, but less repulsive than Dionysus Zagreus.

Even among the adventures of Zeus the amour which resulted in the birth of Dionysus Zagreus was conspicuous. "Jupiter ipse filiam incestavit, natum hinc Zagreum."[2] Persephone, fleeing her hateful lover, took the shape of a serpent, and Zeus became the male dragon. The story is on a footing with the Brahmanic myth of Prajapati and his daughter as buck and doe. The Platonists explained the legend, as usual, by their "absurd symbolism".[3]

The child of two serpents, Zagreus, was born, curious as it may seem, with horns on his head. Zeus brought him up in secret, but Hera sent the Titans to kill him. According to Clemens Alexandrinus[4] and other authorities, the Titans won his heart with toys, including the bull-roarer or turn-dun of the Australians.[5] His enemies, also in Australian fashion, daubed themselves over with pipeclay.[6] By these hideous foes the child was torn to pieces, though, according to Nonnus, he changed himself into as many beasts as Proteus by the Nile, or Tamlane by the Ettrick. In his bull-

[1] Roscher's *Lexikon*, p. 1046.

[2] Lobeck, *Aglaoph.*, p. 547, quoting Callimachus and Euphorio.

[3] *Ibid.*, p. 550.

[4] *Admon.*, p. 11; Nonnus, xxiv. 43; ap. *Aglaoph.*, p. 555.

[5] *Custom and Myth*, p. 39.

[6] *Cf.* Demosthenes, *Pro. Or.*, 313; Lobeck, pp. 556, 646, 700.

shape, Zagreus was finally chopped up small, cooked (except the heart), and eaten by the Titans.[1] Here we are naturally reminded of the dismemberment of Osiris, Ymir, Purusha, Chokanipok and so many other gods and beasts in Egypt, India, Scandinavia and America. This point must not be lost sight of in the controversy as to the origin and date of the story of Dionysus Zagreus. Nothing can be much more repulsive than these hideous incidents to the genius, for example, of Homer. He rarely tells anything worse about the gods than the tale of Ares' imprisonment in the large bronze pot, an event undignified, indeed, but not in the ferocious taste of the Zagreus legend. But it need not, therefore, be decided that the story of Dionysus and the Titans is later than Homer because it is inconsistent with the tone of Homeric mythology, and because it is found in more recent authorities. Details like the use of the "turndun" (ῥόμβος) in the Dionysiac mysteries, and the bodies of the celebrants daubed with clay, have a primitive, or at least savage, appearance. It was the opinion of Lobeck that the Orphic poems, in which the legend first comes into literature, were the work of Onomacritus.[2] On the other hand, Müller argued that the myth was really archaic, although it had passed through the hands of Onomacritus. On the strength of the boast of the Delphian priests that they possessed the grave in which the fragments of the god were buried, Müller believed that Onomacritus received the story from Delphi.[3] Müller writes, "The way in

[1] Proclus *in Crat.*, p. 115.

[2] *Aglaoph.*, p. 616. "Onomacritum architectum istius mythi."

[3] Müller's Proleg., English transl., p. 319.

which these Orphics went to work with ancient myths can be most distinctly seen in the mythus of the *tearing asunder of Bacchus*, which, at all events, passed *through* the hands of Onomacritus, an organiser of Dionysian orgies, according to Pausanias, an author of Orphean poems also, and therefore, in all probability, an Orphic".

The words of Pausanias are (viii. 37, 3), "Onomacritus, taking from Homer the name of the Titans, established Dionysiac orgies, and represented the Titans as the authors of the sorrows of the god".

Now it is perhaps impossible to decide with certainty whether, as Lobeck held, Onomacritus "adapted" the myth, and the Delphians received it into their religion, with rites purposely meant to resemble those of Osiris in Egypt, or whether Müller more correctly maintains that Onomacritus, on the other hand, brought an old temple mystery and "sacred chapter" into the light of literature. But it may very plausibly be maintained that a myth so wild, and so analogous in its most brutal details to the myths of many widely scattered races, is more probably ancient than a fresh invention of a poet of the sixth century. It is much more likely that Greece, whether at Delphi or elsewhere, possessed a legend common to races in distant continents, than that Onomacritus either invented the tale or borrowed it from Egypt and settled it at Delphi. O. Müller could not appeal to the crowd of tales of divine dismemberment in savage and civilised lands, because with some he was unacquainted, and others (like the sacrifice of Purusha, the cutting up of Omorca, the rending of Ymir) do not seem to have occurred to his memory. Though the majority of these legends of divine dismemberment are connected with the making of the world, yet in essentials they do resemble the tale of Dionysus and the Titans. Thus the balance of probability is in favour of the theory that the myth is really old, and was borrowed, not invented, by Onomacritus.[1] That very shifty person may have made his own alterations in the narrative, but it cannot be rash to say with O. Müller, "If it has been supposed that he was the inventor of the entire fable, which Pausanias by no means asserts, I must confess that I cannot bring myself to think so. According to the notions of the ancients, it must have been an unholy, an accursed man who could, from a mere caprice of his own, represent the ever-young Dionysus, the god of joy, as having been torn to pieces by the Titans." A reply to this might, no doubt, be sought in the passages describing the influx of new superstitions which are cited by Lobeck.[2] The Greek comic poets especially derided these religious novelties, which corresponded very closely to our "Esoteric Buddhism" and similar impostures. But these new mysteries and trumpery cults of the decayed civilisation were things very different from the worship of Dionysus Zagreus and his established sacrifices of oxen in the secret penetralia of Delphi.[3] It may be determined, therefore, that the tale and the mystery-play of Dionysus and the Titans are, in essentials, as old as the savage state of religion, in which their analogues abound, whether at Delphi they were or were not of foreign origin,

[1] Lobeck, *Aglaoph.*, p. 671. [2] *Aglaoph.*, 625-630.
[3] *Lycophron*, 206, and the Scholiast.

and introduced in times comparatively recent. The fables, wherever they are found, are accompanied by savage rites, in which (as in some African tribes when the chief is about to declare war) living animals were torn asunder and eaten raw. These horrors were a kind of representation of the sufferings of the god. O. Müller may well observe,[1] "We can scarcely take these rites to be new usages and the offspring of a post-Homeric civilisation". These remarks apply to the custom of *nebrismus*, or tearing fawns to pieces and dancing about draped in the fawn-skins. Such rites were part of the Bacchic worship, and even broke out during a pagan revival in the time of Valens, when dogs were torn in shreds by the worshippers.[2]

Whether the antiquity of the Zagrean ritual and legend be admitted or not, the problem as to their original significance remains. Although the majority of heathen rites of this kind were mystery-plays, setting forth in action some story of divine adventure or misadventure,[3] yet Lobeck imagines the story of Zagreus and the Titans to have been invented or adapted from the Osiris legend, as an account of the mystic performances themselves. What the myth meant, or what the furious actions of the celebrants intended, it is only possible to conjecture. Commonly it is alleged that the sufferings of Dionysus are the

[1] *Lycophron*, p. 322.

[2] Theodoretus, ap. Lobeck, p. 653. Observe the number of examples of daubing with clay in the mysteries here adduced by Lobeck, and compare the Mandan tribes described by Catlin in *O-Kee-Pa*, London, 1867, and by Theal in *Kaffir Folk-Lore*.

[3] Lactantius, v. 19, 15; Ovid, *Fasti*, iv. 211.

ruin of the summer year at the hands of storm and winter, while the revival of the child typifies the vernal resurrection; or, again, the slain Dionysus is the vintage. The old English song tells how "John Barleycorn must die," and how potently he came back to life and mastered his oppressors. This notion, too, may be at the root of "the passion of Dionysus," for the grapes suffer at least as many processes of torture as John Barleycorn before they declare themselves in the shape of strong drink.[1] While Preller talks about the *tiefste Erd-und Naturschmerz* typified in the Zagrean ritual, Lobeck remarks that Plato would be surprised if he could hear these "drunken men's freaks" decoratively described as *ein erhabene Naturdienst*. Lobeck looks on the wild acts, the tearing of fawns and dogs, the half-naked dances, the gnawing of raw bleeding flesh, as the natural expression of fierce untutored folk, revelling in freedom, leaping and shouting. But the odd thing is that the most civilised of peoples should so long have retained the manners of *ingenia inculta et indomita*. Whatever the original significance of the Dionysiac revels, that significance was certainly expressed in a ferocious and barbaric fashion, more worthy of Australians than Athenians.

On this view of the case it might perhaps be maintained that the germ of the myth is merely the sacrifice itself, the barbaric and cruel dismembering of an animal victim, which came to be identified with the god. The sufferings of the victim would

[1] Decharme, *Mythologie de la Grece*, p. 437. Compare Preller, i. 572 on *tiefste Naturschmerz*, and so forth.

thus finally be transmuted into a legend about the passion of the deity. The old Greek explanation that the ritual was designed "in imitation of what befel the god" would need to be reversed. The truth would be that the myth of what befel the god was borrowed from the actual torture of the victim with which the god was identified. Examples of this mystic habit of mind, in which the slain beast, the god, and even the officiating celebrant were confused in thought with each other, are sufficiently common in ritual.[1]

The sacrifices in the ritual of Dionysus have a very marked character, and here, more commonly than in other Hellenic cults, the god and the victim are recognised as essentially the same. The sacrifice, in fact, is a sacrament, and in partaking of the victim the communicants eat their god. This detail is so prominent that it has not escaped the notice even of mythologists who prefer to take an ideal view of myths and customs, to regard them as symbols in a nature-worship originally pure. Thus M. Decharme says of the bull-feast in the Dionysiac cult, "Comme le taureau est un des formes de Dionysos, c'était le corps du dieu dont se repaissaient les initiés, c'était son sang dont ils s'abreuvaient dans ce banquet mystique". Now it was the peculiarity of the Bacchici who maintained these rites, that, as a rule, they abstained from the flesh of animals altogether, or at least their conduct took this shape when adopted into

[1] As to the torch-dances of the Mænads, compare Roscher, *Lexikon*, p. 1041, and Mannhardt *Wald und Feld Kultus*, i. 534, for parallels in European folk-lore.

the Orphic discipline.[1] This ritual, therefore, has points in common with the usages which appear also to have survived into the cult of the ram-god in Egypt.[2] The conclusion suggested is that where Dionysus was adored with this sacrament of bull's flesh, he had either been developed out of, or had succeeded to, the worship of a bull-totem, and had inherited his characteristic ritual. Mr. Frazer, however, proposes quite a different solution.[3] Ours is rendered plausible by the famous Elean chant in which the god was thus addressed: "Come, hero Dionysus, come with the Graces to thy holy house by the shores of the sea; hasten with thy bull-foot". Then the chorus repeated, "Goodly bull, goodly bull".[4] M. Decharme publishes a cameo[5] in which the god is represented as a bull, with the three Graces standing on his neck, and seven stars in the field. M. Decharme decides that the stars are the Pleiades, the Graces the rays of the vernal sun, and Dionysus as a bull the symbol of the vernal sun itself. But all such symbolical explanations are apt to be mere private conjectures, and they are of no avail in face of the ritual which, on the other hypothesis, is to be expected, and is actually found, in connection with the bull Dionysus. Where Dionysus is not absolutely called a bull, he is addressed as the "horned deity," the "bull-horned," the "horned child".[6] A still more curious incident

[1] Lobeck, *Aglaoph.*, i. 244; Plato, *Laws*, vi. 782; Herodot., ii. 81. Porphyry says that this also was the rule of Pythagoras (*Vita Pyth.*, 1630, p. 22).

[2] Herodot., ii. 42.

[3] *Golden Bough*, vol. ii.

[4] Plutarch, *Qu. Gr.*, 36.

[5] *Op. cit.*, p. 431.

[6] Clemens Alex., *Adhort.*, ii. 15-18; Nonnus, vi. 264; Diodorus, iv. 4, 3. 64.

of the Dionysiac worship was the sacrifice of a booted calf, a calf with cothurns on its feet.[1] The people of Tenedos, says Ælian, used to tend their goodliest cow with great care, to treat it, when it calved, like a woman in labour, to put the calf in boots and sacrifice it, and then to stone the sacrificer and drive him into the sea to expiate his crime. In this ceremony, as in the Diipolia at Athens, the slain bull is, as it were, a member of the blood-kindred of the man who immolates him, and who has to expiate the deed as if it were a murder.[2] In this connection it is worth remarking that Dionysus Zagreus, when, according to the myth, he was attacked by the Titans, tried to escape his enemies by assuming various forms. It was in the guise of a bull that he was finally captured and rent asunder. The custom of rending the living victims of his cult was carried so far that, when Pentheus disturbed his mysteries, the king was torn piecemeal by the women of his own family.[3] The pious acquiescence of the author of the so-called Theocritean idyll in this butchery is a curious example of the conservatism of religious sentiment. The connection of Dionysus with the bull in particular is attested by various ritual epithets, such as "the bull," "bull-born,"[4] "bull-horned," and "bull-browed".[5] He was also worshipped with sacrifice of he-goats; according to the popular explanation, because the goat gnaws the vine, and therefore is odious to the god.

[1] Ælian., *H. A.*, xii. 34.

[2] O. Müller, *Proleg.*, Engl. transl., 322, attributes the Tenedos Dionysus rites to "the Bœotic Achæan emigrants". *Cf. Aglaoph.*, 674-677.

[3] Theocritus, *Idyll*, xxvi.

[4] Pollux, iv. 86.

[5] Athenæus, xi. 466, A.

The truth is, that animals, as the old commentator on Virgil remarks, were sacrificed to the various gods, *aut per similitudinem aut per contrarietatem,"* either because there was a community of nature between the deity and the beast, or because the beast had once been sacred in a hostile clan or tribe.[1] The god derived some of his ritual names from the goat as well as from the bull. According to one myth, Dionysus was changed into a kid by Zeus, to enable him to escape the jealousy of Hera.[2] "It is a peculiarity," says Voigt, "of the Dionysus ritual that the god is one of his offering." But though the identity of the god and the victim is manifest, the phenomenon is too common in religion to be called peculiar.[3] Plutarch[4] especially mentions that "many of the Greeks make statues of Dionysus in the form of a bull".

Dionysus was not only an animal-god, or a god who absorbed in his rights and titles various elder forms of beast-worship. Trees also stood in the same relation to him. As *Dendrites*, he is, like Artemis, a tree-god, and probably succeeded to the cult of certain sacred trees; just as, for example, St. Bridget, in Ireland, succeeded to the cult of the fire-goddess and to her ceremonial.[5] Dionysus was even called ἔνδενδρος, "the

[1] *Cf.* Roscher, *Lexikon*, p. 1059; Robertson Smith on "Sacrifice," *Encyc. Brit.*

[2] Appolodorus, iii. 4, 9.

[3] "Dionysos selber. Stier Zicklein ist, und als Zagreus-kind selber, den Opfertod erleidet." Ap. Roscher, p. 1059.

[4] *De Is. et Os.*

[5] Elton, *Origins of English History*, p. 280, and the authorities there quoted.

god in the tree,"[1] reminding us of Artemis Dendritis, and of the village gods which in India dwell in the *peepul* or the *bo* tree.[2] Thus Pausanias[3] tells us that, when Pentheus went to spy on the Dionysiac mysteries, the women found him hidden in a tree, and there and then tore him piecemeal. According to a Corinthian legend, the Delphic oracle bade them seek this tree and worship it with no less honour than the god (Dionysus) himself. Hence the wooden images of Dionysus were made of that tree, the fig tree, *non ex quovis ligno*, and the god had a ritual name, "The fig-tree Dionysus". In the idols the community of nature between the god and the fig tree was expressed and commemorated. An unhewn stump of wood was the Dionysus idol of the rustic people.[4]

Certain antique elements in the Dionysus cult have now been sketched; we have seen the god in singularly close relations with animal and plant worship, and have noted the very archaic character of certain features in his mysteries. Doubtless these things are older than the bright anthropomorphic Dionysus of the poets—the beautiful young deity, vine-crowned, who rises from the sea to comfort Ariadne in Tintoretto's immortal picture. At his highest, at his best, Dionysus is the spirit not only of Bacchic revel and of dramatic poetry, but of youth, health and gaiety. Even in this form he retains something tricksy and enigmatic, the survival perhaps of earlier ideas; or, again, it may be the result of a more or less conscious symbolism. The god of the vine and of the juice of the vine maketh

[1] Hesychius.
[2] *Cf.* Roscher, p. 1062.
[3] ii. 2, 5.
[4] Max. Tyr., 8, 1.

glad the heart of man; but he also inspires the kind of metamorphosis which the popular speech alludes to when a person is said to be "disguised in drink". For this reason, perhaps, he is now represented in art as a grave and bearded man, now as a manly youth, and again as an effeminate lad of girlish loveliness. The bearded type of the god is apparently the earlier; the girlish type may possibly be the result merely of decadent art, and its tendency to a sexless or bisexual prettiness.[1]

Turning from the ritual and local cults of the god, which, as has been shown, probably retain the earlier elements in his composite nature, and looking at his legend in the national literature of Greece, we find little that throws any light on the origin and primal conception of his character In the *Iliad* Dionysus is not one of the great gods whose politics sways Olympus, and whose diplomatic or martial interference is exercised in the leaguer of the Achæans or in the citadel of Ilios. The longest passage in which he is mentioned is *Iliad*, vi. 130, a passage which clearly enough declares that the worship of Dionysus, or at least that certain of his rites were brought in from without, and that his worshippers endured persecution. Diomedes, encountering Glaucus in battle, refuses to fight him if he is a god in disguise. "Nay, moreover, even Dryas' son, mighty Lykourgos, was not for long when he strove with heavenly gods; he that erst chased through the goodly land of Nysa the nursing mothers of frenzied Dionysus; and they all cast their wands upon the ground, smitten with murderous Lykourgos'

[1] See Thræmer, in Roscher, pp. 1090-1143.

ox-goad. Then Dionysus fled, and plunged beneath the salt sea-wave, and Thetis took him to her bosom, affrighted, for mighty trembling had seized him at his foe's rebuke. But with Lykourgos the gods that live at ease were wroth, and Kronos's son made him blind, and he was not for long, because he was hated of all the immortal gods."

Though Dionysus is not directly spoken of as the wine-god here, yet the gear (*θύσθλα*) of his attendants, and his own title, "the frenzied," seem to identify him with the deity of orgiastic frenzy. As to Nysa, volumes might be written to little or no purpose on the learning connected with this obscure place-name, so popular in the legend of Dionysus. It has been identified as a mountain in Thrace, in Bœotia, in Arabia, India, Libya and Naxos, as a town in Caria or the Caucasus, and as an island in the Nile. The flight of Dionysus into the sea may possibly recall the similar flight of Agni in Indian myth.

The *Odyssey* only mentions Dionysus [1] in connection with Ariadne, whom Artemis is said to have slain "by reason of the witness of Dionysus," [2] and where the great golden urn of Thetis is said to have been a present from the god. The famous and beautiful hymn proves, as indeed may be learned from Hesiod,[3] that the god was already looked on as the patron of the vine. When the pirates had seized the beautiful young man with the dark-blue eyes, and had bound him in their ship, he "showed marvels among them," changed into the shape of a bear, and turned his

[1] xi. 325. [2] xxiv. 74.
[3] *Works and Days*, 614.

captors into dolphins, while wine welled up from the timbers of the vessel, and vines and ivy trees wreathed themselves on the mast and about the rigging.

Leaving aside the Orphic poems, which contain most of the facts in the legend of Dionysus Zagreus, the *Bacchæ* of Euripides is the chief classical record of ideas about the god. Dionysus was the patron of the drama, which itself was an artistic development of the old rural songs and dances of his Athenian festival. In the *Bacchæ*, then, Euripides had to honour the very patron of his art. It must be said that his praise is but half-hearted. A certain ironical spirit, breaking out here and there (as when old Cadmus dances, and shakes a grey head and a stiff knee) into actual burlesque, pervades the play. Tradition and myth doubtless retained some historical truth when they averred that the orgies of the god had been accepted with reluctance into state religion. The tales about Lycurgus and Pentheus, who persecuted the Bacchæ in Thebes, and was dismembered by his own mother in a divine madness, are survivals of this old distrust of Dionysus. It was impossible for Euripides, a sceptic, even in a sceptical age, to approve sincerely of the god whom he was obliged to celebrate. He falls back on queer etymological explanations of the birth of Dionysus from the thigh of Zeus. This myth, as Cadmus very learnedly sets forth, was the result of forgetfulness of the meaning of words, was born of a *Volks-etymologie*. Zeus gave a hostage (ὅμηρος) to Hera, says Cadmus, and in "process of time" (a very short time) men forgot what they meant when they said this, and supposed that Dionysus had been sewn up in the thigh (ὁ μηρός) of his father.[1] The explanation is absurd, but it shows how Euripides could transfer the doubt and distrust of his own age, and its attempt at a philological interpretation of myth, to the remote heroic times. Throughout the play the character and conduct of the god, and his hideous revenge on the people who reject his wild and cruel rites, can only be justified because they are articles of faith. The chorus may sing—"Ah! blessed he who dwelleth in happiness, expert in the rites of the gods, and so hallows his life, fulfilling his soul with the spirit of Dionysus, revelling on the hills with charms of holy purity".[2] This was the interpretation which the religious mind thrust upon rites which in themselves were so barbarously obscene that they were feigned to have been brought by Dionysus from the barbaric East,[3] and to be the invention of Rhea, an alien and orgiastic goddess.[4] The bull-horned, snake-wreathed god,[5] the god who, when bound, turns into a bull (618); who manifests himself as a bull to Pentheus (920), and is implored by the chorus to appear "as bull, or burning lion, or many-headed snake" (1017-19), this god is the ancient barbarous deity of myth, in manifest contrast with the artistic Greek conception of him as "a youth with clusters of golden hair, and in his dark eyes the grace of Aphrodite" (235, 236).

The *Bacchæ*, then, expresses the sentiments of a moment which must often have occurred in Greek religion. The Greek reverence accepts, hallows and

[1] *Bacchæ*, 291, 296. [2] *Ibid.*, 73, 76.
[3] *Ibid.*, 10-20. [4] *Ibid.*, 59. [5] *Ibid.*, 100, 101.

adorns an older faith, which it feels to be repugnant and even alien, but none the less recognises as human and inevitable. From modern human nature the ancient orgiastic impulse of savage revelry has almost died away. In Greece it was dying, but before it expired it sanctified and perpetuated itself by assuming a religious form, by draping its naked limbs in the fawn-skin or the bull-skin of Dionysus. In precisely the same spirit Christianity, among the Negroes of the Southern States, has been constrained to throw its mantle over what the race cannot discard. The orgies have become camp-meetings; the Voodoo-dance is consecrated as the "Jerusalem jump". In England the primitive impulse is but occasionally recognised at "revivals". This orgiastic impulse, the impulse of Australian corroboree and Cherokee fetish-dances, and of the "dancing Dervishes" themselves, occasionally seizes girls in modern Greece. They dance themselves to death on the hills, and are said by the peasants to be victims of the Nereids. In the old classic world they would have been saluted as the nurses and companions of Dionysus, and their disease would have been hallowed by religion. Of that religion the "bull-horned," "bull-eating," "cannibal" Dionysus was the deity; and he was refined away into the youth with yellow-clustered curls, and sleepy eyes, and smiling lips, the girlish youth of the art of Praxiteles. So we see him in surviving statues, and seeing him, forget his ghastly rites, and his succession to the rites of goats, and deer, and bulls.

ATHENE.

Among deities for whom an origin has been sought in the personification of elemental phenomena, Athene is remarkable. Perhaps no divine figure has caused more diverse speculations. The study of her legend is rather valuable for the varieties of opinion which it illustrates than for any real contribution to actual knowledge which it supplies. We can discover little, if anything, about the rise and development of the conception of Athene. Her local myths and local *sacra* seem, on the whole, less barbaric than those of many other Olympians. But in comparing the conjectures of the learned, one lesson comes out with astonishing clearness. It is most perilous, as this comparison demonstrates, to guess at an origin of any god in natural phenomena, and then to explain the details of the god's legend with exclusive reference to that fancied elemental origin.

As usual, the oldest literary references to Athene are found in the *Iliad* and *Odyssey*. It were superfluous to collect and compare texts so numerous and so familiar. Athene appears in the *Iliad* as a martial maiden, daughter of Zeus, and, apparently, of Zeus alone without female mate.[1] She is the patron of valour and the inspirer of counsel; she arrests the hand of Achilles when his sword is half drawn from the sheath in his quarrel with Agamemnon; she is the constant companion and protector of Odysseus; and though she is worshipped in the citadel of Troy,

[1] *Iliad*, v. 875, 880. This is stated explicitly in the Homeric Hymn to Apollo, where Athene is said to have been born from the head of Zeus (Pindar, *Olympic Odes*, vii.).

she is constant to the cause of the Achæans. Occasionally it is recorded of her that she assumed the shape of various birds; a sea-bird and a swallow are among her metamorphoses; and she could put on the form of any man she pleased; for example, of Deiphobus.[1] It has often been observed that among the lower races the gods habitually appear in the form of animals. "Entre ces facultés qui possèdent les immortels, l'une des plus frappantes est celle de se metamorphoser, de prendre des apparences non seulement animales, mais encore de se transformer en objets inanimes."[2] Of this faculty, inherited from the savage stage of thought, Athene has her due share even in Homer. But in almost every other respect she is free from the heritage of barbarism, and might very well be regarded as the ideal representative of wisdom, valour and manfulness in man, of purity, courage and nobility in woman, as in the Phæacian maid Nausicaa.

In Hesiod, as has already been shown, the myth of the birth of Athene retains the old barbaric stamp. It is the peculiarity of the Hesiodic poems to preserve the very features of religious narrative which Homer disregards. According to Hesiod, Zeus, the youngest child of child-swallowing Cronus, married Metis after he had conquered and expelled his father. Now Metis, like other gods and goddesses, had the power of transforming herself into any shape she pleased. Her husband learned that her child—for she was pregnant—would be greater than its father, as in the case of the child of Thetis. Zeus, therefore,

[1] *Iliad*, xxii. 227, xvii. 351, *Od.* iii. 372, v. 353; *Iliad*, vii. 59.

[2] Maury, *Religion de la Grece*, i. 256.

persuaded Metis to transform herself into a fly. No sooner was the metamorphosis complete than he swallowed the fly, and himself produced the child of Metis out of his head.[1] The later philosophers explained this myth[2] by a variety of metaphysical interpretations, in which the god is said to contain the all in himself, and again to reproduce it. Any such ideas must have been alien to the inventors of a tale which, as we have shown, possesses many counterparts among the lowest and least Platonic races.[3] C. O. Müller remarks plausibly that "the figure of the swallowing is employed in imitation of still older legends," such as those of Africa and Australia. This leaves him free to imagine a philosophic explanation of the myth based on the word Metis.[4] We may agree with Müller that the "swallow-myth" is extremely archaic in character, as it is so common among the backward races. As to the precise amount, however, of philosophic reflection and allegory which was present to the cosmogonic poet's mind when he used Metis as the name of the being who could become a fly, and so be swallowed by her husband, it is impossible to speak with confidence. Very probably the poet meant to read a moral and speculative meaning into a barbaric *märchen* surviving in religious tradition.

To the birth of Athene from her father's head savage parallels are not lacking. In the legends of the South Pacific, especially of Mangaia, Tangaroa is fabled to have been born from the head of Papa.[5] In the

[1] Hesiod, *Theog.*, 886, and the Scholiast.

[2] Lobeck, i. 613, note 2.

[3] See the Cronus myth.

[4] *Proleg.*, Engl. transl., p. 308.

[5] Gill, *Myths and Songs*, p. 10.

Vafthrudismal (31) a maid and a man-child are born from under the armpits of a primeval gigantic being. The remarks of Lucian on miraculous birth have already been quoted.[1]

With this mythical birth for a starting-point, and relying on their private interpretations of the *cognomina* of the goddess, of her *sacra*, and of her actions in other parts of her legend, the modern mythologists have built up their various theories. Athene is now the personification of wisdom, now the dawn, now the air or æther, now the lightning as it leaps from the thunder-cloud; and if she has not been recognised as the moon, it is not for lack of opportunity.[2] These explanations rest on the habit of twisting each detail of a divine legend into conformity with aspects of certain natural and elemental forces, or they rely on etymological conjecture. For example, Welcker[3] maintains that Athene is "a feminine personification of the upper air, daughter of Zeus, the dweller in æther". Her name Tritogenia is derived[4] from an ancient word for water, which, like fire, has its source in æther.[5] Welcker presses the title of the goddess, "Glaucopis," the "grey-green-eyed," into the service. The heaven in Attica *oft ebenfalls wunderbar grun ist*.[6] Moreover, there was a temple at Methone of Athene of the Winds (Anemotis), which would be a

[1] *Cf.* Dionysus.

[2] Welcker, i. 305.

[3] *Griechische Götterlehre*, Göttingen, 1857, i. 303.

[4] *Op. cit.*, 311.

[5] The ancients themselves were in doubt whether Trito were the name of a river or mere, or whether the Cretan for the head was intended. See *Odyssey*, Butcher and Lang, note 10, p. 415.

[6] *Op. cit.*, i. 303.

better argument had there not been also temples of Athene of the Pathway, Athene of the Ivy, Athene of the Crag, Athene of the Market-place, Athene of the Trumpet, and so forth. Moreover, the olive trêe is one of the sacred plants of Athene. Now why should this be? Clearly, thinks Welcker, because olive-oil gives light from a lamp, and light also comes from æther.[1] Athene also gives Telemachus a fair wind in the *Odyssey*, and though any Lapland witch could do as much, this goes down to her account as a goddess of the air.[2]

Leaving Welcker, who has many equally plausible proofs to give, and turning to Mr. Max Müller, we learn that Athene was the dawn. This theory is founded on the belief that Athene = Ahanâ, which Mr. Max Müller regards as a Sanskrit word for dawn. "Phonetically there is not one word to be said against, Ahanâ = Athene, and that the morning light offers the best starting-point for the later growth of Athene has been proved, I believe, beyond the reach of doubt, or even of cavil." Mr. Müller adds that "nothing really important could be brought forward against my equation Ahanâ = Athene".

It is no part of our province here to decide between the conjectures of rival etymologists, nor to pronounce on their relative merits. But the world cannot be expected to be convinced by philological scholars before they have convinced each other. Mr. Max Müller had not convinced Benfey, who offered another etymology of Athene, as the feminine of the Zend *Thrœtana*

[1] *Op. cit.* i. 318.

[2] Mr. Ruskin's *Queen of the Air* is full of similar ingenuities.

athwyana, an etymology of which Mr. Müller remarks that "whoever will take the trouble to examine its phonetic foundation will be obliged in common honesty to confess that it is untenable".[1] Meanwhile Curtius[2] is neither for Ahanâ and Sanskrit and Mr. Max Müller, nor for Benfey and Zend. He derives Athene from the root ἀθ, "whence perhaps comes Athene, the blooming one" = the maiden. Preller, again,[3] finds the source of the name Athene in αἰθ, whence αἴθηρ, "the air," or ἀνθ, whence ἄνθος, "a flower". He does not regard these etymologies as certain, though he agrees with Welcker that Athene is the clear height of æther.

Manifestly no one can be expected to accept as matter of faith an etymological solution which is rejected by philologists. The more fashionable theory for the moment is that maintained some time since by Lauer and Schwartz, and now by Furtwängler in Roscher's *Lexikon*, that Athene is the "cloud-goddess," or the goddess of the lightning as it springs from the clouds.[4] As the lightning in mythology is often a serpent, and as Athene had her sacred serpent, "which might be Erichthonios,"[5] Schwartz conjectures that the serpent is the lightning and Athene the cloud. A long list of equally cogent reasons for identifying Athene with the lightning and the thunder-cloud has been compiled by Furtwängler, and deserves some attention. The passage excellently illustrates the

[1] *Nineteenth Century*, October, 1885, pp. 636, 639.

[2] *Gr. Et.*, Engl. transl., i. 300. [3] Preller, i. 151.

[4] *Cf.* Lauer, *System der Griesch. Myth.*, Berlin, 1853, p. 220; Schwartz *Ursprung der Mythol.*, Berlin, 1863, p. 38.

[5] Paus., xxiv. 7.

error of taking poetic details in authors as late as Pindar for survivals of the absolute original form of an elemental myth.

Furtwängler finds the proof of his opinion that Athene is originally the goddess of the thunder-cloud and the lightning that leaps from it in the Olympic ode.[1] "By Hephaistos' handicraft beneath the bronze-wrought axe from the crown of her father's head Athene leapt to light, and cried aloud an exceeding cry, and heaven trembled at her coming, and earth, the mother." The "cry" she gave is the thunder-peal; the spear she carried is the lightning; the ægis or goat-skin she wore is the cloud again, though the cloud has just been the head of Zeus.[2] Another proof of Athene's connection with storm is the miracle she works when she sets a flame to fly from the head of Diomede or of Achilles,[3] or fleets from the sky like a meteor.[4] Her possession, on certain coins, of the thunderbolts of Zeus is another argument. Again, as the Trumpet-Athene she is connected with the thunder-peal, though it seems more rational to account for her supposed invention of a military instrument by the mere fact that she is a warlike goddess. But Furtwängler explains her martial attributes as those of a thunder-goddess, while Preller finds it just as easy to explain her moral character as goddess of wisdom by her elemental character as goddess, not at all of the cloud, but of the clear sky.[5] "Lastly, as goddess of the

[1] *Ode*, vii. 35, Myers.
[2] *Cf.* Schwartz, *Ursprung*, etc., pp. 68, 83.
[3] *Iliad*, v. 7, 18, 203.
[4] *Ibid*, iv. 74.
[5] Preller, i. 183.

heavenly clearness, she is also goddess of spiritual clearness." Again, "As goddess of the cloudless heaven, she is also goddess of health".[1] There could be no more instructive examples of the levity of conjecture than these, in which two scholars interpret a myth with equal ease and freedom, though they start from diametrically opposite conceptions. Let Athene be lightning and cloud, and all is plain to Furtwängler. Let Athene be cloudless sky, and Preller finds no difficulties. Athene as the goddess of woman's work as well as of man's, Athene Ergane, becomes clear to Furtwängler as he thinks of the *fleecy* clouds. Probably the storm-goddess, when she is not thundering, is regarded as weaving the fleeces of the upper air. Hence the myth that Arachne was once a woman, changed by Athene into a spider because she contended with her in spinning.[2] The metamorphosis of Arachne is merely one of the half-playful ætiological myths of which we have seen examples all over the world. The spider, like the swallow, the nightingale, the dolphin, the frog, was once a human being, metamorphosed by an angry deity. As Preller makes Athene goddess of wisdom because she is goddess of clearness in the sky, so Furtwängler derives her intellectual attributes from her skill in weaving clouds. It is tedious and unprofitable to examine these and similar exercises of facile ingenuity. There is no proof that Athene was ever a nature-goddess at all, and if she was, there is nothing to show what was her department of nature. When we meet her in Homer,

[1] Preller, i. 179.

[2] Ovid, *Metamorph.*, vi. 5-145.

she is patroness of moral and physical excellence in man and woman. Manly virtue she typifies in her martial aspect, the armed and warlike maid of Zeus; womanly excellence she protects in her capacity of *Ergane*, the toiler. She is the companion and guardian of Perseus no less than of Odysseus.[1]

The sacred animals of Athene were the owl, the snake (which accompanies her effigy in Athens, and is a form of her foster-child Erechtheus), the cock,[2] and the crow.[3] Probably she had some connection with the goat, which might not be sacrificed in her fane on the Acropolis, where she was settled by Ægeus ("goat-man"?). She wears the goat-skin, *ægis*, in art, but this is usually regarded as another type of the storm-cloud.[4]

Athene's maiden character is stainless in story, despite the brutal love of Hephæstus. This characteristic perhaps is another proof that she neither was in her origin nor became in men's minds one of the amorous deities of natural phenomena. In any case, it is well to maintain a sceptical attitude towards explanations of her myth, which only agree in the determination to make Athene a "nature power" at all costs, and which differ destructively from each other as to whether she was dawn, storm, or clear heaven. Where opinions are so radically divided and so slenderly supported, suspension of belief is natural and necessary.

[1] Pindar, *Olymp.*, x. *ad fin.*

[2] Paus., vi. 262. [3] *Ibid.*, iv. 34, 6.

[4] Roscher, in his *Lexikon*, *s.v.* *Ægis*, with his arguments there. Compare, on this subject of Athene as the goddess of a goat-stock. Robertson Smith on "Sacrifice" in the *Encycl. Brit.*

APHRODITE.

No polytheism is likely to be without a goddess of love, and love is the chief, if not the original, department of Aphrodite in the Greek Olympus. In the *Iliad* and *Odyssey* and the Homeric Hymn she is already the queen of desire, with the beauty and the softness of the laughter-loving dame. Her cestus or girdle holds all the magic of passion, and is borrowed even by Hera when she wishes to win her fickle lord. She disturbs the society of the gods by her famous amours with Ares, deceiving her husband, Hephæstus, the lord of fire; and she even stoops to the embraces of mortals, as of Anchises. In the Homeric poems the charm of "Golden Aphrodite" does not prevent the singer from hinting a quiet contempt for her softness and luxury. But in this oldest Greek literature the goddess is already thoroughly Greek, nor did later ages make any essential changes in her character. Concerning her birth Homer and Hesiod are not in the same tale; for while Homer makes her a daughter of Zeus, Hesiod prefers, as usual, the more repulsive, and probably older story, which tells how she sprang from the sea-foam and the mutilated portions of Cronus.[1] But even in the Hesiodic myth it is remarkable that the foam-born goddess first landed at Cythera, or again "was born in wave-washed Cyprus". Her ancient names—the Cyprian and the Cytherean—with her favoured seats in Paphos, Idalia and the Phœnician settlement of Eryx in Sicily, combine with historical traditions to show that the Greek Aphrodite was, to

[1] *Iliad*, v. 312; *Theog.*, 188-206.

some extent, of Oriental character and origin. It is probable, or rather certain, that even without foreign influence the polytheism of Greece must have developed a deity of love, as did the Mexican and Scandinavian polytheisms. But it is equally certain that portions of the worship and elements in the myth of Aphrodite are derived from the ritual and the legends of the Oriental queen of heaven, adored from old Babylon to Cyprus and on many other coasts and isles of the Grecian seas. The Greeks themselves recognised Asiatic influence. Pausanias speaks of the temple of heavenly Aphrodite in Cythera as the holiest and most ancient of all her shrines among the Hellenes.[1] Herodotus, again, calls the fane of the goddess in Askalon of the Philistines "the oldest of all, and the place whence her worship travelled to Cyprus," as the Cyprians say, and the Phœnicians planted it in Cythera, being themselves emigrants from Syria. The Semitic element in this Greek goddess and her cult first demand attention.

Among the Semitic races with whose goddess of love Aphrodite was thus connected the deity had many names. She was regarded as at once the patroness of the moon, and of fertility in plants beasts, and women. Among the Phœnicians her title is Astarte; among the Assyrians she was Istar; among the Syrians, Aschera; in Babylon, Mylitta.[2] Common practices in the ritual of the Eastern and Western goddesses were the licence of the temple-girls, the sacrifices of animals supposed to be peculiarly amorous (sparrows, doves, he-goats), and, above all, the festivals and fasts for Adonis. There

[1] Paus., iii. 23, 1.

[2] So Roscher, *Ausführ. Lexik.*, pp. 391, 647. See also *Astarte*, p. 655.

can scarcely be a doubt that Adonis—the young hunter beloved by Aphrodite, slain by the boar, and mourned by his mistress—is a symbol of the young season, the *renouveau*, and of the spring vegetation, ruined by the extreme heats, and passing the rest of the year in the underworld. Adonis was already known to Hesiod, who called him, with obvious meaning, the son of *Phœnix* and Alphesibœa, while Pausanias attributed to him, with equal significance, Assyrian descent.[1] The name of Adonis is manifestly a form of the Phœnician ADON, "Lord". The nature of his worship among the Greeks is most familiar from the fifteenth Idyll of Theocritus, with its lively picture of dead Adonis lying in state, of the wailing for him by Aphrodite, of the little "gardens" of quickly-growing flowers which personified him, and with the beautiful nuptial hymn for his resurrection and reunion to Aphrodite. Similar rites were customary at Athens.[2] Mannhardt gives the main points in the ritual of the Adonis-feast thus: The fresh vegetation is personified as a fair young man, who in ritual is represented by a kind of idol, and also by the plants of the "Adonis-gardens". The youth comes in spring, the bridegroom to the bride, the vernal year is their honeymoon. In the heat of summer the bridegroom perishes for the nonce, and passes the winter in the land of the dead. His burial is bewailed, his resurrection is rejoiced in. The occasions of the rite are spring and midsummer. The idol and the plants are finally cast into the sea, or into well-water. The

[1] Apollod., *Bibliothec.*, iii. 14, 4.

[2] Aristoph., *Lysistrata*, 389; Mannhardt, *Feld und Wald Kultus*, ii. 276.

union of the divine lovers is represented by pairing of men and maidens in bonds of a kindly sentimental sort, —the flowery bonds of valentines.

The Oriental influence in all these rites has now been recognised; it is perfectly attested both by the Phœnican settlements, whence Aphrodite-worship spread, and by the very name of her lover, the spring. But all this may probably be regarded as little more than the Semitic colouring of a ritual and a belief which exist among Indo-European peoples, quite apart from Phœnican influence. Mannhardt traces the various points in the Aphrodite cult already enumerated through the folk-lore of the German peasants. The young lover, the spring, is the *Maikönig* or *Laubmann*; his effigy is a clothed and crowned idol or puppet, or the *Maibaum*. The figure is thrown into the water and bewailed in Russia, or buried or burned with lamentations.[1] He is wakened and kissed by a maiden, who acts as the bride.[2] Finally, we have the "May-pairs," a kind of valentines united in a nominal troth.

The probable conclusion seems to be that the Adonis ritual expresses certain natural human ways of regarding the vernal year. It is not unlikely that the ancestors of the Greeks possessed these forms of folk-lore previous to their contact with the Semitic races, and their borrowing of the very marked Semitic features in the festivals.

For the rest, the concern of Aphrodite with the passion of love in men and with general productiveness in nature is a commonplace of Greek literature.

[1] i. 418; ii. 287. [2] i. 435.

It would be waste of space to recount the numerous and familiar fables in which she inspires a happy or an ill-fated affection in gods or mortals. Like most other mythical figures, Aphrodite has been recognised by Mr. Max Müller as the dawn; but the suggestion has not been generally accepted.[1] If Aphrodite retains any traces of an elemental origin, they show chiefly in that part of her legend which is peculiarly Semitic in colour. For the rest, though she, like Hermes, gives good luck in general, she is a recognised personification of passion and the queen of love.

HERMES.

Another child of Zeus whose elemental origin and character have been much debated is Hermes. The meaning of the name[2] (Ἑρμείας, Ἑρμέας, Ἑρμῆς) is confessedly obscure.

Opinion, then, is divided about the elemental origin of Hermes and the meaning of his name. His character must be sought, as usual, in ancient poetic myth and in ritual and religion. Herodotus recognised his rites as extremely old, for that is the meaning of his remark[3] that the Athenians borrowed them from the

[1] Roscher, *Lexikon*, p. 406.

[2] Preller, i. 307. The name of Hermes is connected by Welcker (*Griesch. Göt.*, i. 342) with ὁρμᾶν, and he gives other examples of the Æolic use of ο for ε. Compare Curtius's *Greek Etymology*, English translation, 1886, vol. i. p. 420. Kuhn compares ὁρμή with Indic *Saramā*, and *Sārāmējās*, the son of the latter, with Ἑρμείας, ascribing to both the same meaning, "storm". Mr. Max Müller, on the other hand (*Lectures*, ii. 468), takes Hermes to be the son of the Dawn. Curtius reserves his opinion. Mr. Max Müller recognises Saramejas and Hermes as deities of twilight. Preller (i. 309) takes him for a god of dark and gloaming.

[3] Herod., ii. 51.

Pelasgians, who are generally recognised as prehistoric Greeks. In the rites spoken of, the images of the god were in one notable point like well-known Bushmen and Admiralty Island divine representations, and like those of Priapus.[1] In Cyllene, where Hermes was a great resident god, Artemidorus [2] saw a representation of Hermes which was merely a large phallus, and Pausanias beheld the same sacred object, which was adored with peculiar reverence.[3] Such was Hermes in the Elean region, whence he derived his name, Cyllenian.[4] He was a god of "the liberal shepherds," conceived of in the rudest aspect, perhaps as the patron of fruitfulness in their flocks. Manifestly he was most unlike the graceful swift messenger of the gods, and guide of the ghosts of men outworn, the giver of good fortune, the lord of the crowded market-place, the teacher of eloquence and of poetry, who appears in the literary mythology of Greece. Nor is there much in his Pelasgian or his Cyllenian form to suggest the elemental deity either of gloaming, or of twilight, or of the storm.[5] But whether the pastoral Hermes of the Pelasgians was refined into the messenger-god of Homer, or whether the name and honours of that god were given to the rude Priapean patron of the shepherds by way of bringing him into the Olympic circle, it seems impossible to

[1] Can the obscene story of Cicero (*De Nat. Deor.*, iii. 22, 56) be a repetition of the sacred chapter, *ἱρόν τινα λόγον*, by which Herodotus says the Pelasgians explained the attribute of the image?

[2] Artem., i. 45.

[3] Paus., vi. 26, 3.

[4] Homeric Hymns, iii. 2.

[5] But see Welcker, i. 343, for connection between his name and his pastoral functions.

ascertain. These combinations lie far behind the ages of Greece known to us in poetry and history. The province of the god as a deity of flocks is thought to be attested by his favourite companion animal the ram, which often stood beside him in works of art.[1] In one case, where he is represented with a ram on his shoulder, the legend explained that by carrying a ram round the walls he saved the city of Tanagra from a pestilence.[2] The Arcadians also represented him carrying a ram under his arm.[3] As to the phallic Hermæ, it is only certain that the Athenian taste agreed with that of the Admiralty Islanders in selecting such unseemly images to stand beside every door. But the connection of Hermes with music (he was the inventor of the lyre, as the Homeric Hymn sets forth) may be explained by the musical and poetical character of old Greek shepherd life.

If we could set aside the various elemental theories of Hermes as the storm-wind, the twilight, the child of dawn, and the rest, it would not be difficult to show that one moral conception is common to his character in many of its varied aspects. He is the god of luck, of prosperity, of success, of fortunate adventure. This department of his activity is already recognised in Homer. He is giver of good luck.[4] He is "Hermes, who giveth grace and glory to all the works of men". Hence comes his Homeric name, ἐριούνιος, the luck-bringer. The last cup at a feast is drunk to his honour "for luck". Where we cry

[1] Pausanias, ii. 3, 4.

[2] For Hermes, god of herds and flocks, see Preller, i. 322-325.

[3] Pausanias, v. 27, 5.

[4] *Iliad*, xiv. 491; *Od.* 15, 319.

"Shares!" in a lucky find, the Greek cried "Hermes in common!" A godsend was ἕρμαιον. Thus among rough shepherd folk the luck-bringing god displayed his activity chiefly in making fruitful the flocks, but among city people he presided over the mart and the public assembly, where he gave good fortune, and over musical contests.[1] It is as the lucky god that Hermes holds his "fair wand of wealth and riches, three-leafed and golden, which wardeth off all evil".[2] Hermes has thus, among his varied departments, none better marked out than the department of luck, a very wide and important province in early thought. But while he stands in this relation to men, to the gods he is the herald and messenger, and, in some undignified myths, even the pander and accomplice. In the Homeric Hymn this child of Zeus and Maia shows his versatile character by stealing the oxen of Apollo, and fashioning the lyre on the day of his birth. The theft is sometimes explained as a solar myth; the twilight steals the bright days of the sun-god. But he could only steal them day by day, whereas Hermes lifts the cattle in an hour.[3] The surname of Hermes, Ἀργειφόντης, is usually connected with the slaying of Argus, a supernatural being with many eyes, set by Hera to watch Io, the mistress of Zeus.[4] Hermes lulled the creature to sleep with his music and cut off his head. This myth yields a very natural explanation if Hermes be the twilight of dawn, and if Argus be

[1] See also Preller, i. 326, note 3.

[2] Hymn, 529. See *Custom and Myth*, "The Divining Rod".

[3] Preller, i. 316, note 2; Welcker, *Gr. Göt.*, i. 338, and note 11.

[4] Æsch., *Prom. Vinct.*, 568.

the many-eyed midnight heaven of stars watching Io, the moon. If Hermes be the storm-wind, it seems just as easy to say that he kills Argus by driving a cloud over the face of heaven. In his capacity as the swift-winged messenger, who, in the *Odyssey*, crosses the great gulf of the sea, and scarce brushes the brine with his feathers, Hermes might be explained, by any one so minded, either as lightning or wind. Neither hypothesis suits very well with his duties as guide of the ghosts, whom he leads down darkling ways with his wand of gold.[1] In this capacity he and the ghosts were honoured at the Athenian All-Souls' day, in February.[2]

Such are the chief mythic aspects of Hermes. He has many functions; common to all of them is the power of bringing all to a happy end. This resemblance to twilight, "which bringeth all things good," as Sappho sang, may be welcome to interpreters who see in Hermes a personification of twilight. How ingeniously, and even beautifully, this crepuscular theory can be worked out, and made to explain all the activities of Hermes, may be read in an essay of Paul de St. Victor.[3] "What is the dawn? The passage from night to day. Hermes therefore is the god of all such fleet transitions, blendings, changes. The messenger of the gods, he flits before them, a heavenly ambassador to mortals. Two light wings quiver on his rounded cap, *the vault of heaven in little*. . . . The

[1] *Odyssey*, xxiv. 1-14.

[2] Preller, i. 330, and see the notes on the passage. The ceremonies were also reminiscent of the Deluge.

[3] *Les Deux Masques*, i. 316-326.

highways cross and meet and increase the meetings of men; so Hermes, the ceaseless voyager, is their protecting genius. . . . Who should guide the ghosts down the darkling ways but the deity of the dusk; sometimes he made love to fair ghostly maids whom he attended." So easy is it to interpret all the functions of a god as reflections of elemental phenomena. The origin of Hermes remains obscure; but he is, in his poetical shape, one of the most beautiful and human of the deities. He has little commerce with the beasts; we do not find him with many animal companions, like Apollo, nor adored, like Dionysus, with a ritual in which are remnants of animal-worship. The darker things of his oldest phallic forms remain obscure in his legends, concealed by beautiful fancies, as the old wooden phallic figure, the gift of Cecrops, which Pausanias saw in Athens, was covered with myrtle boughs. Though he is occasionally in art represented with a beard, he remains in the fancy as the Odysseus met him, "Hermes of the golden wand, like unto a young man, with the first down on his cheek, when youth is loveliest".

Demeter.

The figure of Demeter, the *mater dolorosa* of paganism, the sorrowing mother seated on the stone of lamentation, is the most touching in Greek mythology. The beautiful marble statue found by Mr. Newton at Cnidos, and now in the British Museum, has the sentiment and the expression of a Madonna. Nowhere in ancient religion was human love, regret, hope and *desiderium* or wistful longing typified so clearly as in the myth and ritual of Demeter. She is severed from her daughter, Persephone, who goes down among the dead, but they are restored to each other in the joy of the spring's renewal. The mysteries of Eleusis, which represented these events in a miracle-play, were certainly understood by Plato and Pindar and Æschylus to have a mystic and pathetic significance. They shadowed forth the consolations that the soul has fancied for herself, and gave promise of renewed and undisturbed existence in the society of all who have been dear on earth. Yet Aristophanes, in the *Frogs*, ventures even here to bring in his raillery, and makes Xanthias hint that the mystæ, the initiate, "smell of roast-pig". No doubt they had been solemnly sacrificing, and probably tasting the flesh of the pig, the sacred animal of Demeter, whose bones, with clay or marble *figurines* representing him, are found in the holy soil of her temples. Thus even in the mystery of Demeter the grotesque, the barbaric element appears, and it often declares itself in her legend and in her ritual.

A scientific study of Demeter must endeavour to disentangle the two main factors in her myth and cult, and to hold them apart. For this purpose it is necessary to examine the development of the cult as far as it can be traced.

As to the *name* of the goddess, for once there is agreement, and even certainty. It seems hardly to be disputed that Demeter is Greek, and means *mother-earth* or *earth the mother.*[1] There is nothing

[1] Welcker, *Griech. Gött.*, i. 385-387; Preller, i. 618, note 2; Maury, *Rel. des Grècs*, i. 69. Apparently Δὲ still means earth in Albanian; Max Müller, *Selected Essays*, ii. 428. Mannhardt is all for "Corn-mother," Corn being *his* mythological panacea.

peculiarly Hellenic or Aryan in the adoration of earth. A comparative study of earth-worship would prove it to be very widely diffused, even among non-European tribes. The Demeter cult, however, is distinct enough from the myth of Gæa, the Earth, considered as, in conjunction with Heaven, the parent of the gods. Demeter is rather the fruitful soil regarded as a person than the elder Titanic formless earth personified as Gæa. Thus conceived as the foster-mother of life, earth is worshipped in America by the Shawnees and Potawatomies as *Me-suk-kum-mik-o-kwi*, the "mother of earth". It will be shown that this goddess appears casually in a Potawatomie legend, which is merely a savage version of the sacred story of Eleusis.[1] Tacitus found that Mother Hertha was adored in Germany with rites so mysterious that the slaves who took part in them were drowned. "Whereof ariseth a secret terror and an holy ignorance what that should be which they only see who are a-perishing."[2] It is curious that in the folk-lore of Europe, up to this century, food-offerings to the earth were *buried* in Germany and by Gipsies; for the same rite is practised by the Potawatomies.[3] The Mexican Demeter, Centeotl, is well known, and Acosta's account of religious ceremonies connected with harvest in Mexico and Peru might almost be taken for a description of the Greek *Eiresionê*. The god of agriculture among the Tongan Islanders has one very curious point of resemblance to

[1] Compare Maury, *Religions de la Grèce*, i. 72.

[2] *Germania*, 40, translation of 1622.

[3] Compare Tylor, *Prim. Cult.*, ii. 273, with Father De Smet, *Oregon Missions*, New York, 1847, p. 351.

Demeter. In the *Iliad* (v. 505) we read that Demeter presides over the fanning of the grain. "Even as a wind carrieth the chaff about the sacred threshing-floors when men are winnowing, *what time golden Demeter, in rush of wind*, maketh division of grain and chaff." . . . Now the name of the "god of wind, and weather, rain, harvest and vegetation in general" in the Tongan Islands is *Álo-Álo*, literally "*to fan*".[1] One is reminded of Joachim Du Bellay's poem, "To the Winnowers of Corn". Thus from all these widely diffused examples it is manifest that the idea of a divinity of earth, considered as the mother of fruits, and as powerful for good or harm in harvest-time, is anything but peculiar to Greece or to Aryan peoples. In her character as potent over this department of agriculture, the Greek goddess was named "she of the rich threshing-floors," "of the corn heaps," "of the corn in the ear," "of the harvest-home," "of the sheaves," "of the fair fruits," "of the goodly gifts," and so forth.[2]

In popular Greek religion, then, Demeter was chiefly regarded as the divinity of earth at seed-time and harvest. Perhaps none of the gods was worshipped in so many different cities and villages, or possessed so large a number of shrines and rustic chapels. There is a pleasant picture of such a chapel, with its rural disorder, in the *Golden Ass* of Apuleius. Psyche, in her search for Cupid, "came to the temple and went

[1] Mariner's *Tonga Islands*, 1827, ii. 107. The Attic *Eiresionê* may be studied in Mannhardt, *Wald und Feld Cultus*, ii. 312, and Aztec and Peruvian harvest rites of a similar character in *Custom and Myth*, pp. 17-20. See also *Prim. Cult.*, ii. 306, for other examples.

[2] Welcker, ii, 468-470, a collection of such titles.

in, whereas behold she espied sheaves of corn lying on a heap, blades with withered garlands, and reeds of barley. Moreover, she saw hooks, scythes, sickles and other instruments to reape, but everie thing laide out of order, and as it were cast in by the hands of labourers; which when Psyche saw she gathered up and put everything in order." The chapel of Demeter, in short, was a tool-house, dignified perhaps with some rude statue and a little altar. Every village, perhaps every villa, would have some such shrine.

Behind these observances, and behind the harvest-homes and the rites—half ritual, half folk-lore—which were expected to secure the fertility of the seed sown, there lurked in the minds of priests and in the recesses of sanctuaries certain mystic and secret practices of adoration. In these mysteries Demeter was doubtless worshipped in her *Chthonian* character as a goddess of earth, powerful over those who are buried in her bosom, over death and the dead. In these hidden mysteries of her cult, moreover, survived ancient legends of the usual ugly sort, tales of the amours of the goddess in bestial guise. Among such rites Pausanias mentions, at Hermione of Dryopian Argolis, the *fête* of Chthonian Demeter, a summer festival. The procession of men, women, boys and priests dragged a struggling heifer to the doors of the temple, and thrust her in unbound. Within the fane she was butchered by four old women armed with sickles. The doors were then opened, and a second and third heifer were driven in and slain by the old women. "This marvel attends the sacrifice, that all the heifers fall on the same side as the first that was slain." There remains somewhat undivulged.

"The things which they specially worship, I know not, nor any man, neither native or foreigner, but only the ancient women concerned in the rite."[1] In Arcadia there was a temple of Demeter, whose priests boasted a connection with Eleusis, and professed to perform the mysteries in the Eleusinian manner. Here stood two great stones, with another over them, probably (if we may guess) a prehistoric dolmen. Within the dolmen, which was so revered that the neighbours swore their chief oath by it ("by the πέτρωμα"), were kept certain sacred scriptures. These were read aloud once a year to the initiated by a priest who covered his face with a mask of Demeter. At the same time he smote the earth with rods, and called on the folk below the earth. Precisely the same practice, smiting the earth with rods, is employed by those who consult diviners among the Zulus.[2] The Zulu woman having a spirit of divination says, "Strike the ground for them" (the spirits). "See, they say you came to inquire about something." The custom of wearing a mask of the deity worshipped is common in the religions of animal-worship in Egypt, Mexico, the South Seas and elsewhere. The Aztec celebrant, we saw, wore a mask made of the skin of the thigh of the human victim. Whether this Arcadian Demeter was represented with the head of a beast does not appear; she had a mare's head in Phigalia. One common point between this Demeter of the Pheneatæ and the Eleusinian is her *taboo* on beans, which are so strangely mystical a vegetable in Greek and Roman ritual.[3]

[1] Paus., ii. 35. [2] Callaway, *Izinyanga Zokubula*, p. 362.
[3] For a collection of passages see *Aglaophamus*, 251-254.

The Black Demeter of the Phigalians in Arcadia was another most archaic form of the goddess. In Phigalia the myth of the wrath and reconciliation of the goddess assumed a brutal and unfamiliar aspect. The common legend, universally known, declares that Demeter sorrowed for the *enlèvement* of her daughter, Persephone, by Hades. The Phigalians added another cause; the wandering Demeter had assumed the form of a mare, and was violently wooed by Poseidon in the guise of a stallion.[1] The goddess, in wrath at this outrage, attired herself in black mourning raiment, and withdrew into a cave, according to the Phigalians, and the fruits of the earth perished. Zeus learned from Pan the place of Demeter's retreat, and sent to her the Mœræ or Fates, who persuaded her to abate her anger. The cave became her holy place, and there was set an early wooden *xoanon*, or idol, representing

[1] The same story was told of Cronus and Philyra, of Agni and a cow in the *Satapatha Brahmana* (English translation, i. 326), of Saranyu, daughter of Tvashtri, who "fled in the form of a mare". Visvasvat, in like manner, assumed the shape of a horse, and followed her. From their intercourse sprang the two Asvins. See Muir, *Sanskrit Texts*, v. 227, or *Rig-Veda*, x. 17, 1. Here we touch a very curious point. Erinnys was an Arcadian cognomen of the Demeter who was wedded as a mare (Paus., viii. 25). Now, Mr. Max Müller says that "Erinnys is the Vedic Saranyu, the Dawn," and we have seen that both Demeter Erinnys and Saranyu were wooed and won in the form of mares (*Select Essays*, i. 401, 492-622). The curious thing is that, having so valuable a proof in his hand as the common bestial amours of both Saranyu and Erinnys Demeter, Mr. Max Müller does not produce it. The Scandinavian horse-loves of Loki also recur to the memory. Prajapati's loves in the shape of a deer are familiar in the Brahmanas. If Saranyu=Erinnys, and both=Dawn, then a dawn-myth has been imported into the legend of Demeter, whom nobody, perhaps, will call a dawn-goddess. Schwartz, as usual, makes the myth a storm-myth, and Demeter a goddess of storms (*Ursprung der Myth.*, p. 164).

the goddess in the shape of a woman with the head and mane of a mare, in memory of her involuntary intrigue in that shape. Serpents and other creatures were twined about her head, and in one hand, for a mystic reason undivulged, she held a dolphin, in the other a dove. The wooden image was destroyed by fire, and disasters fell on the Phigalians. Onatas was then employed to make a bronze statue like the old idol, wherof the fashion was revealed to him in a dream. This restoration was made about the time of the Persian war. The sacrifices offered to this Demeter were fruits, grapes, honey and uncarded wool; whence it is clear that the black goddess was a true earth-mother, and received the fruits of the earth and the flock. The image by Onatas had somewhat mysteriously disappeared before the days of Pausanias.[1]

Even in her rude Arcadian shape Demeter is a goddess of the fruits of earth. It is probable that her most archaic form survived from the "Pelásgian" days in remote mountainous regions. Indeed Herodotus, observing the resemblance between the Osirian mysteries in Egypt and the Thesmophoria of Demeter in Greece, boldly asserts that the Thesmophoria were Egyptian, and were brought to the Pelasgians from Egypt (ii. 171). The Pelasgians were driven out of Peloponnesus by the Dorians, and the Arcadians, who were not expelled, retained the rites. As Pelasgians also lingered long in Attica, Herodotus recognised the Thesmophoria as in origin Egyptian. In modern language this theory means that the Thesmophoria were

[1] Paus., viii. 42. Compare viii. 25, 4, for the horse Arion, whom Demeter bore to Poseidon.

thought to be a rite of prehistoric antiquity older than the Dorian invasion. Herodotus naturally explained resemblances in the myth and ritual of distant peoples as the result of borrowing, usually from Egypt, an idea revived by M. Foucart. These analogies, however, are more frequently produced by the working out of similar thoughts, presenting themselves to minds similarly situated in a similar way. The mysteries of Demeter offer an excellent specimen of the process. While the Greeks, not yet collected into cities, lived in village settlements, each village would possess its own feasts, mysteries and "medicine-dances," as the Red Indians say, appropriate to seed-time and harvest. For various reasons, certain of these local rites attained high importance in the development of Greek civilisation The Eleusinian performances, for instance, were adopted into the state ritual of a famous city, Athens, and finally acquired a national status, being open to all not disqualified Hellenes. In this development the old local ritual for the propitiation of Demeter, for the fertility of the seed sown, and for the gratification of the dead ancestors, was caught up into the religion of the state, and was modified by advancing ideas of religion and morality. But the local Athenian mystery of the Thesmophoria probably retained more of its primitive shape and purpose.

The Thesmophoria was the feast of seed-time, and Demeter was adored by the women as the patroness of human as well as of universal fertility. Thus a certain jocund and licentious element was imparted to the rites, which were not to be witnessed by men.

The Demeter of the Thesmophoria was she who introduced and patronised the *θεσμός* of marriage.

> οἱ μὲν ἔπειτα
> Ἀσπάσιοι λέκτροιο παλαιοῦ θεσμὸν ἵκοντο

as Homer says of Odysseus and Penelope.[1] What was done at the Thesmophoria Herodotus did not think fit to tell. A scholiast on Lucian's *Dialogues of Courtesans* let out the secret in a much later age. He repeats the story of the swineherd Eubuleus, whose pigs were swallowed up by the earth when it opened to receive Hades and Persephone. In honour and in memory of Eubuleus, pigs were thrown into the cavern (*χάσματα*) of Demeter. Then certain women brought up the decaying flesh of the dead pigs, and placed it on the altar. It was believed that to mix this flesh with the seed-corn secured abundance of harvest. Though the rite is magical in character, perhaps the decaying flesh might act as manure, and be of real service to the farmer. Afterwards images of pigs, such as Mr. Newton found in a hole in the holy plot of Demeter at Cnidos, were restored to the place whence the flesh had been taken. The practice was believed to make marriage fruitful; its virtues were for the husband as well as for the husbandman.[2]

However the Athenians got the rite, whether they evolved it or adapted it from some "Pelasgian" or other prehistoric people, similar practices occur among the Khonds in India and the Pawnees in America. The Khonds sacrifice a pig and a human victim, the Pawnees a girl of a foreign tribe. The fragments of

[1] *Odyssey*, xxiii. 295.

[2] Newton, *Halicarnassus*, plate lv. pp. 331, 371-391.

flesh are not mixed with the seed-corn, but buried on the borders of the fields.[1]

The ancient, perhaps "Pelasgian," ritual of Demeter had thus its savage features and its savage analogues. More remarkable still is the Pawnee version, as we may call it, of the Eleusinia. Curiously, the Red Indian myth which resembles that of Demeter and Persephone is *not* told about Me-suk-kum-mik-o-kwi, the Red Indian Mother Earth, to whom offerings are made, valuable objects being buried for her in brass kettles.[2] The American tale is attached to the legend of Manabozho and his brother Chibiabos, not to that of the Earth Mother and her daughter, if in America she had a daughter.

The account of the Pawnee mysteries and their origin is worth quoting in full, as it is among the most remarkable of mythical coincidences. If we decline to believe that Père De Smet invented the tale for the mere purpose of mystifying mythologists, we must, apparently, suppose that the coincidences are due to the similar workings of the human mind in the Prairies as at Eleusis. We shall first give the Red Indian version. It was confided to De Smet, as part of the general tradition of the Pawnees, by an old chief, and was first published by De Smet in his *Oregon Mission*.[3] Tanner speaks of the legend as one that the Indians chant in their "medicine-songs," which record the sacred beliefs of the race.[4] He adds

[1] De Smet, *Oregon Missions*, p. 359; Mr. Russell's, "Report" in Major Campbell's *Personal Narrative*, 1864, pp. 55, 113.

[2] Tanner's *Narrative*, 1830, p. 115.

[3] New York, 1847.

[4] *Ibid.*, New York, 1830, pp. 192, 193.

that many of these songs are noted down, by a method probably peculiar to the Indians, on birch-bark or small flat pieces of wood, the ideas being conveyed by emblematical figures. When it is remembered that the *luck* of the tribe depends on these songs and rites, it will be admitted that they are probably of considerable antiquity, and that the Indians probably did not borrow the story about the origin of their ritual from some European conversant with the Homeric hymn to Demeter.

Here follows the myth, as borrowed (without acknowledgment) by Schoolcraft from De Smet:—[1]

"The Manitos (powers or spirits) were jealous of Manabozho and Chibiabos. Manabozho warned his brother never to be alone, but one day he ventured on the frozen lake and was drowned by the Manitos. Manabozho wailed along the shores. He waged a war against all the Manitos. . . . He called on the dead body of his brother. He put the whole country in dread by his lamentations. He then besmeared his face with black, and sat down six years to lament, uttering the name of Chibiabos. The Manitos consulted what to do to assuage his melancholy and his wrath. The oldest and wisest of them, who had had no hand in the death of Chibiabos, offered to undertake the task of reconciliation. They built a sacred lodge close to that of Manabozho, and prepared a sumptuous feast. They then assembled in order, one behind the other, each carrying under his arm a sack of the skin of some favourite animal, as a beaver, an otter, or a lynx, and filled with precious and curious

[1] Schoolcraft, i. 318.

medicines culled from all plants. These they exhibited, and invited him to the feast with pleasing words and ceremonies. He immediately raised his head, uncovered it, and washed off his besmearments and mourning colours, and then followed them. They offered him a cup of liquor prepared from the choicest medicines, at once as a propitiation and an initiatory rite. He drank it at a single draught, and found his melancholy departed. They then commenced their dances and songs, united with various ceremonies. All danced, all sang, all acted with the utmost gravity, with exactness of time, motion and voice. Manabozho was cured; he ate, danced, sang and smoked the sacred pipe.

"In this manner the mysteries of the great medicine-dance were introduced.

"The Manitos now united their powers to bring Chibiabos to life. They did so, and brought him to life, but it was forbidden to enter the lodge. They gave him, through a chink, a burning coal, and told him to go and preside over the country of souls and reign over the land of the dead.

"Manabozho, now retired from men, commits the care of medicinal plants to Misukumigakwa, or the Mother of the Earth, to whom he makes offerings."

In all this the resemblance to the legend of the Homeric hymn to Demeter is undeniable. The hymn is too familiar to require a long analysis. We read how Demeter had a fair daughter, Persephone; how the Lord of the Dead carried her off as she was gathering flowers; how Demeter sought her with burning torches; and how the goddess came to Eleusis and the house of Celeus in the guise of an old wife. There she dwelt in sorrow, neither eating nor drinking, till she tasted of a mixture of barley and water (*cyceon*), and was moved to smile by the mirth of Iambe. Yet she still held apart in wrath from the society of the gods, and still the earth bore not her fruits, till the gods bade Hermes restore Persephone. But Persephone had tasted one pomegranate-seed in Hades, and therefore, according to a world-wide belief, she was under bonds to Hades. For only half the year does she return to earth; yet by this Demeter was comforted; the soil bore fruits again, and Demeter showed forth to the chiefs of Eleusis her sacred mysteries and the ritual of their performance.[1]

The Persephone myth is not in Homer, though in Homer Persephone is Lady of the Dead. Hesiod alludes to it in the *Theogony* (912-914); but the chief authority is the Homeric hymn, which Matthæus found (1777) in a farmyard at Moscow. "Inter pullos et porcos latuerat"—the pigs of Demeter had guarded the poem of her mysteries.[2] As to the date and authorship of the hymn, the learned differ in opinion. Probably most readers will regard it as a piece of poetry, like the hymn to Aphrodite, rather than as a "mystic chain of verse" meant solely for hieratic purposes. It is impossible to argue with safety that the Eleusinian mysteries and legend were later than Homer, because Homer does not allude to them. He

[1] The superstition about the food of the dead is found in New Zealand, Melanesia, Scotland, Finland and among the Ojibbeways. Compare "Wandering Willie's" tale in *Redgauntlet*.

[2] Ruhnken, *ap.* Hignard, *Les Hymnes Homériques*, p. 292, Paris 1864.

has no occasion to speak of them. Possibly the mysteries were, in his time, but the rites of a village or little town; they attained celebrity owing to their adoption by Athens, and they ended by becoming the most famous national festival. The meaning of the legend, in its origin, was probably no more than a propitiation of earth, and a ceremony that imitated, and so secured, the return of spring and vegetation. This early conception, which we have found in America, was easily combined with doctrines of the death and revival, not of the year, not of the seed sown, but of the human soul. These ideas were capable of endless illustration and amplification by priests; and the mysteries, by Plato's time, and even by Pindar's, were certainly understood to have a purifying influence on conduct and a favourable effect on the fortunes of the soul in the next world.

"Happy whosoever of mortal men has looked on these things; but whoso hath had no part nor lot in this sacrament hath no equal fate when once he hath perished and passed within the pall of darkness."[1] Of such rites we may believe that Plato was thinking when he spoke of "beholding apparitions innocent and simple, and calm and happy, *as in a mystery*".[2] Nor is it strange that, when Greeks were seeking for a sign, and especially for some creed that might resist the new worship of Christ, Plutarch and the Neo-Platonic philosophers tried to cling to the promise of the mysteries of Demeter. They regarded her secret things as "a dreamy shadow of that spectacle and that rite," the spectacle and rite of the harmonious

[1] *Homeric Hymn*, 480-482. [2] Phædrus, 250.

order of the universe, some time to be revealed to the souls of the blessed.[1] It may not have been a drawback to the consolations of the hidden services that they made no appeal to the weary and wandering reason of the later heathens. Tired out with endless discourse on fate and free will, gods and demons, allegory and explanation, they could repose on mere spectacles and ceremonies and pious ejaculations, "without any evidence or proof offered for the statements". Indeed, writers like Plutarch show almost the temper of Pascal, trying to secure rest for their souls by a wise passiveness and pious contemplation, and participation in sacraments not understood.

As to the *origin* of these sacraments, we may believe, with Lobeck, that it was no priestly system of mystic and esoteric teaching, moral or physical. It was but the "medicine-dance" of a very old Greek tribal settlement, perhaps from the first with an ethical element. But from this, thanks to the genius of Hellas, sprang all the beauty of the Eleusinian ritual, and all the consolation it offered the bereaved, all the comfort it yielded to the weary and heavy laden.[2] That the popular religious excitement caused by the mysteries and favoured by the darkness often produced scenes of lustful revelry, may be probable enough. "Revivals" everywhere have this among other consequences. But we may share Lobeck's scepticism as to the wholesale charges of iniquity (*ἔρωτες ἄτοποι καὶ παίδων ὕβρεις καὶ γάμων διαφθοραὶ*) brought by the Fathers.

[1] Plutarch, *De Def. Orac.*, xxii.
[2] Lobeck, *Aglaoph.*, 133.

In spite of survivals and slanders, the religion of Demeter was among the most natural, beautiful and touching of Greek beliefs. The wild element was not lacking; but a pious contemporary of Plato, when he bathed in the sea with his pig before beholding the mystery-play, probably made up his mind to blink the barbaric and licentious part of the performances.

Conclusion.

This brief review of Greek divine myths does not of course aim at exhausting the subject. We do not pretend to examine the legends of all the Olympians. But enough has been said to illustrate the method of interpretation, and to give specimens of the method at work. It has been seen that there is only agreement among philologists as to the origin and meaning of two out of nearly a dozen divine names. Zeus is admitted to be connected with *Dyaus*, and to have originally meant "sky". Demeter is accepted as Greek, with the significance of "Mother Earth". But the meaning and the roots of Athene, Apollo, Artemis, Hermes, Cronus, Aphrodite, Dionysus—we might add Poseidon and Hephæstus—are very far from being known. Nor is there much more general agreement as to the original elemental phenomena or elemental province held by all of these gods and goddesses. The moon, the wind, the twilight, the sun, the growth and force of vegetation, the dark, the night, the atmosphere, have been shuffled and dealt most variously to the various deities by learned students of myth. This complete diversity of opinion must be accepted as a part in the study.

The learned, as a rule, only agree in believing (1) that the names hold the secret of the original meaning of the gods; and (2) that the gods are generally personifications of elements or of phenomena, or have been evolved out of such personifications. Beyond this almost all is confusion, doubt, "the twilight of the gods".

In this darkness there is nothing to surprise. We are not wandering in a magical mist poured around us by the gods, but in a fog which has natural causes. First, there is the untrustworthiness of attempts to analyse proper names. "With every proper name the etymological operation is by one degree more difficult than with an appellative. . . . We have to deal with two unknown quantities," origin and meaning; whereas in appellatives we know the meaning and have only to hunt for the origin. And of all proper names mythological names are the most difficult to interpret. Curtius has shown how many paths may be taken in the analysis of the name Achilles. The second part may be of the stem λαο = people, or the stem λασ = stone. Does the first part of the word mean "water" (cf. *aqua*), or is it equivalent to Ἐχε, as in Ἐχέλαος ("bulwark" or "the people")? Or is it akin to Ἀχι, as in ἄχος ("one who causes pain")? Or is the ἀ "prothetic"? and is χελ the root, and does it mean "clear-shining"? Or is the word related to ἀχλύς, and does it mean "dark"?

All these and other explanations are offered by the learned, and are chosen by Curtius to show the uncertainty and difficulty of the etymological process as applied to names in myth. Cornutus remarked long ago that the great antiquity of the name of Athene made its etymology difficult. Difficult it remains.[1] Whatever the science of language may accomplish in the future, it is baffled for the present by the divine names of Greece, or by most of them, and these the most important.[2]

There is another reason for the obscurity of the topic besides the darkness in which the origin of the names has been wrapped by time. The myths had been very long in circulation before we first meet them in Homer and Hesiod. We know not whence the gods came. Perhaps some of them were the chief divine conceptions of various Hellenic clans before the union of clans into states. However this may be, when we first encounter the gods in Homer and Hesiod, they have been organised into a family, with regular genealogies and relationships. Functions have been assigned to them, and departments. Was Hermes always the herald? Was Hephæstus always the artisan? Was Athene from the first the well-beloved daughter of Zeus? Was Apollo from the beginning the mediator with men by oracles? Who can reply? We only know that the divine ministry has been thoroughly organised, and departments assigned, as in a cabinet, before we meet the gods on Olympus. What they were in the ages before this organisation, we can only conjecture. Some may have been adopted from clans whose chief deity they were. If any one

[1] *Cf.* Curtius, *Greek Etym.*, Engl. transl., i. 137-139.

[2] Gruppe, *Griech. Culte und Mythus*, p. 169, selects Iapetos, Kadmos, Kabeiros, Adonis, Baitylos, Typhon, Nysos (in Dionysos), Acheron, Kimmerians and Gryps, as certainly Phœnician. But these are not the names of the high gods.

took all the Samoan gods, he could combine them into a family with due functions and gradations. No one man did this, we may believe, for Greece: though Herodotus thought it was done by Homer and Hesiod. The process went on through centuries we know not of; still less do we know what or where the gods were before the process began.

Thus the obscurity in which the divine origins are hidden is natural and inevitable. Our attempt has been to examine certain birth-marks which the gods bear from that hidden antiquity, relics of fur and fin and feather, inherited from ancestral beasts like those which ruled Egyptian, American and Australian religions. We have also remarked the brilliant divinity of beautiful form which the gods at last attained, in marble, in gold, in ivory and in the fancy of poets and sculptors. Here is the truly Hellenic element, here is the ideal—Athene arming, Hera with the girdle of Aphrodite, Hermes with his wand, Apollo with the silver bow—to this the Hellenic intellect attained; this ideal it made more imperishable than bronze. Finally, the lovely shapes of gods "defecate to a pure transparency" in the religion of Aristotle and Plutarch. But the gods remain beautiful in their statues, beautiful in the hymns of Pindar and the plays of Sophocles; hideous, often, in temple myth, and ancient *xoanon*, and secret rite, till they are all, good and evil, cast out by Christianity. The most brilliant civilisation of the world never expelled the old savage from its myth and its ritual. The lowest savagery scarcely ever, if ever, wholly loses sight of a heavenly Father.

In conclusion, we may deprecate the charge of

exclusivism. The savage element is something, nay, is much, in Greek myth and ritual, but it is not everything. The truth, grace and beauty of the myths are given by "the clear spirit" of Hellas. Nor is all that may be deplored necessarily native. We may well believe in borrowing from Phœnicians, who in turn may have borrowed from Babylon. Examples of this process have occasionally been noted. It will be urged by some students that the wild element was adopted from the religion of prehistoric races, whom the Greeks found in possession when first they seized the shores of the country. This may be true in certain cases, but historical evidence is not to be obtained. We lose ourselves in theories of Pelasgians and Pre-Pelasgians, and "la Grèce avant les Grecs". In any case, the argument that the more puzzling part of Greek myth is a "survival" would not be affected. Borrowed, or inherited, or imitated, certain of the stories and rites are savage in origin, and the argument insists on no more as to that portion of Greek mythology.

CHAPTER XIX.

HEROIC AND ROMANTIC MYTHS.

A new class of myths—Not explanatory—Popular tales—Heroic and romantic myths—(1) Savage tales—(2) European *Contes*—(3) Heroic myths—Their origin—Diffusion—History of their study—Grimm's theory—Aryan theory—Benfey's theory—Ancient Egyptian stories examined—*Wanderung's theorie*—Conclusion.

THE myths which have hitherto been examined possess, for the most part, one common feature. All, or almost all of them, obviously aim at satisfying curiosity about the causes of things, at supplying gaps in human knowledge. The nature-myths account for various aspects of Nature, from the reed by the river-side that once was a fair maiden pursued by Pan, to the remotest star that was a mistress of Zeus; from the reason why the crow is black, to the reason why the sun is darkened in eclipse. The divine myths, again, are for the more part essays in the same direction. They try to answer these questions: "Who made things?" "How did this world begin?" "What are the powers, felt to be greater than ourselves, which regulate the order of events and control the destinies of men?" Myths reply to all these questionings, and the answers are always in accordance with that early nebulous condition of thought and reason where observation lapses into superstition, religion into science, science into fancy, knowledge into fable. In the same manner the myths which we do not treat of here—the myths of the origin of death, of man's first possession of fire, and of the nature of his home among the dead—are all tentative contributions to knowledge. All seek to satisfy the eternal human desire to *know*. "Whence came death?" man asks, and the myths answer him with a story of Pandora, of Maui, of the moon and the hare, or the bat and the tree. "How came fire to be a servant of ours?" The myths tell of Prometheus the fire-stealer, or of the fire-stealing wren, or frog, or coyote, or cuttlefish. "What manner of life shall men live after death? in what manner of home?" The myth answers with tales of Pohjola, of Hades, of Amenti, of all that, in the Australian black fellow's phrase, "lies beyond the Rummut," beyond the surf of the Pacific, beyond the "stream of Oceanus," beyond the horizon of mortality. To these myths, and to the more mysterious legend of the Flood, we may return some other day. For the present, it must suffice to repeat that all these myths (except, perhaps, the traditions of the Deluge) fill up gaps in early human knowledge, and convey information as to matters outside of practical experience.

But there are classes of tales, or *märchen*, or myths which, as far as can be discovered, have but little of the explanatory element. Though they have been interpreted as broken-down nature-myths, the variety of the interpretations put upon them proves that, at least, their elemental meaning is dim and uncertain, and makes it very dubious whether they ever had any such significance at all. It is not denied here that some of these myths and tales *may* have been *suggested* by elemental and meteorological phenomena. For example, when we find almost everywhere among European peasants, and among Samoyeds and Zulus, as in Greek heroic-myths of the Jason cycle, the story of the children who run away from a cannibal or murderous mother or step-mother, we are reminded of certain nature-myths. The stars are often said[1] to be the children of the sun, and to flee away at dawn, lest he or their mother, the moon, should devour them. This early observation *may* have started the story of flight from the cannibal parents, and the legend *may* have been brought down from heaven to earth. Yet this were, perhaps, a far-fetched hypothesis of the origin of a tale which may readily have been born wherever human beings have a tendency (as in North America and South Africa) to revert to cannibalism.

The peculiarity, then, of the myths which we propose to call "Heroic and Romantic Tales" (*märchen contes populaires*), is the absence, as a rule, of any obvious explanatory purpose. They are romances or novels, and if they do explain anything, it is rather the origin or sanction of some human law or custom than the cause of any natural phenomenon that they expound.

The kind of traditional fictions here described as heroic and romantic may be divided into three main categories.

(1) First we have the popular tales of the lower and

[1] *Nature-Myths*, vol. i. p. 130. The story is "Asterinos und Pulja" in Von Hahn's *Griech. und Alban. Märchen.* Compare *Samojedische Märchen*, Castren, *Vorles. über die Alt. Volk*, p. 164; Callaway, *Uzembeni.*

more backward races, with whom may be reckoned, for our present purpose, the more remote and obscure peoples of America. We find popular tales among the Bushmen, Kaffirs, Zulus, Samoans, Maoris, Hurons, Samoyeds, Eskimos, Crees, Blackfeet and other so-called savage races. We also find tales practically identical in character, and often in plot and incident, among such a people as the Huarochiris, a civilised race brought under the Inca Empire some three generations before the Spanish conquest. The characteristics of these tales are the presence of talking and magically helpful beasts; the human powers and personal existence of even inanimate objects; the miraculous accomplishments of the actors; the introduction of beings of anothor race, usually hostile; the power of going to and returning from Hades—always described in much the same imaginative manner. The persons are sometimes anonymous, sometimes are named while the name is not celebrated; more frequently the tribal culture-hero, demiurge, or god is the leading character in these stories. In accordance with the habits of savage fancy, the chief person is often a beast, such as Ananzi, the West African spider; Cagn, the Bushman grasshopper; or Michabo, the Algonkin white hare. Animals frequently take parts assigned to men and women in European *märchen*.

(2) In the second place, we have the *märchen*, or *contes*, or household tales of the modern European, Asiatic and Indian peasantry, the tales collected by the Grimms, by Afanasief, by Von Hahn, by Miss Frere, by Miss Maivé Stokes, by M. Sébillot, by Campbell of Islay, and by so many others. Every

reader of these delightful collections knows that the characteristics, the machinery, all that excites wonder, are the same as in the savage heroic tales just described. But it is a peculiarity of the popular tales of the peasantry that the *places* are seldom named; the story is not localised, and the characters are anonymous. Occasionally our Lord and his saints appear, and Satan is pretty frequently present, always to be defeated and disgraced; but, as a rule, the hero is "a boy," "a poor man," "a fiddler," "a soldier," and so forth, no names being given.

(3) Thirdly, we have in epic poetry and legend the romantic and heroic tales of the great civilised races, or races which have proved capable of civilisation. These are the Indians, the Greeks, Romans, Celts, Scandinavians and Germans. These have won their way into the national literatures and the region of epic. We find them in the *Odyssey*, the *Edda*, the Celtic poems, the *Ramayana*, and they even appear in the *Veda*. They occur in the legends and pedigrees of the royal heroes of Greece and Germany. They attach themselves to the dim beginnings of actual history, and to real personages like Charlemagne. They even invade the legends of the saints. The characters are national heroes, such as Perseus, Jason, Œdipus and Olympian gods, and holy men and women dear to the Church, and primal heroes of the North, Sigurd and Signy. Their paths and places are not in dim fairy-land, but in the fields and on the shores we know—at Roland's Pass in the Pyrenees, on the enchanted Colchian coast, or among the blameless Ethiopians, or in Thessaly, or in Argos.

Now, in all these three classes of romance, savage fables, rural *märchen*, Greek or German epics, the ideas and incidents are analogous, and the very conduct of the plot is sometimes recognisably the same. The moral ideas on which many of the *märchen*, sagas, or epic myths turn are often identical. Everywhere we find doors or vessels which are not to be opened, regulations for the conduct of husband and wife which are not to be broken; everywhere we find helpful beasts, birds and fishes; everywhere we find legends proving that one cannot outwit his fate or evade the destiny prophesied for him.

The chief problems raised by these sagas and stories are—(1) How do they come to resemble each other so closely in all parts of the world? (2) Were they invented once for all, and transmitted all across the world from some centre? (3) What was that centre, and what was the period and the process of transmission?

Before examining the solutions of those problems, certain considerations may be advanced.

The supernatural *stuff* of the stories, the threads of the texture, the belief in the life and personality of all things—in talking beasts and trees, in magical powers, in the possibility of visiting the dead—must, on our theory as already set forth, be found wherever men have either passed through savagery, and retained survivals of that intellectual condition, or wherever they have borrowed or imitated such survivals.

By this means, without further research, we may account for the similarity of the stuff of heroic myths and *märchen*. The stuff is the same as in nature myths and divine myths.

But how is the similarity of the arrangement of the incidents and ideas into *plots* to be accounted for? The sagas, epic myths, and *märchen* do not appear to resemble each other everywhere (as the nature-myths do), because they are the same ideas applied to the explanation of the same set of natural facts. The sagas, epics and *märchen* seem to explain nothing, but to be told, in the first instance, either to illustrate and enforce a moral, or for the mere pleasure of imaginative narration.

We are thus left, provisionally, with the notion that occasionally the resemblance of plot and arrangement may be *accidental*. In shaking the mental kaleidoscope, which contains a given assortment of ideas, analogous combinations may not impossibly be now and then produced everywhere. Or the story may have been invented once for all in one centre, but at a period so incalculably remote that it has filtered, in the exchanges and contacts of prehistoric life, all over the world, even to or from the Western Pacific and the lonely Oceanic Islands. Or, once more, the story may have had a centre in the Old World, say, in India; may have been carried to Europe by oral tradition or in literary vehicles, like the *Pantschatantra* or the *Hitopadesa*, or by gypsies; may have reached the sailors, and trappers, and miners of civilisation, and may have been communicated by them (in times subsequent to the discovery of America by Columbus) to the backward races of the world.

These are preliminary statements of possibilities, and theories more or less based on those ideas are now to be examined.

The best plan may be to trace briefly the history of the study of popular tales. As early as Charles Perrault's time (1696), popular traditional tales had attracted some curiosity, more or less scientific. Mademoiselle L'Héritier, the Abbé Villiers, and even the writer of the dedication of Perrault's *Contes* to MADEMOISELLE, had expressed opinions as to the purposes for which they were first told, and the time and place where they probably arose. The Troubadours, the Arabs, and the fanciful invention of peasant nurses were vaguely talked of as possible first authors of the popular tales. About the same time, Huet, Bishop of Avranches, had remarked that the Hurons in North America amused their winter leisure with narratives in which beasts endowed with speech and reason were the chief characters.

Little was done to secure the scientific satisfaction of curiosity about traditional folk-tales, *contes* or *märchen* till the time when the brothers Grimm collected the stories of Hesse. The Grimms became aware that the stories were common to the peasant class in most European lands, and that they were also known in India and the East. As they went on collecting, they learned that African and North American tribes also had their *märchen*, not differing greatly in character from the stories familiar to German firesides.

Already Sir Walter Scott had observed, in a note to the *Lady of the Lake*, that "a work of great interest might be compiled upon the origin of popular fiction, and the transmission of similar tales from age to age, and from country to country. The mythology of one period would then appear to pass into the romance of the next, and that into the nursery tales of subsequent ages." This opinion has long been almost universal. Thus, if the story of Jason is found in Greek myths, and also, with a difference, in popular modern *märchen*, the notion has been that the *märchen* is the last and youugest form, the *detritus* of the myth. Now, as the myth is only known from literary sources (Homer, Mimnermus, Apollonius Rhodius, Euripides, and so on), it must follow, on this theory, that the people had borrowed from the literature of the more cultivated classes. As a matter of fact, literature has borrowed far more from the people than the people have borrowed from literature, though both processes have been at work in the course of history. But the question of the relations of *märchen* to mýths, and of both to romance, may be left unanswered for the moment. More pressing questions are, what is the *origin*, and where the original home of the *märchen* or popular tales, and how have they been so widely diffused all over the world?

The answers given to these questions have naturally been modified by the widening knowledge of the subject. One answer seemed plausible when only the common character of European *contes* was known; another was needed when the Aryan peoples of the East were found to have the same stories; another, or a modification of the second, was called for when *märchen* like those of Europe were found among the Negroes, the Indians of Brazil, the ancient Huarochiri of Peru, the people of Madagascar, the Samoyeds, the Samoans, the Dènè Hareskins of the extreme American

North-west, the Zulus and Kaffirs, the Bushmen, the Finns, the Japanese, the Arabs, and the Swahilis.

The Grimms, in the appendix to their *Household Tales*,[1] give a list of the stories with which they were acquainted. Out of Europe they note first the literary collections of the East, the *Thousand and One Nights* and the *Hitopadesa*, which, with the *Book of Sindabad*, and the *Pantschatantra*, and the *Katharit Sagara*, contain almost all of the Oriental tales that filtered into Western literature through written translations. The Grimms had not our store of folk-tales recently collected from the lips of the Aryan and non-Aryan natives of Hindostan, such as the works of Miss Maivé Stokes, of Miss Frere, of Captain Steel, of Mr. Lal Behar Day, and the few Santal stories. But the Grimms had some Kalmuck stories.[2] One or two Chinese and Japanese examples had fallen into their hands, and all this as early as 1822. In later years they picked up a Malay story, some Bechuana tales, Koelle's Kanuri or Bornu stories, Schoolcraft's and James Athearn Jones's North American legends, Finnish, Esthonian and Mongolian narratives, and an increasing store of European *contes*. The Grimms were thus not unaware that the *märchen*, with their surprising resemblances of plot and incident, had a circulation far beyond the limits of the Ayran peoples. They were specially struck, as was natural, by the reappearance of incidents analogous to those of the German *contes* (such as *Machandelboom* and the

[1] Mrs. Hunt's translation, London, 1884.

[2] "The relations of Ssidi Kür," in Bergmann's *Nomadische Streifereien* vol. i.

Singing Bone, 47, 28) among the remote Bechuanas of South Africa. They found, too, that in Sierra Leone beasts and birds play the chief parts in *märchen*. "They have a much closer connection with humanity, . . . nay, they have even priests," as the animals in Guiana have *peays* or sorcerers of their own. "Only the beasts of the country itself appear in the *märchen*." Among these Bornu legends they found several tales analogous to *Faithful John* (6), and to one in Straparola's *Piacevoli Notti* (Venice, 1550), a story, by the way, which recurs among the Santals, an "aboriginal" tribe of India. It is the tale of the man who knows the language of animals, and is warned by them against telling secrets to women. Among the Indians of North America Grimm found the analogue of his tale (182) of the *Elves' Gifts*, which, by the way, also illustrates a proverb in Japan. Finnish, Tartar and Indian analogues were discovered in plenty.

Such were Grimm's materials; much less abundant than ours, indeed, but sufficient to show him that "the resemblance existing between the stories, not only of nations widely removed from each other by time and distance, but also between those which lie near together, consists partly in the underlying idea and the delineation of particular characters, and partly in the weaving together and unravelling of incidents". How are these resemblances to be explained? That is the question. Grimm's answer was, as ours must still be, only a suggestion. "There are situations so simple and natural that they reappear everywhere, just like the isolated words which are produced in a nearly or entirely identical form in languages which have no connection with each other, by the mere imitation of natural sounds." Thus to a certain, but in Grimm's opinion to a very limited extent, the existence of similar situations in the *märchen* of the most widely separated peoples is the result of the common facts of human thought and sentiment.

To repeat a convenient illustration, if we find talking and rational beasts and inanimate objects, and the occurrence of metamorphosis and of magic, and of cannibals and of ghosts (as we do), in the *märchen* as in the higher myths of all the world, and if we also find certain curious human customs in the *contes, these* resemblances may be explained as born of the same early condition of human fancy, which regards all known things as personal and animated, which believes in ghosts and magic, while men also behave in accordance with customs now obsolete and forgotten in civilisation. These common facts are the threads (as we have said) in the cloth of myth and *märchen.* They were supplied by the universal early conditions of the prescientific human intellect. Thus the *stuff* of *märchen* is everywhere the same. But why are the *patterns*—the situations, and the arrangements, and sequence of incidents—also remarkably similar in the *contes* of unrelated and unconnected tribes and races everywhere?

Here the difficulty begins in earnest.

It is clearly not enough to force the analogy, and reply that the patterns of early fabrics and the decorations of early weapons, of pottery, tattooing marks, and so forth, are also things universally human.[1] The

[1] See *Custom and Myth,* "The Art of Savages," p. 288.

close resemblances of undeveloped Greek and Mexican and other early artistic work are interesting, but may be accounted for by similarity of materials, of instruments, of suggestions from natural objects, and of inexperience in design. The selections of similar situations and of similar patterns into which these are interwoven in *märchen*, by Greeks, Huarochiris of Peru, and Samoans or Eskimos, is much more puzzling to account for.

Grimm gives some examples in which he thinks that the ideas, and their collocations in the story, can only have originally occurred to one mind, once for all. How is the wide distribution of such a story to be accounted for? Grimm first admits *as rare exceptions* "the probability of a story's passing from one people to another, and firmly rooting itself in foreign soil". But such cases, he says, are "one or two solitary exceptions," whereas the diffusion of stories which, in his opinion, could only have been invented once for all is an extensive phenomenon. He goes on to say, "We shall be asked where the outermost lines of common property in stories begin, and how the lines of affinity are gradated". His answer was not satisfactory even to himself, and the additions to our knowledge have deprived it of any value. "The outermost lines are coterminous with those of the great race which is called Indo-Germanic." Outside of the Indo-Germanic, or "Aryan" race, that is to say, are found none of the *märchen* which are discovered within the borders of that race. But Grimm knew very well himself that this was an erroneous belief. "We see with amazement in such of the stories of the Negroes of Bornu and the Bechuanas (a wandering tribe in South Africa) as we have become acquainted with *an undeniable connection with the German ones*, while at the same time their peculiar composition distinguishes them from these." So Grimm, though he found "no decided resemblance" in North American stories, admitted that the boundaries of common property in *märchen* did include more than the "Indo-Germanic" race. Bechuanas, and Negroes, and Finns, as he adds, and as Sir George Dasent saw,[1] are certainly within the fold.

There William Grimm left the question in 1856. His tendency apparently was to explain the community of the *märchen* on the hypothesis that they were the original common store of the undivided Aryan people, carried abroad in the long wanderings of the race. But he felt that the presence of the *märchen* among Bechuanas, Negroes and Finns was not thus to be explained. At the same time he closed the doors against a theory of borrowing, except in "solitary exceptions," and against the belief in frequent, separate and independent evolution of the same story in various unconnected regions. Thus Grimm states the question, but does not pretend to have supplied its answer.

The solutions offered on the hypothesis that the *märchen* are exclusively Aryan, and that they are the *detritus* or youngest and latest forms of myths, while these myths are concerned with the elemental phenomena of Nature, and arose out of the decay of language, have been so frequently criticised that they

[1] *Popular Tales from the Norse*, 1859, pp. liv., lv.

need not long detain us.[1] The most recent review of the system is by M. Cosquin.[2] In place of repeating objections which have been frequently urged by the present writer, an abstract of M. Cosquin's reasons for differing from the "Aryan" theory of Von Hahn may be given. Voh Hahn was the collector and editor of stories from the modern Greek,[3] and his work is scholarly and accomplished. He drew up comparative tables showing the correspondence between Greek and German *märchen* on the one side, and Greek and Teutonic epics and higher legends or sagas on the other. He also attempted to classify the stories in a certain number of recurring *formulæ* or plots. In Von Hahn's opinion, the stories were originally the myths of the undivided Aryan people in its central Asian home. As the different branches scattered and separated, they carried with them their common store of myths, which were gradually worn down into the *detritus* of popular stories, "the youngest form of the myth". The same theory appeared (in 1859) in Mr. Max Müller's *Chips from a German Workshop*.[4] The undivided Aryan people possessed, in its mythological and proverbial phraseology, the seeds or germs, more or less developed, which would flourish, under any sky, into very similar plants—that is, the popular stories.

Against these ideas M. Cosquin argues that if the Aryan people before its division preserved the myths only in their *earliest germinal form*, it is incredible

[1] See our Introduction to Mrs. Hunt's translation of Grimm's *Household Tales*.

[2] *Contes Populaire de Lorraine*, Paris, 1886, pp. i., xv.

[3] *Grieschische und Albanesische Märchen*, 1864.

[4] Vol. ii. p. 226.

that, when the separated branches had lost touch of each other, the *final* shape of their myths, the *märchen*, should have so closely resembled each other as they do. The Aryan theory (as it may be called for the sake of brevity) rejects, as a rule, the idea that tales can, as a rule, have been *borrowed*, even by one Aryan people from another.[1] "Nursery tales are generally the last things to be borrowed by one nation from another."[2] Then, says M. Cosquin, as the undivided Aryan people had only the myths in their least developed state, and as the existing peasantry have only the *detritus* of these myths—the *märchen*—and as you say borrowing is out of the question, how do you account for a coincidence like *this?* In the Punjaub, among the Bretons, the Albanians, the modern Greeks and the Russians we find a *conte* in which a young man gets possession of a magical ring. This ring is stolen from him, and recovered by the aid of certain grateful beasts, whom the young man has benefited. His foe keeps the ring in his mouth, but the grateful mouse, insinuating his tail into the nose of the thief, makes him sneeze, and out comes the magical ring!

Common sense insists, says M. Cosquin, that this detail was invented once for all. It must have first occurred, not in a myth, but in a *conte* or *märchen*, from which all the others alike proceed. Therefore, if you wish the idea of the mouse and the ring and the sneeze to be a part of the store of the undivided Aryans, you must admit that they had *contes*, *märchen*, popular stories, what you call the *detritus* of myths,

[1] Cox, *Mythol. of Aryan Nations*, i. 109.
[2] Max Müller, *Chips*, ii. 216.

as well as myths themselves, before they left their cradle in Central Asia. "Nos ancêtres, les pères des nations européennes, auraient, de cette façon, emporté dans leurs fourgons la collection complete de contes bleus actuels." In short, if there was no borrowing, myths have been reduced (on the Aryan theory) to the condition of *detritus*, to the diamond dust of *märchen*, before the Aryan people divided. But this is contrary to the hypothesis.

M. Cosquin does not pause here. The *märchen*—mouse, ring, sneeze and all—is found among *non-Aryan* tribes, "the inhabitants of Mardin in Mesopotamia and the Kariaines of Birmanie".[1] Well, if there was no borrowing, how did the non-Aryan peoples get the story?

M. Cosquin concludes that the theory he attacks is untenable, and determines that, "after having been invented in this place or that, which we must discover" [if we can], "the popular tales of the various European nations (to mention these alone) have spread all over the world from people to people by way of borrowing".

In arriving at this opinion, M. Cosquin admits, as is fair, that the Grimms, not having our knowledge of non-Aryan *märchen* (Mongol, Syrian, Arab, Kabyle, Swahili, Annamite—he might have added very many more), could not foresee all the objections to the theory of a store common to Aryans alone.

Were we constructing an elaborate treatise on *märchen*, it would be well in this place to discuss the Aryan theory at greater length. That theory turns on the belief that popular stories are the *detritus* of

[1] Cosquin, i, xi., xii., with his authorities in note 1.

Aryan myths. It would be necessary then to discuss the philological hypothesis of the origin and nature of these original Aryan myths themselves; but to do so would lead us far from the study of mere popular tales.[1]

Leaving the Aryan theory, we turn to that supported by M. Cosquin himself—the theory, as he says, of Benfey.[2]

Inspired by Benfey, M. Cosquin says: "The method must be to take each type of story successively, and to follow it, if we can, from age to age, from people to people, and see where this voyage of discovery will lead us. Now, travelling thus from point to point, often by different routes, we always arrive at the same centre, namely, at India, *not the India of fabulous times*, but the India of actual history."

The theory of M. Cosquin is, then, that the popular stories of the world, or rather the vast majority of them, were *invented* in India, and that they were carried from India, during the historical period, by various routes, till they were scattered over all the races among whom they are found.

This is a venturesome theory, and is admitted, apparently, to have its exceptions. For example, we possess ancient Egyptian popular tales corresponding to those of the rest of the world, but older by far than historical India, from which, according to M. Cosquin, the stories set forth on their travels.[3]

[1] It has already been attempted in our *Custom and Myth*; Introduction to Mrs. Hunt's *Grimm*; *La Mythologie*, and elsewhere.

[2] For M. Benfey's notions, see *Bulletin de l'Académie de Saint Petersbourg*, September 4-16, 1859, and *Pantschatantra*, Leipzig, 1859.

[3] See M. Maspero's collection, *Contes Populaires de l'Egypte Ancienne*, Paris, 1882.

One of these Egyptian tales, *The Two Brothers*, was actually written down on the existing manuscript in the time of Rameses II., some 1400 years before our era, and many centuries before India had any known history. No man can tell, moreover, how long it had existed before it was copied out by the scribe Ennànà. Now this tale, according to M. Cosquin himself, has points in common with *märchen* from Hesse, Hungary, Russia, modern Greece, France, Norway, Lithuania, Hungary, Servia, Annam, modern India, and, we may add, with Samoyed *märchen*, with Hottentot *märchen*, and with *märchen* from an "aboriginal" people of India, the Santals.

We ask no more than this one *märchen* of ancient Egypt to upset the whole theory that India was the original home of the *contes*, and that from *historic* India they have been carried by oral transmission, and in literary vehicles, all over the world. First let us tell the story briefly, and then examine its incidents each separately, and set forth the consequences of that examination.

According to the story of *The Two Brothers*—

Once upon a time there were two brothers; Anapou was the elder, the younger was called Bitiou. Anapou was married, and Bitiou lived with him as his servant. When he drove the cattle to feed, he heard what they said to each other, and drove them where they told him the pasture was best. One day his brother's wife saw him carrying a very heavy burden of grain, and she fell in love with his force, and said, "Come and lie with me, and I will make thee goodly raiment".

But he answered, "Art thou not as my mother, and my brother as a father to me? Speak to me thus no more, and never will I tell any man what a word thou hast said."

Then she cast dust on her head, and went to her husband,

saying, "Thy brother would have lain with me; slay him or I die".

Then the elder brother was like a panther of the south, and he sharpened his knife, and lay in wait behind the door. And when the sun set, Bitiou came driving his cattle; but the cow that walked before them all said to him, "There stands thine elder brother with his knife drawn to slay thee".

Then he saw the feet of his brother under the door, and he fled, his brother following him; and he cried to Ra, and Ra heard him, and between him and his brother made a great water flow full of crocodiles.

Now in the morning the younger brother told the elder all the truth, and he mutilated himself, and cast it into the water, and the *calmar* fish devoured it. And he said, "I go to the Valley of Acacias" (possibly a mystic name for the next world), "and in an acacia tree I shall place my heart; and if men cut the tree, and my heart falls, thou shalt seek it for seven years, and lay it in a vessel of water. Then shall I live again and requite the evil that hath been done unto me. And the sign that evil hath befallen me shall be when the cup of beer in thy hand is suddenly turbid and troubled."

Then the elder brother cast dust on his head and besmeared his face, and went home and slew his wicked wife.

Now the younger brother dwelt in the Valley of Acacias, and all the gods came by that way, and they pitied his loneliness, and Chnum made for him a wife.[1] And the seven Hathors came and prophesied, saying, "*She shall die an ill death and a violent*". And Bitiou loved her, and told her the secret of his life, and that he should die when his heart fell from the acacia tree.

Now, a lock of the woman's hair fell into the river, and it floated to the place where Pharaoh's washermen were at work. And the sweet lock perfumed all the raiment of Pharaoh, and the washermen knew not wherefore, and they were rebuked. Then Pharaoh's chief washerman went to the water and found the hair of the wife of Bitiou; and Pharaoh's magicians went to him and said, "Our lord, thou must marry the woman from whose head this tress of hair hath floated hither". And Pharaoh hearkened unto them, and he sent messengers even to the Valley of Acacias, and they came unto the wife of Bitiou. And she said, "First you must slay my

[1] Chnum is the artificer among the gods.

husband" ; and she showed them the acacia tree, and they cut the flower that held the heart of Bitiou, and he died.

Then it so befel that the brother of Bitiou held in his hand a cup of beer, and, lo! the beer was troubled. And he said, "Alas, my brother!" and he sought his brother's heart, and he found it in the berry of the acacia. Then he laid it in a cup of fresh water, and Bitiou drank of it, and his heart went into his own place, and lived again.

Then said Bitiou, "Lo! I shall become the bull, even Apis" (Hapi); and they led him to the king, and all men rejoiced that Apis was found. But the bull went into the chamber of the king's women, and he spake to the woman that had been the wife of Bitiou. And she was afraid, and said to Pharaoh, "Wilt thou swear to give me my heart's desire ?" and he swore it with an oath. And she said, "Slay that bull that I may eat his liver". Then felt Pharaoh sick for sorrow, yet for his oath's sake he let slay the bull. And there fell of his blood two quarts on either side of the son of Pharaoh, and thence grew two persea trees, great and fair, and offerings were made to the trees, as they had been gods.

Then the wife of Pharaoh went forth in her chariot, and the tree spake to her, saying, "I am Bitiou". And she let cut down that tree, and a chip leaped into her mouth, and she conceived and bare a son. And that child was Bitiou ; and when he came to full age and was prince of that land, he called together the councillors of the king, and accused the woman, and they slew her. And he sent for his elder brother, and made him a prince in the land of Egypt.

We now propose to show, not only that the incidents of this tale—far more ancient than historic India as it is—are common in the *märchen* of many countries, but that they are inextricably entangled and intertwisted with the chief plots of popular tales. There are few of the main cycles of popular tales which do not contain, as essential parts of their machinery, one or more of the ideas and situations of this legend. There is thus at least a presumption that these cycles of story may have been in existence in the reign of

Rameses II., and for an indefinite period earlier; while, if they were not, and if they are made of borrowed materials, it may have been from the Egypt of an unknown antiquity, not from much later Indian sources, that they were adapted.

The incidents will now be analysed and compared with those of *märchen* in general.

To this end let us examine the incidents in the ancient Egyptian tale of *The Two Brothers.* These incidents are:—

(1) The *spretæ injuria formæ* of the wedded woman, who, having offered herself in vain to a man, her brother-in-law, accuses him of being her assailant. This incident, of course, occurs in Homer, in the tale of Bellerophon, before we know anything of historic India. This, moreover, seems one of the notions (M. Cosquin admits, with Benfey, that there are such notions) which are "universally human," and *might* be invented anywhere.

(2) The Egyptian Hippolytus is warned of his danger by his cow, which speaks with human voice. Every one will recognise the ram which warns Phrixus and Helle in the Jason legend.[1] In the Albanian *märchen*,[2] a *dog*, not a cow nor a ram, gives warning of the danger. Animals, in short, often warn of danger by spoken messages, as the fish does in the Brahmanic deluge-myth, and the dog in a deluge-myth from North America.

(3) The accused brother is pursued by his kinsman,

[1] The authority cited by the scholiast (Apoll. Rhod., *Argon.*, i. 256) is Hecatæus. Scholiast on *Iliad*, vii. 86, quotes Philostephanus.

[2] Von Hahn, i. 65.

and about to be slain, when Ra, at his prayer, casts between him and the avenger a stream full of crocodiles. This incident is at least not very unlike one of the most widely diffused of all incidents of story—the *flight*, in which the runaways cause magical rivers or lakes suddenly to cut off the pursuer. This narrative of the flight and the obstacles is found in Scotch, Gaelic, Japanese (no water obstacle), Zulu, Russian, Samoan, and in "The Red Horse of the Delawares," a story from Dacotah, as well as in India and elsewhere.[1] The difference is, that in the Egyptian *conte*, as it has reached us in literary form, the fugitive appeals to Ra to help him, instead of magically making a river by throwing water or a bottle behind him, as is customary. It may be conjectured that the substitution of divine intervention in response to prayer for magical self-help is the change made by a priestly scribe in the traditional version.[2]

(4) Next morning the brothers parley across the stream. The younger first mutilates himself (Atys) then says he is going to the vale of the acacia, according to M. Maspero probably a name for the other world. Meanwhile the younger brother will put his *heart* in a high acacia tree. If the tree is cut down, the elder brother must search for the *heart*, and place it in a jar of water, when the younger brother will revive. Here we have the idea which recurs in the Samoyed *märchen*, where the men lay aside their *hearts*, in which are their separable *lives*. As Mr.

[1] See *Folk-Lore Journal*, April, 1886, review of Clouston's *Popular Stories*, for examples of the magic used in the flight.

[2] Maspero, *Contes*, p. 13, note 1.

Ralston says,[1] "This heart-breaking episode occurs in the tales of many lands". In the Russian the story is Koschchei the deathless, whose "death" (or *life*) lies in an egg, in a duck, on a log, in the ice.[2] As Mr. Ralston well remarks, a very singular parallel to the revival of the Egyptian brother's heart in water is the Hottentot tale of a girl eaten by a lion. Her *heart* is extracted from the lion, is placed in a calabash of milk, and the girl comes to life again.[3]

(5) The younger brother gives the elder a sign magical, whereby he shall know how it fares with the heart. When a cup of beer suddenly grows turbid, then evil has befallen the heart. This is merely one of the old *sympathetic signs* of story—the opal that darkens; the comb of Lemminkainen in the *Kalewala* that drops blood when its owner is in danger; the stick that the hero erects as he leaves home, and which will fall when he is imperilled. In Australia the natives practise this magic with a stick, round which they bind the hair of the distant person about whose condition they want to be informed.[4] This incident, turning on the belief in *sympathies*, might perhaps be regarded as "universally human" and capable of being invented anywhere.

M. Cosquin has found in France the trait of the blood that boils in the glass when the person concerned is in danger.

[1] *Russian Folk-Tales*, 109.

[2] In Norse, Asbjornsen and Moe, 36; Dasent, 9. Gaelic, Campbell, i. 4, p. 81. Indian, "Punchkin," *Old Deccan Days*, pp. 13-16. Samoyed, Castren, *Ethnol. Vorles über die Altaischen Völker.*, p. 174.

[3] Bleek, *Reynard the Fox of South Africa*, p. 57.

[4] Dawson, *Australian Aborigines*, p. 36, 1881. The stick used is the "throwing stick" wherewith the spear is hurled.

(6) The elder brother goes home and kills his wife. The gods pity the younger Bitiou in the Valley of Acacias, and make him a wife.

(7) The three Hathors come to her creation, and prophesy for her a violent death. For this incident compare Perrault's *The Sleeping Beauty* and Maury's work on *Les Fées*. The spiritual midwives and prophetesses at the hour of birth are familiar in *märchen* as *Fairies*, and *Fates*, and *Mœræ*.

(8) The river carries a tress of the hair of Bitiou's wife to the feet of Pharaoh's washermen; the scent perfumes all the king's linen. Pharaoh falls in love with the woman from whose locks this tress has come. For this incident compare *Cinderella*. In Santal and Indian *märchen* a tress of hair takes the place of the glass-slipper, and the amorous prince or princess will only marry the person from whose head the lock has come. Here M. Cosquin himself gives Siamese, Mongol, Bengali (Lal Behar Day, p. 86), and other examples of the lock of hair doing duty for the slipper with which the lover is smitten, and by which he recognises his true love.

(9) The wife of Bitiou reveals the secret of his heart. The people of Pharaoh cut down the acacia tree.

(10) His brother reads in the turbid beer the death of Bitiou. He discovers the *heart* and *life* in a berry of the acacia.

It is superfluous to give modern parallels to the various transformations of the life of Bitiou. He becomes an Apis bull, and his faithless wife desires his death, and wishes to eat his liver, but his life goes on in other forms. This is merely the familiar situation of the ass in *Peau d'Ane* (the ass who clearly, before Perrault's time, had been human).

Demandez lui la peau de ce rare animal!

In most traditional versions of *Cinderella* will be found examples of the beast, once human, slain by an enemy, yet potent after death. This beast takes the part given by Perrault to the fairy godmother. The idea is also familar in Grimm's *Machandelboom* (47), and was found by Casalis among the Bechuanas.

(11) The wicked wife obtains the bull Apis's death by virtue of a *hasty oath* of Pharaoh's (*Jephtha*, *Herodias*).

(12) The blood of the bull grows into two persea trees.

Here M. Cosquin himself supplies parallels of blood turning into trees from Hesse (Wolf, p. 394) and from Russian. We may add the ancient Lydian myth. When the gods slew Agdistis, a drop of his blood became an almond tree, the fruit of which made women pregnant.[1]

(13) The persea tree is also cut down by the wicked wife of Bitiou. A chip from its boughs is swallowed by the wicked wife, who conceives, like Margata in the *Kalewala*, and bears a son.

The story of Agdistis, just quoted, is in point, but the topic is of enormous range, and the curious may consult *Le Fils de Vierge* by M. H. De Charencey. Compare also Surya Bay in *Old Deccan Days* (6). The final resurrection of Surya Bay is exactly like that in the Hottentot tale already quoted. Surya is drowned

[1] Pausanias, vii. 17.

by a jealous rival, becomes a golden flower, is burned, becomes a mango; one of the fruits falls into a calabash of milk, and out of the calabash, like the Hottentot girl, comes Surya!

(14) The son of the persea tree *was* Bitiou, born of his own faithless wife; and when he grew up he had her put to death.

Even a hasty examination of these incidents from old Egypt proves that before India was heard of in history the people of the Pharaohs possessed a large store of incidents perfectly familiar in modern *märchen*. Now, if one single Egyptian tale yields this rich supply, it is an obvious presumption that the collection of an Egyptian Grimm might, and probably would, have furnished us with the majority of the situations common in popular tales. M. Cosquin himself remarks that these ideas cannot be invented more than once (I. lxvii.). The other Egyptian *contes*, as that of *Le Prince Prédestiné* (twentieth dynasty), and the noted *Master Thief* of Herodotus (ii. 121), are merely familiar *märchen* of the common type, and have numerous well-known analogues.

From all these facts M. Cosquin draws no certain conclusions. He asks: Did Egypt borrow these tales from India, or India from Egypt? *And were there Aryans in India in the time of Rameses II.?*

These questions are beyond conjecture. We know nothing of Egyptian relations with prehistoric India. We know not how many æons the tale of *The Two Brothers* may have existed in Egypt before Ennànà, the head librarian, wrote it out for Pharaoh's treasurer, Qagabou.

What we do know is, that if we find a large share of the whole stock of incident of popular tale fully developed in one single story long before India was historic, it is perfectly vain to argue that all stories were imported from historic India. It is impossible to maintain that the single centre whence the stories spread was not the India of fable, but the India of history, when we discover such abundance of story material in Egypt before, as far as is known, India had even become the India of fable.

The topic is altogether too obscure for satisfactory argument. Certainly the *märchen* were at home in Egypt before we have even reason to believe that Egypt and India were conscious of each other's existence. The antiquity of *märchen* by the Nile-side touches geological time, if we agree with M. Maspero that Bitiou is a form of Osiris, that is, that the Osiris myth may have been developed out of the Bitiou *märchen*.[1] The Osiris myth is as old as the Egypt we know, and the story of Bitiou may be either the *detritus* or the germ of the myth. This gives it a dateless antiquity; and with this *märchen* the kindred and allied *märchen* establish a claim to enormous age. But it is quite impossible to say *when* these tales were first invented. We cannot argue that the cradle of a story is the place where it first received literary form. We know not whence the Egyptians came to Nile-side; we know not whether they brought the story with them, or found it among some nameless earlier people, fugitives from Kôr, perhaps, or anywhere else. We know not whether the remote ancestors of modern

[1] Maspero, *op. cit.*, p. 17, note 1.

peoples, African, or European, or Asiatic, who now possess forms of the tale, borrowed it from a people more ancient than Egypt, or from Egypt herself. These questions are at present insoluble. We only know for certain that, when we find anywhere any one of the numerous incidents of the story of *The Two Brothers*, we can be certain that their original home was *not* historic India. There is also the presumption that, if we knew more of the tales of ancient Egypt, we could as definitely refuse to regard historic India as the cradle of many other *märchen*.

Thus, in opposition to the hypothesis of borrowing from India, we reach some distinct and assured, though negative, truths.

1. So far as the ideas in *The Two Brothers* are representative of *märchen* (and these ideas are inextricably interwoven with some of the most typical legends), *historic* India is certainly and demonstrably *not* the cradle of popular tales. These are found far earlier already in the written literature of Egypt.

2. As far as these ideas are representative of *märchen*, there is absolutely no evidence to show that *märchen* sprang from India, whether historical or prehistoric ; nor is any connection proved between ancient Egypt and prehistoric India.

3. As far as *märchen* are represented by the ideas in *The Two Brothers* and the *Predestined Prince*, there is absolutely no evidence to show in what region or where they were originally invented.

The Bellerophon story rests on a *donnée* in *The Two Brothers ;* the *Flight* rests on another ; *Cinderella* reposes on a third ; the giant with no heart in his body depends on a fourth ; the *Milk-White Dove* on the same ; and these incidents occur in Hottentot, Bechuana, Samoyed, Samoan, as well as in Greek, Scotch, German, Gaelic. Now, as all these incidents existed in Egyptian *märchen* fourteen hundred years before Christ, they *may* have been dispersed without Indian intervention. One of the white raiders from the Northern Sea may have been made captive, like the pseud-Odysseus, in Egypt ; may have heard the tales ; may have been ransomed, and carried the story to Greece or Libya, whence a Greek got it. Southwards it may have passed up the Nile to the Great Lakes, and down the Congo and Zambesi, and southward ever with the hordes of T'Chaka's ancestors. All these processes are possible and even probable, but absolutely nothing is known for certain on the subject. It is only as manifest as facts can be that all this might have occurred if the Indian peninsula did not exist.

Another objection to the hypothesis of distribution from historic India is the existence of sagas or epic legends corresponding to *märchen* in pre-Homeric Greece. The story of Jason, for example, is in its essential features, perhaps, the most widely diffused of all.[1] The story of the return of the husband, and of his difficult recognition by his wife, the central idea of the *Odyssey*, is of wide distribution, and the *Odyssey* (as Fénelon makes the ghost of Achilles tell Homer in Hades) is *un amas de contes de vieilles.* The Cyclops, the Siren, Scylla, and the rest,[2] these

[1] *Custom and Myth*, "A Far-Travelled Tale".

[2] Gerland, *Alt Griechische Märchen in der Odyssee.*

tales did not reach Greece from historic India at least, and we have no reason for supposing that India before the dawn of history was their source.

The reasons for which India has been regarded as a great centre and fountain-head of popular stories are, on the other hand, excellent, if the theory is sufficiently limited. The cause is *vera causa*. *Märchen* certainly did set out from mediæval India, and reached mediæval Europe and Asia in abundance. Not to speak of oral communications in the great movements, missions and migrations, Tartar, crusading, Gypsy, commercial and Buddhistic—in all of which there must have been "swopping of stories"—it is certain that Western literature was actually invaded by the *contes* which had won a way into the literature of India.[1] These are facts beyond doubt, but these facts must not be made the basis of too wide an inference. Though so many stories have demonstrably been borrowed from India in the historical period, it is no less certain that many existed in Europe before their introduction. Again, as has been ably argued by a writer in the *Athenæum* (April 23, 1887), the literary versions of the tales probably had but a limited influence on the popular narrators, the village gossips and grandmothers. Thus no collection of published tales has ever been more popular than that of Charles Perrault, which for many years has been published not only in cheap books, but in cheaper broadsheets. Yet M. Sébillot and other French

[1] Cosquin, *op. cit.*, I. xv., xxiv.; Max Müller, "The Migrations of Fables," *Selected Essays*, vol. ii., Appendix; Benfey, *Pantschatantra;* Comparetti, Introduction to *Book of Sindibad*, English translation of the Folk-Lore Society.

collectors gather from the lips of peasants versions of *Cinderella*, for example, quite unaffected by Perrault's version, and rich in archaic features, such as the presence of a miracle-working beast instead of a fairy godmother. That detail is found in Kaffir, and Santhal, and Finnish, as well as in Celtic, and Portuguese, and Scottish variants, and has been preserved in popular French traditions, despite the influence of Perrault. In the same way, M. Carnoy finds only the faintest traces of the influence of a collection so popular as the *Arabian Nights*. The peasantry regard tales which they read in books as quite apart from their inherited store of legend.[1]

If printed literature has still so little power over popular tradition, the manuscript literature of the Middle Ages must have had much less, though sometimes *contes* from India were used as parables by preachers. Thus we must beware of over-estimating the effect of importation from India, even where it distinctly existed. Even the versions that were brought in the Middle Ages by oral tradition must have encountered versions long settled in Europe—versions which may have been current before any scribe of Egypt perpetuated a legend on papyrus.

Once more, the Indian theory has to account for the presence of tales in Africa and America among populations which are not known to have had any contact with India at all. Where such examples are urged, it is usual to say that the stories either do not really resemble our *märchen*, or are quite recent

[1] Sébillot's popular *Cendrillon* is *Le Taureau Bleu* in *Contes de la Haute Bretagne*. See also M. Carnoy's *Contes Français*, 1885, p. 9.

importations by Europeans, Dutch, French, English and others.[1] Here we are on ground where proof is difficult, if not impossible. Assuredly French influence declares itself in certain narratives collected from the native tribes of North America. On the other hand, when the *märchen* is interwoven with the national traditions and poetry of a remote people, and with the myths by which they account to themselves for the natural features of their own country, the hypothesis of recent borrowing from Europeans appears insufficient. A striking example is the song of Siati (a form of the Jason myth) among the people of Samoa.[2] Even more remarkable is the presence of a crowd of familiar *märchen* in the national traditions of the Huarochiri, a pre-Inca civilised race of Southern Peru. These were published, or at least collected and written down, by Francisco de Avila, a Spanish priest, about 1608. He remarks that "these traditions are deeply rooted in the hearts of the people of this province".[3] These traditions refer to certain prehistoric works of engineering or accidents of soil, whereby the country was drained. The Huarochiri explained them by a series of *märchen* about Huthiacuri, Pariaca (culture-heroes), and about friendly animals which aided them in the familiar way. In the same manner exactly the people of the Marais of Poitou have to account for the drainage of the country, a work of the twelfth century. They attribute the old works to the local

[1] Cosquin, *op. cit.*, 1, xix.

[2] Turner's *Samoa*, p. 102.

[3] *Rites of the Incas.* Hakluyt Society. The third document in the book. The *märchen* have been examined by me in *The Marriage of Cupid and Psyche*, p. lxxii.

hero, Gargantua, who "drank up all the water".[1] No one supposes that this legend is borrowed from Rabelais, and it seems even more improbable that the Huarochiri hastily borrowed *märchen* from the Spaniards, and converted them before 1600 into national myths.

We have few opportunities of finding examples of remote American *märchen* recorded so early as this, and generally the hypothesis of recent borrowing from Europeans, or from Negroes influenced by Europeans, is at least possible, and it would be hard to prove a negative. But the case of the Huarochiri throws doubt on the hypothesis of recent borrowing as the invariable cause of the diffusion of *märchen* in places beyond the reach of historic India.

The only way (outside of direct evidence) to prove borrowing would be to show that ideas and customs peculiarly Indian (for example) occur in the *märchen* of people destitute of these ideas. But it would be hard to ask believers in the Indian theory to exhibit such survivals. In the first place, if *contes* have been borrowed, it seems that a new "local colour" was given to them almost at the moment of transference. The Zulu and Kaffir *märchen* are steeped in Zulu and Kaffir colour, and the life they describe is rich in examples of rather peculiar native rites and ceremonies, seldom if ever essential to the conduct of the tale. Thus, if stories are "adapted" (like French plays) in the moment of borrowing, it will be cruel to ask supporters of the Indian theory for traces of Indian traits and ideas in European *märchen*. Again, apart

[1] *Revue des Traditions Populaires*, April 25, 1887, p. 186.

from special yet non-essential matters of etiquette (such as the ceremonies with which certain kinsfolk are treated, or the initiation of girls at the marriageable age), the ideas and customs found in *märchen* are practically universal. As has been shown, the supernatural *stuff*—metamorphosis, equality of man, beasts and things, magic and the like—*is* universal. Thus little remains that could be fixed on as especially the custom or idea of any one given people. For instance, in certain variants of *Puss in Boots*, Swahili, Avar, Neapolitan, the beast-hero makes it a great point that, when he dies, he is to be *honourably buried*. Now what peoples give beasts honourable burial? We know the cases of ancient Egyptians, Samoans, Arabs and Athenians (in the case, at least, of the wolf), and probably there are many more. Thus even so peculiar an idea or incident as this cannot be proved to belong to a definite region, or to come from any one original centre.[1]

By the very nature of the case, therefore, it is difficult for M. Cosquin and other supporters of the Indian theory to prove the existence of Indian ideas in European *märchen*. Nor do they establish this point. They urge that *charity to beasts* and the *gratitude of beasts*, as contrasted with human lack of gratitude, are Indian, and perhaps Buddhist ideas. Thus the Buddha gave his own living body to a famished tigress. But so, according to Garcilasso, were the subjects of the Incas wont to do, and they were not Buddhists. The beasts in *märchen*, again,

[1] See Deulin, *Contes de ma Mère l'Oye*, and Reinhold Köhler in Gonzenbach's *Sicilianische Märchen*, No. 65.

are just as often, or even more frequently, helpful to men without any motive of gratitude; nor would it be fair to argue that the notion of gratitude has dropped out, because we find friendly beasts all the world over, totems and manitous, who have never been benefited by man. The favours are all on the side of the totems. It is needless to adduce again the evidence on this topic. M. Cosquin adds that the belief in the equality and interchangeability of attributes and aspect between man and beast is "une idée bien indienne," and derived from the doctrine of metempsychosis, "qui efface la distinction entre l'homme et l'animal, et qui en tout vivant voit un frère". But it has been demonstrated that this belief in the equality and kinship not only of all animate, but all inanimate nature, is the very basis of Australian, Zuñi and all other philosophies of the backward races. No idea can be less peculiar to India; it is universal. Once more, the belief that shape-shifting (metamorphosis) can be achieved by skin-shifting, by donning or doffing the hide of a beast, is no more "peculiarly Indian" than the other conceptions. Benfey, to be sure, laid stress on this point;[1] but it is easy to produce examples of skin-shifting and consequent metamorphosis from Roman, North American, Old Scandinavian, Thlinkeet, Slav and Vogul ritual and myths.[2] There remains only a trace of polygamy in European *märchen* to speak of specially Indian influence.[3] But polygamy

[1] *Pantschatantra*, i. 265.

[2] *Marriage of Cupid and Psyche*, pp. lx., lxiv., where examples and authorities are given.

[3] Cosquin, *op. cit.*, i. xxx.

is not peculiar to India, nor is monogamy a recent institution in Europe.

Thus each "peculiarly Indian" idea supposed to be found in *märchen* proves to be practically universal. So the whole Indian hypothesis is attacked on every side. *Contes* are far older than *historic* India. Nothing raises even a presumption that they first arose in *prehistoric* India. They are found in places where they could hardly have travelled from historic India. Their ideas are not peculiarly Indian, and though many reached Europe and Asia in literary form derived from India during the Middle Ages, and were even used as parables in sermons, yet the majority of European folk-tales have few traces of Indian influence. Some examples of this influence, as when the "frame-work" of an Oriental collection has acquired popular circulation, will be found in Professor Crane's interesting book, *Italian Popular Tales*, pp. 168, 359. But to admit this is very different from asserting that German *Hausmärchen* are all derived from "Indian and Arabian originals, with necessary changes of costume and manners," which is, apparently, the opinion of some students.

What remains to do is to confess ignorance of the original centre of the *märchen*, and inability to decide dogmatically which stories must have been invented only once for all, and which may have come together by the mere blending of the universal elements of imagination. It is only certain that no limit can be put to a story's power of flight *per ora virum*. It may wander wherever merchants wander, wherever captives are dragged, wherever slaves are sold, wherever the custom of exogamy commands the choice of alien wives. Thus the story flits through the whole race and over the whole world. Wherever human communication is or has been possible, there the story may go, and the space of time during which the courses of the sea and the paths of the land have been open to story is dateless and unknown. Here the story may dwindle to a fireside tale; there it may become an epic in the mouth of Homer or a novel in the hands of Madame D'Aulnoy or Miss Thackeray. The savage makes the characters beasts or birds; the epic poet or saga-man made them heroic kings, or lovely, baleful sorceresses, daughters of the Sun; the French Countess makes them princesses and countesses. Like its own heroes, the popular story can assume every shape; like some of them, it has drunk the waters of immortality.[1]

[1] A curious essay by Mr. H. E. Warner, on "The Magical Flight," urges that there is no *plot*, but only a fortuitous congeries of story-atoms (*Scribner's Magazine*, June, 1887). There is a good deal to be said, in this case, for Mr. Warner's conclusions.

APPENDICES.

APPENDIX A.

FONTENELLE'S FORGOTTEN COMMON SENSE.

In the opinion of Aristotle, most discoveries and inventions have been made time after time and forgotten again. Aristotle may not have been quite correct in this view; and his remarks, perhaps, chiefly applied to politics, in which every conceivable and inconceivable experiment has doubtless been attempted. In a field of less general interest—namely, the explanation of the absurdities of mythology—the true cause was discovered more than a hundred years ago by a man of great reputation, and then was quietly forgotten. Why did the ancient peoples—above all, the Greeks—tell such extremely gross and irrational stories about their Gods and heroes? That is the riddle of the mythological Sphinx. It was answered briefly, wittily and correctly by Fontenelle; and the answer was neglected, and half a dozen learned but impossible theories have since come in and out of fashion. Only within the last ten years has Fontenelle's idea been, not resuscitated, but rediscovered. The followers of Mr. E. B. Taylor, Mannhardt, Gaidoz, and the rest, do not seem to be aware that they are only repeating the notions of the nephew of Corneille.

The Academician's theory is stated in a short essay, *De l'Origine des Fables* (Œuvres: Paris, 1758, vol. iii. p.

270). We have been so accustomed from childhood, he says, to the absurdities of Greek myth, that we have ceased to be aware that they are absurd. Why are the legends of men and beasts and Gods so incredible and revolting? Why have we ceased to tell such tales? The answer is, that early men were in "a state of almost inconceivable savagery and ignorance," and that the Greek myths are inherited from people in that condition. "Look at the Kaffirs and Iroquois," says Fontenelle, "if you wish to know what early men were like; and remember that even the Iroquois and Kaffirs are people with a long past, with knowledge and culture (*politesse*) which the first men did not enjoy." Now the more ignorant a man is, the more prodigies he supposes himself to behold. Thus the first narratives of the earliest men were full of monstrous things, "parce qu'ils etoient faits par des gens sujets à voir bien des choses qui n'etaient pas". This condition answers, in Mr. Tylor's system, to the confusion the savage makes between dreams and facts, and to the hallucinations which beset him when he does not get his regular meals. Here, then, we have a groundwork of irresponsible fancy.

The next step is this: even the rudest men are curious, and ask "the reason why" of phenomena. "Il y a eu de la philosophie même dans ces siècles grossiers;" and this rude philosophy "greatly contributed to the origin of myths". Men looked for causes of things. "'Whence comes this river?' asked the reflective man of those ages—a queer philosopher, yet one who might have been a Descartes did he live to-day. After long meditation, he concluded that some one had always to keep filling the source whence the stream springs. And whence came the water? Our philosopher did not consider so curiously. He had evolved the myth of a water-nymph or naïad, and there he stopped."

The characteristic of these mythical explanations—as of all philosophies, past, present and to come—was that they were limited by human experience. Early man's experience showed him that effects were produced by conscious, sentient, personal causes like himself. He sprang to the conclusion that all hidden causes were also persons. These persons are the *dramatis personæ* of myth. It was a person who caused thunder, with a hammer or a mace; or it was a bird whose wings produced the din.

"From this rough philosophy which prevailed in the early ages were born the gods and goddesses"—deities made not only in the likeness of man, but of savage man as he, in his ignorance and superstition, conceived himself to be. Fontenelle might have added that those fancied personal causes who became gods were also fashioned in the likeness of the beasts, whom early man regarded as his equals or superiors. But he neglects this point. He correctly remarks that the gods of myth appear immoral to us because they were devised by men whose morality was all unlike ours—who prized justice less than power, especially (he might have added) magical power. As morality ripened into self-consciousness, the gods improved with the improvement of men; and "the gods known to Cicero are much better than those known to Homer, because better philosophers have had a hand at their making". Moreover, in the earliest speculations an imaginative and hair-brained philosophy explained all that seemed extraordinary in nature; while the sphere of philosophy was filled by fanciful narratives about facts. The constellations called the Bears were accounted for as metamorphosed men and women. Indeed, "all the metamorphoses are the physical philosophy of these early times," which accounted for every fact by what we now call ætiological nature-myths. Even the peculiarities of birds and beasts were thus explained. The partridge flies low because Dædalus (who had seen his son Icarus perish through a lofty flight) was changed into a partridge. This habit of mind, which finds a story for the solution of every problem, survives, Fontenelle remarks, in what we now call folk-lore —popular tradition. Thus, the elder tree is said to have borne as good berries as the vine does till Judas Iscariot hanged himself from its branches. This story must be later than Christianity; but it is precisely identical in character with those ancient metamorphoses which Ovid collected. The kind of fancy that produced these and other prodigious myths is not peculiar, Fontenelle maintains, to Eastern peoples. "It is common to all men," at a certain mental stage—"in the tropics or in the regions of eternal ice." Thus the world-wide similarities of myths are, on the whole, the consequence of a world-wide uniformity of intellectual development.

Fontenelle hints at his proof of this theory. He compares the myths of America with those of Greece, and shows that distance in space and difference of race do not hinder Peruvians and Athenians from being "in the same tale". "For the Greeks, with all their intelligence, did not, in their beginnings, think more rationally than the savages of America, who were also, apparently, a rather primitive people (*assez nouveau*)." He concludes that the Americans might have become as sensible as the Greeks if they had been allowed the leisure.

With an exception in the Israelites, Fontenelle decides that all nations made the astounding part of their myths while they were savages, and retained them from custom and religious conservatism. But myths were also borrowed and interchanged between Phœnicia, Egypt and Greece. Further, Greek misunderstandings of the meanings of Phœnician and other foreign words gave rise to myths. Finally, myths were supposed to contain treasures of antique mysterious wisdom; and mythology was explained by systems which themselves are only myths, stories told by the learned to themselves and to the public.

"It is not science to fill one's head with the follies of Phœnicians and Greeks, but it is science to understand what led Greeks and Phœnicians to imagine these follies." A better and briefer system of mythology could not be devised; but the Mr. Casaubons of this world have neglected it, and even now it is beyond their comprehension.

APPENDIX B.

REPLY TO OBJECTIONS.

In a work which perhaps inevitably contains much controversial matter, it has seemed best to consign to an Appendix the answers to objections against the method advocated. By this means the attention is less directed from the matter in hand, the exposition of the method itself. We have announced our belief that a certain element in mythology is derived from the mental condition of savages. To this it is replied, with perfect truth, that there are savages and savages; that a vast number of shades of culture and of nascent or retrograding civilisation exist among the races to whom the term "savage" is commonly applied. This is not only true, but its truth is part of the very gist of our theory. It is our contention that myth is sensibly affected by the varieties of culture which prevail among so-called savage tribes, as they approach to or decline from the higher state of barbarism. The anthropologist is, or ought to be, the last man to lump all savages together, as if they were all on the same level of culture.

When we speak of "the savage mental condition," we mean the mental condition of all uncultivated races who still fail to draw any marked line between man and the animate or inanimate things in the world, and who explain physical phenomena on a vague theory, more or less consciously held, that all nature is animated and endowed with human attributes. This state of mind is nowhere absolutely extinct; it prevails, to a limited extent, among untutored European peasantry, and among the children of the educated classes. But this intellectual condition is most marked and most powerful among the races which ascend from the condition of the Australian Murri and the Bushmen, up to the comparatively advanced Maoris of New Zealand and Algonkins or Zuñis of North America. These are the sorts of people who, for our present purpose, must be succinctly described as still in the savage condition of the imagination.

Again, it is constantly objected to our method that we have no knowledge of the past of races at present in the savage status. "The savage are as old as the civilised races, and can as little be named primitive," writes Dr. Fairbairn.[1] Mr. Max Müller complains with justice of authors who "speak of the savage of to-day as if he had only just been sent into the world, forgetting that, as a living species, he is probably not a day younger than ourselves".[2] But Mr. Max Müller has himself admitted all we want, namely, *that savages or nomads represent an earlier stage of culture than even the ancient Sanskrit-speaking Aryans*. This follows from the learned writer's assertion that savage tongues, Kaffir and so forth, are still in the childhood which Hebrew and the most ancient Sanskrit had long left behind them.[3] "We see in them" (savage languages) "what we can no longer expect to see even in the most ancient Sanskrit or Hebrew. We watch the childhood of language with all its childish pranks." These "pranks" are the result of the very habits of savage thought which we regard as earlier than "the most ancient Sanskrit". Thus Mr. Max Müller has

[1] *Academy*, 20th July, 1878. [2] *Hibb. Lect.*, p. 66.
[3] *Lectures on Science of Language*, 2nd series, p. 41.

admitted all that we need—admitted that savage language (and therefore, in his view, savage thought) is of an earlier stratum than, for example, the language of the Vedas. No more valuable concession could be made by a learned opponent.

Objections of an opposite character, however, are pushed, along with the statement that we have no knowledge of the past of savages. Savages were not always what they are now; they may have degenerated from a higher condition; their present myths may be the corruption of something purer and better; above all, savages are not *primitive.*

All this contention, whatever its weight, does not affect the thesis of the present argument. It is quite true that we know nothing directly of the condition, let us say, of the Australian tribes a thousand years ago except that it has left absolutely no material traces of higher culture. But neither do we know anything directly about the condition of the Indo-European peoples five hundred years before Philology fancies that she gets her earliest glimpse of them. We must take people as we find them, and must not place too much trust in our attempts to reconstruct their "dark backward". As to the past of savages, it is admitted by most anthropologists that certain tribes have probably seen better days. The Fuegians and the Bushmen and the Digger Indians were probably driven by stronger races out of seats comparatively happy and habits comparatively settled into their present homes and their present makeshift wretchedness.[1] But while degeneration is admitted as

[1] The Fuegians are not (morally and socially) so black as they have occasionally been painted. But it is probable that they "have seen better days". If the possession of a language with, apparently, a very superfluous number of words is a proof of high civilisation in the past, then the Fuegians

an element in history, there seems no tangible reason for believing that the highest state which Bushmen, Fuegians, or Diggers ever attained, and from which they can be thought to have fallen, was higher than a rather more comfortable savagery. There are ups and downs in savage as in civilised life, and perhaps "crowned races may degrade," but we have no evidence to show that the ancestors of the Diggers or the Fuegians were a "crowned race". Their descent has not been comparatively a very deep one; their presumed former height was not very high. As Mr. Tylor observes, "So far as history is to be our criterion, progression is primary and degradation secondary; culture must be gained before it can be lost". One thing about the past of savages we do know: it must have been a long past, and there must have been a period in it when the savage had even less of what Aristotle calls χορηγία, even less of the equipment and provision necessary for a noble life than he possesses at present. His past must have been long, because great length of time is required for the evolution of his exceedingly complex customs, such as his marriage laws and his minute etiquette. Mr. Herbert Spencer has deduced from the multiplicity, elaborateness and wide diffusion of Australian marriage laws the inference that the Australians were once more civilised than they are now, and had once a kind of central government and police. But to reason thus is to fall back on the old Greek theory which for every traditional custom imagined an early legislative hero, with a genius for devising laws, and with power to secure their being obeyed. The more generally accepted view of modern science is that law

are degraded indeed. But the finding of one piece of native pottery in an Australian burial-mound would prove more than a wilderness of irregular verbs.

and custom are things slowly evolved under stress of human circumstances. It is certain that the usual process is from the extreme complexity of savage to the clear simplicity of civilised rules of forbidden degrees. Wherever we see an advancing civilisation, we see that it does not put on new, complex and incomprehensible regulations, but that it rather sloughs off the old, complex and incomprehensible regulations bequeathed to it by savagery.

This process is especially manifest in the laws of forbidden degrees in marriage—laws whose complexity among the Australians or North American Indians "might puzzle a mathematician," and whose simplicity in a civilised country seems transparent even to a child. But while the elaborateness and stringency of savage customary law point to a more, and not a less barbarous past, they also indicate a past of untold duration. Somewhere in that past also it is evident that the savage must have been even worse off materially than he is at present. Even now he can light a fire; he has a bow, or a boomerang, or a blowpipe, and has attained very considerable skill in using his own rough tools of flint and his weapons tipped with quartz. Now man was certainly not born in the possession of fire; he did not come into the world with a bow or a boomerang in his hand, nor with an instinct which taught him to barb his fishing-hooks. These implements he had to learn to make and use, and till he had learned to use them and make them his condition must necessarily have been more destitute of material equipment than that of any races known to us historically. Thus all that can be inferred about the past of savages is that it was of vast duration, and that at one period man was more materially destitute, and so far more struggling and forlorn, than the Murri of

Australia were when first discovered by Europeans. Even then certain races *may* have had intellectual powers and potentialities beyond those of other races. Perhaps the first fathers of the white peoples of the North started with better brains and bodies than the first fathers of the Veddahs of Ceylon; but they all started naked, tool-less, fire-less. The only way of avoiding these conclusions is to hold that men, or some favoured races of man, were created with civilised instincts and habits of thought, and were miraculously provided with the first necessaries of life, or were miraculously instructed to produce them without passing through slow stages of experiment, invention and modification. But we might as well assume, with some early Biblical commentators, that the naked Adam in Paradise was miraculously clothed in a vesture of refulgent light. Against such beliefs we have only to say that they are without direct historical confirmation of any kind.

But if, for the sake of argument, we admit the belief that primitive man was miraculously endowed, and was placed at once in a stage of simple and happy civilisation, our thesis still remains unaffected. Dr. Fairbairn's saying has been quoted, "The savage are as old as the civilised races, and can as little be called primitive". But we do not wish to call savages primitive. We have already said that savages have a far-stretching unknown history behind them, and that (except on the supposition of miraculous enlightenment followed by degradation) their past must have been engaged in slowly evolving their rude arts, their strange beliefs and their elaborate customs. Undeniably there is nothing "primitive" in a man who can use a boomerang, and who must assign each separate joint of the kangaroo he kills to a separate member of his family circle, while to some of those members he is forbidden by law to speak. Men were not born into the world with all these notions. The lowest savage has sought out or inherited many inventions, and cannot be called "primitive". But it never was part of our argument that savages *are* primitive. Our argument does not find it necessary to claim savagery as the state from which all men set forth. About what was "primitive," as we have no historical information on the topic, we express no opinion at all. Man may, if any one likes to think so, have appeared on earth in a state of perfection, and may have degenerated from that condition. Some such opinion, that purity and reasonableness are "nearer the beginning" than absurdity and unreasonableness, appears to be held by Mr. Max Müller, who remarks, "I simply say that in the Veda we have a nearer approach to a beginning, and an intelligible beginning, than in the wild invocations of Hottentots or Bushmen".[1] Would Mr. Müller add, "I simply say that in the arts and political society of the Vedic age we have a nearer approach to a beginning than in the arts and society of Hottentots and Bushmen"? Is the use of chariots, horses, ships—are kings, walled cities, agriculture, the art of weaving, and so forth, all familiar to the Vedic poets, nearer the beginning of man's civilisation than the life of the naked or skin-clad hunter who has not yet learned to work the metals, who acknowledges no king, and has no certain abiding-place? If not, why is the religion of the civilised man nearer the beginning than that of the man who is not civilised? We have already seen that, in Mr. Max Muller's opinion, his language is much farther from the beginning.

Whatever the primitive condition of man may have been, it is certain that savagery was a stage through

[1] *Lectures on India.*

which he and his institutions have passed, or from which he has copiously borrowed. He may have degenerated from perfection, or from a humble kind of harmless simplicity, into savagery. He may have risen into savagery from a purely animal condition. But however this may have been, modern savages are at present in the savage condition, and the ancestors of the civilised races passed through or borrowed from a similar savage condition. As Mr. Tylor says, "It is not necessary to inquire how the savage state first came to be upon the earth. It is enough that, by some means or other, it has actually come into existence."[1] It is a stage through which all societies have passed, or (if that be contested) a condition of things from which all societies have borrowed. This view of the case has been well put by M. Darmesteter.[2] He is speaking of the history of religion. "If savages do not represent religion in its germ, if they do not exemplify that vague and indefinite thing conventionally styled 'primitive religion,' at least they represent a stage through which all religions have passed. The proof is that a very little research into civilised religions discovers a most striking similarity between the most essential elements of the civilised and the non-historic creeds." Proofs of this have been given when we examined the myths of Greece.

We have next to criticise the attempts which have been made to discredit the *evidence* on which we rely for our knowledge of the intellectual constitution of the savage, and of his religious ideas and his myths and legends. If that evidence be valueless, our whole theory is founded on the sand.

The difficulties in the way of obtaining trustworthy information about the ideas, myths and mental processes

[1] *Prim. Cult.*, i. 37. [2] *Revue Critique*, January, 1884.

of savages are not only proclaimed by opponents of the anthropological method, but are frankly acknowledged by anthropologists themselves. The task is laborious and delicate, but not impossible. Anthropology has, at all events, the advantage of studying an actual undeniably existing state of things, to sift the evidence as to that state of things, to examine the opportunites, the discretion, and the honesty of the witnesses, is part of the business of anthropology. A science which was founded on an uncritical acceptance of all the reports of missionaries, travellers, traders, and "beach-combers," would be worth nothing. But, as will be shown, anthropology is fortunate in the possession of a touchstone, "like that," as Theocritus says, "wherewith the money-changers try gold, lest perchance base metal pass for true".

The "difficulties which beset travellers and missionaries in their description of the religious and intellectual life of savages" have been catalogued by Mr. Max Müller. As he is not likely to have omitted anything which tells against the evidence of missionaries and travellers, we may adopt his statement in an abridged shape, with criticisms, and with additional illustrations of our own.[1]

First, "Few men are quite proof against the fluctuations of public opinion". Thus, in Rousseau's time, many travellers saw savages with the eyes Rousseau—that is, as models of a simple "state of nature". In the same way, we may add, modern educated travellers are apt to see savages in the light cast on them by Mr. Tylor or Sir John Lubbock. Mr. Im Thurn, in Guiana, sees with Mr. Tylor's eyes; Messrs. Fison and Howitt, among the Kamilaroi in Australia, see with the eyes of Mr. Lewis Morgan, author of *Systems of Consanguinity*. Very well; we must allow for the bias in each case. But what are

[1] *Hibbert Lectures*, p. 91.

we to say when the travellers who lived long before Regnard report precisely the same facts of savage life as the witty Frenchman who wrote that "next to the ape, the Laplander is the animal nearest to man"? What are we to say when the mariner, or beach-comber, or Indian interpreter, who never heard of Rousseau, brings from Canada or the Marquesas Islands a report of ideas or customs which the trained anthropologist finds in New Guinea or the Admiralty Islands, and with which the Inca, Garcilasso de la Vega, was familiar in Peru? If the Wesleyan missionary in South Africa is in the same tale with the Jesuit in Paraguay or in China, while the Lutheran in Kamtschatka brings the same intelligence as that which they contribute, and all three are supported by the shipwrecked mariner in Tonga and by the squatter in Queensland, as well as by the evidence, from ancient times and lands, of Strabo, Diodorus and Pausanias, what then? Is it not clear that if pagan Greeks, Jesuits and Wesleyans, squatters and anthropologists, Indian interpreters and the fathers of the Christian Church, are all agreed in finding this idea or that practice in their own times and countries, their evidence is at least unaffected by "the fluctuations of public opinion"? This criterion of undesigned coincidence in evidence drawn from Protestants, Catholics, pagans, sceptics, from times classical, mediæval and modern, from men learned and unlearned, is the touchstone of anthropology. It will be admitted that the consentient testimony of persons in every stage of belief and prejudice, of ignorance and learning, cannot agree, as it does agree, by virtue of some "fluctuation of public opinion". It is to be regretted that, in Mr. Max Müller's description of the difficulties which beset the study of savage religious ideas, he entirely omits to mention, on the other side, the corroboration which is derived from the undesigned coincidence of independent testimony. This point is so important that it may be well to quote Mr. Tylor's statement of the value of the anthropological criterion :—

It is a matter worthy of consideration that the accounts of similar phenomena of culture, recurring in different parts of the world, actually supply incidental proof of their own authenticity. Some years since a question which brings out this point was put to me by a great historian, "How can a statement as to customs, myths, beliefs, etc., of a savage tribe be treated as evidence where it depends on the testimony of some traveller or missionary who may be a superficial observer, more or less ignorant of the native language, a careless retailer of unsifted talk, a man prejudiced, or even wilfully deceitful?" This question is, indeed, one which every ethnographer ought to keep clearly and constantly before his mind. Of course he is bound to use his best judgment as to the trustworthiness of all authors he quotes, and if possible to obtain several accounts to certify each point in each locality. But it is over and above these measures of precaution that the test of recurrence comes in. If two independent visitors to different countries, say a mediæval Mohammedan in Tartary and a modern Englishman in Dahomey, or a Jesuit missionary in Brazil and a Wesleyan in the Fiji Islands, agree in describing some analogous art, or rite, or myth among the people they have visited, it becomes difficult or impossible to set down such correspondence to accident or wilful fraud. A story by a bushranger in Australia may perhaps be objected to as a mistake or an invention; but did a Methodist minister in Guinea conspire with him to cheat the public by telling the same story there? The possibility of intentional or unintentional mystification is often barred by such a state of things as that a similar statement is made in two remote lands by two witnesses, of whom A lived a century before B, and B appears never to have heard of A. How distant are the countries, how wide apart the dates, how different the creeds and characters of the observers in the catalogue of facts of civilisation, needs no farther showing to any one who will even glance at the footnotes of the present work. And the more odd the statement, the less likely that several people in several places should have made it wrongly. This being so, it seems reasonable to judge that the statements are in the main truly given, and that their close and regular coincidence is due to the cropping up of similar facts in various districts of culture. Now the most important facts of ethnography are vouched for in this way. Experience leads the student after a while to expect and find that the phenomena of culture, as resulting from widely-acting similar causes, should recur again and again in the world. He even mistrusts isolated statements to which he knows of no parallel elsewhere, and waits for their genuineness to be shown by corresponding accounts from the other side of the earth or the other end of history. So strong indeed is the means of authentication, that the ethnographer in his library may sometimes presume to decide not only whether a particular explorer is a shrewd and honest observer, but also whether what he reports is conformable to the general rules of civilisation. *Non quis, sed quid.*

It must be added, as a rider to Mr. Tylor's remarks, that anthropology is rapidly making the accumulation of fresh and trustworthy evidence more difficult than ever. Travellers and missionaries have begun to read anthropological books, and their evidence is therefore much more likely to be biassed now by anthropological theories than it was of old. When Mr. M'Lennan wrote on "totems" in 1869,[1] he was able to say, "It is some compensation for the completeness of the accounts that we can thoroughly trust them, as the totem has not till now got itself mixed up with speculations, and accordingly the observers have been unbiassed. But as anthropology is now more widely studied, the *naif* evidence of ignorance and of surprise grows more and more difficult to obtain."

We may now assert that, though the evidence of each separate witness may be influenced by fluctuations of opinion, yet the consensus of their testimony, when they are unanimous, remains unshaken. The same argument applies to the private inclination, and prejudice, and method of inquiry of each individual observer.

Travellers in general, and missionaries in particular,

[1] *Fortnightly Review*, October 1869.

are biassed in several distinct ways. The missionary is sometimes anxious to prove that religion can only come by revelation, and that certain tribes, having received no revelation, have no religion or religious myths at all. Sometimes the missionary, on the other hand, is anxious to demonstrate that the myths of his heathen flock are a corrupted version of the Biblical narrative. In the former case he neglects the study of savage myths; in the latter he unconsciously accommodates what he hears to what he calls "the truth". In modern days the missionary often sees with the eyes of Mr. Herbert Spencer. The traveller who is not a missionary may either have the same prejudices, or he may be a sceptic about revealed religion. In the latter case he is perhaps unconsciously moved to put burlesque versions of Biblical stories into the mouths of his native informants, or to represent the savages as ridiculing (Dr. Moffat found that they did ridicule) the Scriptural traditions which he communicates to them. Yet again we must remember that the leading questions of a European inquirer may furnish a savage with a thread on which to string answers which the questions themselves have suggested. "Have you ever had a great flood?" "Yes." "Was any one saved?" The leading question starts the invention of the savage on a Deluge-myth, of which, perhaps, the idea has never before entered his mind.

The last is a source of error pointed out by Mr. Codrington:[1] "The questions of the European are a thread on which the ideas of the native precipitate themselves". Now, as European inquirers are prone to ask much the same questions, a people which, like some Celts and savages, "always answers yes," will everywhere give much the same answers. Mr. Romilly, in his book on

[1] *Journal of Anthrop. Inst.*, February 1881.

the Western Pacific,[1] remarks, "In some parts of New Britain, if a stranger were to ask, 'Are there men with tails in the mountains?' he would probably be answered 'Yes,' that being the answer which the new Briton" (and the North Briton, too, very often) "would imagine was expected of him, and would be most likely to give satisfaction. The train of thought in his mind would be something like this, 'He must know that there are no such men, but he cannot have asked so foolish a question without an object, and therefore he wishes me to say 'Yes!' Of course the first 'Yes' leads to many others, and in a very short time everything is known about these tailed men, and a full account of them is sent home."

What is true of tailed men applies to native answers about myths and customs when the questions are asked by persons who have not won the confidence of the people nor discovered their real beliefs by long and patient observation. This must be borne in mind when missionaries tell us that savages believe in one supreme deity, in a mediator, and the like, and it must be borne in mind when they tell us that savages have no supreme being at all. Always we must be wary! A very pleasing example of inconsistency in reports about the same race may be found in a comparison of the account of the Khonds in the thirteenth volume of the Royal Asiatic Society with the account given by General Campbell in his *Personal Narrative*. The inquirer in the former case did not know the Khond language, and trusted to interpreters, who were later expelled from the public service. General Campbell, on the other hand, believed himself to possess "the confidence of the priests and chiefs," and his description is quite different. In cases of contradictions like these, the anthropologist will do well to leave the subject alone,

[1] *The Western Pacific and New Guinea*, London, 1886, pp. 3-6.

unless he has very strong reasons for believing one or other of the contending witnesses.

We have now considered the objections that may be urged against the bias of witnesses.

Mr. Max Müller founds another objection on "the absence of recognised authorities among savages".[1] This absence of authority is not always complete; the Maoris, for example, have traditional hymns of great authority and antiquity. There are often sacred songs and customs (preserved by the Red Indians in chants recorded by picture-writing on birch bark), and there always is some teaching from the mothers to their children, or in the Mysteries. All these, but, above all, the almost immutable sacredness of *custom*, are sources of evidence. But, of course, the story of one savage informant may differ widely from that of his neighbour. The first may be the black sheep of the tribe, the next may be the saint of the district. "Both would be considered by European travellers as unimpeachable authorities with regard to their religion." This is too strongly stated. Even the inquiring squatter will repose more confidence in the reports about his religion of a black with a decent character, or of a black who has only recently mixed with white men, than in those of a rum-bibbing loafer about up-country stations or a black professional bowler on a colonial cricket-ground. Our best evidence is from linguists who have been initiated into the secret Mysteries. Still more will missionaries and scholars like Bleek, Hahn, Codrington, Castren, Gill, Callaway, Theal, and the rest, sift and compare the evidence of the most trustworthy native informants. The merits of the travellers we have named as observers and scholars are freely acknowledged by Mr. Max Müller himself. To their statements, also, we

[1] *Hibbert Lectures*, p. 92.

can apply the criterion: Does Bleek's report from the Bushmen and Hottentots confirm Castren's from the Finns? Does Codrington in Melanesia tell the same tale as Gill in Mangia or Theal among the Kaffirs? Are all confirmed by Charlevoix, and Lafitau, and Brébeuf, the old Catholic apostles of the North American Indians? If this be so, then we may presume that the inquirers have managed to extract true accounts from some of their native informants. The object of the inquiry, of course, is to find out, not what a few more educated and noble members of a tribe may think, nor what some original speculative thinker among a lower race may have worked out for himself, but to ascertain the general character of the ideas most popular and most widely prevalent among backward peoples.

A third objection is that the priests of savage tribes are not unimpeachable authorities. It is pointed out that even Christian clergy have their differences of opinion. Naturally we expect most shades of opinion where there is most knowledge and most liberty, but the liberty of savage heterodoxy is very wide indeed. We might almost say that (as in the mythology of Greece) there is *no* orthodox mythical doctrine among savages. But, amidst minor diversities, we have found many ideas which are universal both in savage and civilised myths. *Quod semper, quod ubique, quod ab omnibus*. It is on this universal element of faith, not on the discrepancies of local priests, that we must fix our attention. Many a different town in Greece showed the birthplace or tomb of this or that deity. The essential point is that all agreed in declaring that the god was born or died.

Once more—and this is a point of some importance when we are told that priests differ from each other in their statements—we must remember that these very differences are practically universal in all mythology, even in that of civilised races. Thus, if one savage authority declares that men came originally out of trees, while his fellow-tribesman avers that the human race was created out of clay, and a third witness maintains that his first ancestors emerged from a hole in the ground, and a fourth stands to it that his stock is descended from a swan or a serpent, and a fifth holds that humanity was evolved from other animal forms, these savage statements appear contradictory. But when we find (as we do) precisely the same sort of contradictions everywhere recurring among civilised peoples, in Greece, India, Egypt, as well as in Africa, America and Australia, there seems no longer any reason to distrust the various versions of the myth which are given by various priests or chiefs. Each witness is only telling the legend which he has heard and prefers, and it is precisely the coexistence of all these separate monstrous beliefs which makes the enigma and the attraction of mythology. In short, the discrepancies of savage myths are not an argument against the authenticity of our information on the topic, because the discrepancies themselves are repeated in civilised myth. *Semper et ubique, et ab omnibus*. To object to the presence of discrepant accounts is to object to mythology for being mythological.

Another objection is derived from the "unwillingness of savages to talk about religion," and from the difficulty of understanding them when they do talk of it. This hardly applies when Europeans are initiated into savage Mysteries. We may add a fair example of the difficulty of learning about alien religions. It is given by Garcilasso de la Vega, son of an Inca princess, and a companion of Pizarro.[1] "The method that our Spaniards adopted

[1] Garcilasso de la Vega, *Royal Commentaries*, vol. i. 123.

in writing their histories was to ask the Indians in Spanish touching the things they wanted to find out from them. These, from not having a clear knowledge of ancient things, or from bad memories, told them wrong, or mixed up poetical fables with their replies. And the worst of it was that neither party had more than a very imperfect knowledge of the language of the other, so as to understand the inquiry and to reply to it. . . . In this great confusion, the priest or layman who asked the questions placed the meaning to them which was nearest to the desired answer, or which was most like what the Indian was understood to have said. Thus they interpreted according to their pleasure or prejudice, and wrote things down as truths which the Indians never dreamt of." As an example of these comparisons, Garcilasso gives the discovery of the doctrine of the Trinity among the people of Peru. A so-called *Icona* was found answering to the Father, a Son (*Racab*), and a Holy Spirit (*Estrua*); nor was the Virgin lacking, nor even St. Anne. "All these things are fictions of the Spaniards." But no sooner has Garcilasso rebuked the Spaniards and their method, than he hastens to illustrate by his own example another difficulty that besets us in our search for evidence of myths. He says, as if it were a matter of certain fact, that Tlasolteute, a kind of Priapus, god of lust, and Ometoctilti, god of drunkenness, and the god of murder, and the others, "were the names of *men and women* whom the natives of that land worshipped as gods and goddesses". Thus Garcilasso euhemerises audaciously, as also does Sahagun in his account of Mexican religion. We have no right to assume that gods of natural departments (any more than Dionysus and Priapus and Ares) had once been real men and were deified, on evidence like the statement of Garcilasso. He is giving his own euhemeristic guess as if it were matter of fact, and this is a common custom with even the more intelligent of the early missionaries.

Another example of the natural difficulty in studying the myths of savages may be taken from Mr. Sproat's *Scenes of Savage Life* (1868). There is an honesty and candour in Mr. Sproat's work which by itself seems to clear this witness, at least, of charges of haste or prejudice. The religion of savages, says this inquirer, "is a subject as to which a traveller might easily form erroneous opinions, owing to the practical difficulty, even to one skilled in the language, of ascertaining the true nature of their superstitions. This short chapter is the result of more than four years' inquiry, made unremittingly, under favourable circumstances. There is a constant temptation, from which the unbiassed observer cannot be quite free, to fill up in one's mind, without proper material, the gap between what is known of the religion of the natives for certain, and the larger less-known portion, which can only be guessed at; and I frequently found that, under this temptation, I was led on to form, in my own mind, a connected whole, designed to coincide with some ingenious theory which I might wish to be true. Generally speaking, it is necessary, I think, to view with suspicion *any very regular account* given by travellers of the religion of savages." (Yet we have seen the absence of "regularity," the differences of opinion among priests, objected to by Mr. Max Müller as a proof of the untrustworthy nature of our evidence.) "The real religious notions of savages cannot be separated from the vague and unformed, as well as bestial and grotesque, mythology with which they are intermixed. The faint struggling efforts of our natures in so early or so little advanced a stage of moral and intellectual cultivation can produce only a medley of opinions and beliefs, not to be dignified by the epithet religious, which are held loosely by the people themselves, and are neither very easily discovered nor explained." When we came to civilised mythologies, we found that they also are "bestial and grotesque," "loosely held," and a "medley of opinions and beliefs".

Mr. Sproat was "two years among the Ahts, with his mind constantly directed to the subject of their religious beliefs," before he could discover that they had any such beliefs at all. Traders assured him that they had none. He found that the Ahts were "fond of mystification" and of "sells"; and, in short, this inquirer, living with the Ahts like an Aht, discounted every sort of circumstance which could invalidate his statement of their myths.[1] Now, when we find Mr. Codrington taking the same precautions in Melanesia, and when his account of Melanesian myths reads like a close copy of Mr. Sproat's account of Aht legends, and when both are corroborated by the collections of Bleek, and Hahn, and Gill, and Castren, and Rink, in far distant corners of the world, while the modern testimony of these scholarly men is in harmony with that of the old Jesuit missionaries, and of untaught adventurers who have lived for many years with savages, surely it will be admitted that the difficulty of ascertaining savage opinion has been, to a great extent, overcome. If all the evidence be wrong, the coincidences of the witnesses with each other and of the savage myths they report with the myths of Greeks and Aryans of India will be no less than a miracle.

We have now examined the objections urged against a system founded on the comparative study of savage myths. It cannot be said of us (as it has been said of De Brosses), that "whatever we find in the voyages of sailors and

[1] Pp. 203-205.

traders is welcome to us"; that "we have a theory to defend, and whatever seems to support it is sure to be true". Our evidence is based, to a very great extent, on the communications of missionaries who are acknowledged to be scholarly and sober men. It is confirmed by other evidence, Catholic, Dissenting, pagan, scientific, and by the reports of illiterate men, unbiassed by science, and little biassed by religion.

But we have not yet exhausted our evidence, nor had recourse to our ultimate criterion. That evidence, that criterion, is derived from the study of comparative institutions, of comparative ritual, of comparative law, and of comparative customs. In the widely diffused rites and institutions which express themselves in actual practice we have sure evidence for the ideas on which the customs are founded. For example, if a man pays away his wampum, or his yams, or his arrow-heads to a magician for professional services, it follows that he *does* believe in magic. If he puts to death a tribesman for the sin of marrying a woman to whom he was only akin by virtue of common descent from the same beast or plant, it seems to follow that he *does* believe in descent from and kinship with plants and beasts. If he buries food and valuable weapons with his dead, it follows that he *does*, or that his fathers did, believe in the continued life of the dead. At the very least, in all three cases the man is acting on what must once have been actual beliefs, even if the consequent practices be still in force only through custom, after the real faith has dwindled away. Thus the belief, past or present, in certain opinions can be deduced from actual practices, just as we may deduce from our own Coronation Service the fact that oil, anointed on a man's head by a priest, was once believed to have a mysterious efficacy, or the fact that a certain rough block of red sandstone was once supposed to have some kind of sacredness. Of all these sources of evidence, none is more valuable than the testimony of ritual. A moment's reflection will show that ritual, among any people, wild or civilised, is not a thing easily altered. If we take the savage, *his* ritual consists mainly of the magical rites by which he hopes to constrain his gods to answer his prayers, though he may also "reveal" to the neophyte "Our Father". If we examine the Greeks, we discover the same element in such rites as the Attic Thesmophoria, the torch-dance of Demeter, the rainmaking on the Arcadian Mount Lycæus, with many other examples. Meanwhile the old heathen ritual survives in Europe as rural folklore, and we can thus display a chain of evidence, from savage magic to Greek ritual, with the folklore of Germany, France, Russia and Scotland for the link between these and our own time. This is almost our best evidence for the ancient idea about gods and their service. From the evidence of institutions, then, the evidence of reports may be supplemented. "The direct testimony, as M. Darmesteter says, "heureusement peut-être suppleé par le témoignage indirect, celui qui porte sur les usages, les coutumes, l'ordre extérieur de la vie," everything that shows us religious faith embodied in action. Now these actions, also, are only attested by the reports of travellers, missionaries and historians. But it is comparatively easy to describe correctly what is *done*, much more easy than to discover what is *thought*. Yet it will be found that the direct evidence of institutions corroborates the less direct evidence as to thought and opinion. Thus an uncommonly strong texture of testimony is woven by the coincidence of evidence, direct and indirect, ancient and modern, of learned and unlearned men, of Catholics, Protestants, pagans and sceptics. What can be said against that evidence we have heard. We have examined the objections based on "the influence of public opinion on travellers," on "the absence of recognised authorities among savages," on the discrepancies of the authorities who are recognised, on the "unwillingness of savages to talk of their religion," and on the difficulty of understanding them when they do talk of it.

But after allowing for all these drawbacks (as every anthropologist worthy of the name will, in each case, allow), we have shown that there does remain a body of coincident evidence, of authority, now learned and critical, now uncritical and unlearned, which cannot be set aside as "extremely untrustworthy". This authority is accepted in questions of the evolution of art, politics, handicraft; why not in questions of religion? It is usually evidence given by men who did not see its tendency or know its value. A chance word in the Veda shows us that a savage point of marriage etiquette was known to the poet. A sneer of Theophrastus, a denunciation of Ezekiel, an anecdote of Herodotus, reveal to us the practices of contemporary savages as they existed thousands of years ago among races savage or civilised. A traveller's tale of Melville or Mandeville proves to be no mere "yarn," but completes the evidence for the existence in Asia or the Marquesas Islands of belief and rites proved to occur in Europe or India.

Such is the nature of the evidence for savage ideas, and for their survivals in civilisation; and the amount of the evidence is best known to him who has to plod through tracts, histories and missionary reports.

INDEX.

[I am indebted for this Index to my friend Mrs. Ogilby.]